D0089252

Acclaim for

ELAINE PAGELS'S

The Origin of Satan

"Pagels has achieved something important. . . . Thoughtful scholarly works that are also original and adventurous are not common. *The Origin of Satan* is such a work, and we should be correspondingly grateful." —*New York Review of Books*

"Illuminating and rewarding . . . a very readable scholarly work . . . a model of erudition and conciseness." —*Newsday*

"Fascinating and valuable." —*The Nation*

"Lucid and closely reasoned. . . . Pagels remains always a lively writer who discerns the human implications of esoteric texts and scholarly disputes." —*Chicago Tribune*

"One of today's leading interpreters of the world of early Christianity. . . . She brilliantly shows how otherwise arcane theology is related to the social context in which it was conceived." —*Milwaukee Journal Sentinel*

"Succeeds wonderfully." —*San Francisco Chronicle*

THE ORIGIN OF SATAN

THE
ORIGIN OF SATAN

ELAINE PAGELS

Vintage Books
A DIVISION OF RANDOM HOUSE, INC.
NEW YORK

TO SARAH AND DAVID
with love

ACKNOWLEDGMENTS

This book is based upon research originally presented, for the most part, in scholarly publications (cited at the beginning of each chapter's notes) and revised to make it more generally accessible. During the six years of research and writing, I have consulted with many scholars and friends. First I wish to thank John Gager, Rosemary Reuther, and Krister Stendahl, whose research and teaching have contributed so much to illuminate the issues. I especially thank those colleagues and friends who read the manuscript and offered corrections and criticism: Glen Bowersock, Elizabeth Diggs, Howard Clark Kee, Kent Greenawalt, Wayne Meeks, Sharon Olds, Eugene Schwartz, Alan Segal, Peter Stern, and S. David Sperling; and those who offered comments and criticism on portions of the work as it was in progress, including John Gager, Vernon Robbins, and James Robinson, who read the sections on New Testament sources; Steven Mullaney, who read and commented on the sources presented in chapter 1; John Collins, Louis Feldman, Paul Hanson, Martha Himmelfarb, Helmut Koester, Doron Mendels, and George Nickelsburg, who read and commented on the sources presented in chapter 2; and Peter Brown, who read and commented on the article on which part of chapter 6 is based. No doubt each of these colleagues will disagree with some of my conclusions, for which I must take responsibility.

Research for this book began when I was a visitor at the School of Historical Studies at the Institute for Advanced Study in 1990–91 and resumed there in 1994–95. I am most grateful to the members of that school for their gracious hospitality in making available to me, as to many others, the serene and collegial environment the Institute offers. I owe special thanks to Ruth Simmons, Vice Provost of Princeton University, to Jeffrey Stout, Chair of the Department of Religion, and to Robert Gunning, Dean of the Faculty, for making possible a leave to complete the research and writing in 1994–95, and to the National Endowment for the Humanities for the fellowship that supported me during that year.

I wish to thank my colleagues in the Department of Religion at Princeton University, both for conversations that have contributed much to the process and for their grace and understanding during these years, and also to thank the graduate students who struggled through the Greek texts with me in our seminar: Gideon Bohack, Robert Cro, Nicola Denzey, Obery Hendricks, Anne Merideth, Sharon Hefetz, and Joel Walker.

There are certain people without whose participation I cannot imagine having written this book. I am very fortunate and privileged to have worked with Jason Epstein as editor, and deeply appreciate the insight, wit, and passion for clarity he has brought to this process, along with his enthusiastic support. Helaine Randerson has worked on the manuscript through the entire process, offering incisive comments and editorial criticism along with her astonishingly expert manuscript preparation. John Brockman and Katinka Matson have offered encouragement on the project from the beginning, and have contributed in innumerable ways. I am grateful, too, to Anne Merideth for her collaboration in finding research materials, as well as for her excellent judgment on many issues we discussed. I have appreciated and enjoyed working with Virginia Avery, whose editorial suggestions have improved the text; and also thank Joy de Menil for all that she contributed. ·

Finally, I am grateful to the many friends whose presence and personal support in ways known to each of them helped see me through these difficult years since my husband's death, and mention in particular Malcolm Diamond, Elizabeth Diggs, Sarah

Duben-Vaughn, Kent Greenawalt, my brother and sister-in-law, Ralph and Jane Hiesey, Kristin Hughes, Elizabeth and Niccola Khuri, Emily McCulley, Sharon and David Olds, Albert Raboteau, Kathy Murtaugh, and Margot Wilkie.

CONTENTS

INTRODUCTION

In 1988, when my husband of twenty years died in a hiking accident, I became aware that, like many people who grieve, I was living in the presence of an invisible being—living, that is, with a vivid sense of someone who had died. During the following years I began to reflect on the ways that various religious traditions give shape to the invisible world, and how our imaginative perceptions of what is invisible relate to the ways we respond to the people around us, to events, and to the natural world. I was reflecting, too, on the various ways that people from Greek, Jewish, and Christian traditions deal with misfortune and loss. Greek writers from Homer to Sophocles attribute such events to gods and goddesses, destiny and fate—elements as capricious and indifferent to human welfare as the "forces of nature" (which is our term for these forces).

In the ancient Western world, of which I am a historian, many—perhaps most—people assumed that the universe was inhabited by invisible beings whose presence impinged upon the visible world and its human inhabitants. Ancient Egyptians, Greeks, and Romans envisioned gods, goddesses, and spirit beings of many kinds, while certain Jews and Christians, ostensibly monotheists, increasingly spoke of angels, heavenly messengers from God, and some spoke of fallen angels and demons. This was especially true from the first century of the common era onward.

Conversion from paganism to Judaism or Christianity, I realized, meant, above all, transforming one's perception of the invisible world. To this day, Christian baptism requires a person to solemnly "renounce the devil and all his works" and to accept exorcism. The pagan convert was baptized only after confessing that all spirit beings previously revered—and dreaded—as divine were actually only "demons"—hostile spirits contending against the One God of goodness and justice, and against his armies of angels. Becoming either a Jew or a Christian polarized a pagan's view of the universe, and moralized it. The Jewish theologian Martin Buber regarded the moralizing of the universe as one of the great achievements of Jewish tradition, later passed down as its legacy to Christians and Muslims.[1] The book of Genesis, for example, insists that volcanoes would not have destroyed the towns of Sodom and Gomorrah unless all the inhabitants of those towns—all the inhabitants who concerned the storyteller, that is, the adult males—had been evil, "young and old, down to the last man" (Gen. 19:4).

When I began this work, I assumed that Jewish and Christian perceptions of invisible beings had to do primarily with moralizing the natural universe, as Buber claimed, and so with encouraging people to interpret events ranging from illness to natural disasters as expressions of "God's will" or divine judgment on human sin. But my research led me in unexpected directions and disclosed a far more complex picture. Such Christians as Justin Martyr (140 C.E.), one of the "fathers of the church," attributes affliction not to "God's will" but to the malevolence of Satan. His student Tatian allows for accident in the natural world, including disasters, for which, he says, God offers solace but seldom miraculous intervention. As I proceeded to investigate Jewish and Christian accounts of angels and fallen angels, I discovered, however, that they were less concerned with the natural world as a whole than with the particular world of human relationships.

Rereading biblical and extra-biblical accounts of angels, I learned first of all what many scholars have pointed out: that while angels often appear in the Hebrew Bible, Satan, along with other fallen angels or demonic beings, is virtually absent. But among certain first-century Jewish groups, prominently including the Essenes (who saw themselves as allied with angels) and the followers of Jesus, the figure variously called Satan, Beelzebub, or Belial also began to take on central importance. While the gospel of Mark, for example, mentions angels only in the opening frame (1:13) and in the final verses of the original manuscript (16:5–7), Mark deviates from mainstream Jewish tradition by introducing "the devil" into the crucial opening scene of the gospel, and goes on to characterize Jesus' ministry as involving continual struggle between God's spirit and the demons, who belong, apparently, to Satan's "kingdom" (see Mark 3:23–27). Such visions have been incorporated into Christian tradition and have served, among other things, to confirm for Christians their own identification with God and to demonize their opponents—first other Jews, then pagans, and later dissident Christians called heretics. This is what this book is about.

To emphasize this element of the New Testament gospels does not mean, of course, that this is their primary theme. "Aren't the gospels about love?" exclaimed one friend as we discussed this work. Certainly they *are* about love, but since the story they have to tell involves betrayal and killing, they also include elements of hostility which evoke demonic images. This book concentrates on this theme.

What fascinates us about Satan is the way he expresses qualities that go beyond what we ordinarily recognize as human. Satan evokes more than the greed, envy, lust, and anger we identify with our own worst impulses, and more than what we call brutality, which imputes to human beings a resemblance to animals ("brutes"). Thousands of years of tradition have characterized Satan instead as a spirit. Originally he was one of God's angels, but a fallen one. Now he stands in open rebellion against God, and in his frustrated rage he mirrors aspects of our own confrontations with otherness. Many people have claimed to see him embodied at certain times in individuals and groups that seem possessed by an intense spiritual passion, one that engages even our better qualities, like strength, intelligence, and devotion, but turns them toward destruction and takes pleasure in inflicting harm. Evil, then, at its worst, seems to involve the supernatural—what we recognize, with a shudder, as the diabolic inverse of Martin Buber's characterization of God as "wholly other." Yet—historically speaking, at any rate—Satan, along with diabolical colleagues like Belial and Mastema (whose Hebrew name means "hatred"), did not materialize out of the air. Instead, as we shall see, such figures emerged from the turmoil of first-century Palestine, the setting in which the Christian movement began to grow.

I do not intend to do here what other scholars already have done well: The literary scholar Neil Forsyth, in his excellent recent book *The Old Enemy,* has investigated much of the literary and cultural background of the figure of Satan;[2] Walter Wink and the psychoanalyst Carl Gustav Jung and some of his followers have studied Satan's theological and psychological implications.[3] Jeffrey Burton Russell and others have attempted to investigate cross-cultural parallels between the figure of Satan and such figures as the Egyptian god Set or the Zoroastrian evil power Ahriman.[4] What interests me instead are specifically *social* implications of the figure of Satan: how he is invoked to express human conflict and to characterize human enemies within our own religious traditions.

In this book, then, I invite you to consider Satan as a reflection of how we perceive ourselves and those we call "others." Satan has, after all, made a kind of profession out of being the "other"; and so Satan defines negatively what we think of as human. The social and cultural practice of defining certain people as "others" in relation to one's own group may be, of course, as old as humanity itself. The anthropologist Robert Redfield has argued that the worldview of many peoples consists essentially of two pairs of binary oppositions: human/nonhuman and we/they.[5] These two are often correlated, as Jonathan Z. Smith observes, so that "we" equals "human" and "they" equals "not human."[6] The distinction between "us" and "them" occurs within our earliest historical evidence, on ancient Sumerian and Akkadian tablets, just as it exists in the language and culture of peoples all over the world. Such distinctions are charged, sometimes with attraction, perhaps more often with repulsion—or both at once. The ancient Egyptian word for Egyptian simply means "human"; the Greek word for non-Greeks, "barbarian," mimics the guttural gibberish of those who do not speak Greek—since they speak unintelligibly, the Greeks call them *barbaroi*.

Yet this virtually universal practice of calling one's own people human and "dehumanizing" others does not necessarily mean that people actually doubt or deny the humanness of others. Much of the time, as William Green points out, those who so label themselves and others are engaging in a kind of caricature that helps define and consolidate their own group identity:

> A society does not simply discover its others, it fabricates them, by selecting, isolating, and emphasizing an aspect of another people's life, and making it symbolize their difference.[7]

Conflict between groups is, of course, nothing new. What may be new in Western Christian tradition, as we shall see, is how the use of Satan to represent one's enemies lends to conflict a specific kind of moral and religious interpretation, in which "we" are God's people and "they" are God's enemies, and ours as well. Those who adopt this view are encouraged to believe, as Jesus warned his followers, that "whoever kills you will think he is offering a service to God" (John 16:2). Such moral interpretation of conflict has proven extraordinarily effective throughout Western history in consolidating the identity of Christian groups; the same history also shows that it can justify hatred, even mass slaughter.

Research for this book has made me aware of aspects of Christianity I find disturbing. During the past several years, rereading the gospels, I was struck by how their vision of supernatural struggle both expresses conflict and raises it to cosmic dimensions. This research, then, reveals certain fault lines in Christian tradition that have allowed for the demonizing of others throughout Christian history—fault lines that go back nearly two thousand years to the origins of the Christian movement. While writing this book I often recalled a saying of Søren Kierkegaard: "An unconscious relationship is more powerful than a conscious one."

For nearly two thousand years, for example, many Christians have taken for granted that Jews killed Jesus and the Romans were merely their reluctant agents, and that this implicates not only the perpetrators but (as Matthew insists) all their progeny in evil.[8] Throughout the centuries, countless Christians listening to the gospels absorbed, along with the quite contrary sayings of Jesus, the association between the forces of evil and Jesus' Jewish enemies. Whether illiterate or sophisticated, those who heard the gospel stories, or saw them illustrated in their churches, generally assumed both their historical accuracy and their religious validity.

Especially since the nineteenth century, however, increasing numbers of scholars have applied literary and historical analysis to the gospels—the so-called higher criticism. Their critical analysis indicated that the authors of Matthew and Luke used Mark as a source from which to construct their amplified gospels. Many scholars assumed that Mark was the most historically reliable because it was the simplest in style and was written closer to the time of Jesus than the others were. But historical accuracy may not have been the gospel writers' first consideration. Further analysis demonstrated how passages from the prophetic writings and the psalms of the Hebrew Bible were woven into the gospel narratives. Barnabas Lindars and others suggested that Christian writers often expanded biblical passages into whole episodes that "proved," to the satisfaction of many believers, that events predicted by the prophets found their fulfillment in Jesus' coming.[9]

Those who accepted such analysis now realized that the gospel of Mark, as James Robinson shows, is anything but a straightforward historical narrative; rather, it is a theological treatise that assumes the form of historical biography.[10] Recognizing that the authors of Matthew and Luke revised Mark in different ways, scholars have attempted to discriminate between the source materials each accepted from earlier tradition—sayings, anecdotes, and parables—and what each writer added to interpret that material. Some hoped to penetrate the various accounts and to discover the "historical Jesus," recovering his authentic words and deeds from the peripheral material that surrounds them. But others objected to what Albert Schweitzer called the "quest of the historical Jesus,"[11] pointing out that the earliest of the gospels was written more than a generation after Jesus' death, and the others nearly two generations later, and that sorting out "authentic" material in the gospels was virtually impossible in the absence of independent evidence.

Meanwhile, many other scholars introduced historical evidence from the Mishnah, an ancient archive of Jewish tradition, along with other Jewish sources, as well as from Roman history, law, and administrative procedure.[12] One of the primary issues to emerge from these critical studies was the question, What historical basis is there, if any, to the gospels' claim that Jews were responsible for Jesus' death? What makes this question of vital interest is the gospels' claim that this deed was inspired by Satan himself. One group of scholars pointed out discrepancies between Sanhedrin procedure described in the Mishnah and in the gospel accounts of Jesus' "trial before the Sanhedrin," and questioned the accuracy of the accounts in Mark and Matthew. Simon Bernfield declared in 1910 that "the whole trial before the Sanhedrin is nothing but an invention of a later date,"[13] a view that has found recent defenders among Christian literary analysts.[14] Noting that the charge against Jesus and the form of execution are characteristically Roman, many scholars, including Paul Winter in his influential book *On the Trial of Jesus*, published in 1961, argued that it was the Romans who executed Jesus, on political grounds, not religious ones.[15] Others, recently including the Roman historian Fergus Millar, have placed more credence in the accounts of Luke or John, which indicate that the Sanhedrin held only a hearing concerning Jesus, not an actual trial.[16]

Recently, however, one group of scholars has renewed arguments to show that, in Josef Blinzler's words,

> anyone who undertakes to assess the trial of Jesus as a historical and legal event, *reconstructing it from the gospel narratives,*

must come to the same conclusion as the early Christian preachers did themselves, that the main responsibility rests on the Jewish side (emphasis added).[17]

But scholars who take more skeptical views of the historical plausibility of these narratives emphasize Roman responsibility for Jesus' execution, which, they suggest, the gospel writers tended to downplay so as not to provoke the Romans in the aftermath of the unsuccessful Jewish war against Rome.[18]

I agree as a working hypothesis that Jesus' execution was probably imposed by the Romans for activities they considered seditious—possibly for arousing public demonstrations and (so they apparently believed) for claiming to be "king of the Jews." Among his own people, however, Jesus appeared as a radical prophetic figure whose public teaching, although popular with the crowds, angered and alarmed certain Jewish leaders, especially the Temple authorities, who probably facilitated his capture and arrest.

But this book is not primarily an attempt to discover "what really happened"—much less to persuade the reader of this or any other version of "what happened"—since, apart from the scenario briefly sketched above, I find the sources too fragmentary and too susceptible of various interpretations to answer that question definitively. Instead I try to show how the gospels reflect the emergence of the Jesus movement from the postwar factionalism of the late first century. Each author shapes a narrative to respond to particular circumstances, and each uses the story of Jesus to "think with" in an immediate situation, identifying with Jesus and the disciples, and casting those regarded as opponents as Jesus' enemies. To show this, I draw upon a wealth of recent works by historical and literary scholars, many of them discussing (and often disagreeing over) the question of when and how Jesus' followers separated from the rest of the Jewish community.

In this book I add to the discussion something I have not found elsewhere—what I call the social history of Satan; that is, I show how the events told in the gospels about Jesus, his advocates, and his enemies correlate with the supernatural drama the writers use to interpret that story—the struggle between God's spirit and Satan. And because Christians as they read the gospels have characteristically identified themselves with the disciples, for some two thousand years they have also identified their opponents, whether Jews, pagans, or heretics, with forces of evil, and so with Satan.

THE ORIGIN OF SATAN

THE GOSPEL OF MARK AND
THE JEWISH WAR

In 66 C.E., a rebellion against Rome broke out among the Jews of Palestine. Jewish soldiers, recruited at first from the countryside by leaders of the revolt, fought with whatever weapons they could find. But as the revolt spread to towns and cities, the Jewish population divided. Some refused to fight: in Jerusalem, the priestly party and their city-dwelling allies tried to maintain peace with Rome. Among those who joined the revolt, many were convinced that God was on their side: all were passionately intent on ridding their land of foreign domination. Three years into the war, the future emperor Vespasian and his son, the future emperor Titus, marched against Jerusalem with no fewer than sixty thousand well-trained, fully equipped foot soldiers and cavalry and besieged the city.

Some twenty years later, the Jewish historian Joseph ben Matthias, better known by his Romanized name, Flavius Josephus, who had served as governor of Galilee before joining in the fight against Rome, wrote an account of what he calls "not only the greatest war of our own time, but one of the greatest of all recorded wars."[1] Josephus is the only remaining guide to these events. Other accounts of the war have not survived. Although he is a vivid historian, Josephus is also partisan. Born into a wealthy priestly family of royal lineage, Josephus had traveled to Rome when he was about twenty-six—two years before the war—to intervene with the emperor Nero on behalf of several arrested Jewish priests. Rome's wealth and military power impressed the young man, who managed to meet one of Nero's favorite actors—a Jew, as it happened—and, through him, Nero's wife, Poppea. Poppea agreed to help with his mission, and Josephus returned to Palestine. There, he says in his autobiography,

> I found revolutionary movements already begun, and great excitement at the prospect of revolt from Rome. Accordingly, I tried to stop those preaching sedition . . . urging them to place before their eyes those against whom they were fighting; and to remember that they were inferior to the Romans, not only in military skill, but in good fortune. Although earnestly and insistently seeking to dissuade them from their purpose, foreseeing that the results would be disastrous for us, I did not persuade them. The great insanity of those desperate men prevailed.[2]

Wherever he traveled, Josephus says, he found Judea—the Hebrew term for what others called Palestine—in turmoil. Guerrilla leaders such as John of Gischala and his followers dedicated themselves to fight for liberty in the name of God. In the spring of 67, John's fighting men, having routed the Romans from Gischala, their provincial city, burst into Jerusalem. There, urging people to join the revolution, they attracted tens of thousands, Josephus says, and "corrupted a great part of the young men, and stirred them up to war."[3] Others, whom Josephus calls older and wiser, bitterly opposed the revolt. John and other revolutionaries coming into Jerusalem from the countryside escalated the conflict by capturing "the most powerful man in the whole city," the Jewish leader Antipas—the city treasurer—and two other men also connected with the royal dynasty. Accusing their three prisoners of having met with the enemy while plotting to surrender Jerusalem to the Romans, the rebels called them "traitors to our common liberty" and slit their throats.[4]

Josephus says that he himself served at age thirty as governor of Galilee, before joining in the war against Rome under pressure from his countrymen, but doesn't explain why he violated his own principles, though he does say that at first he pretended to agree with the rebels in order not to arouse their suspicion. He describes in detail his own battles against the Romans, and how he barely escaped a Roman massacre at the defeated city of Jotapata. Having managed first to hide and then to survive a suicide pact he made with his fellow refugees, Josephus was captured by the Romans. Brought before Vespasian, the Roman commander, Josephus announced that God had revealed to him that Vespasian would become emperor of Rome. Unimpressed, Vespasian assumed that this was a trick Josephus had contrived to save his life. But after Nero was assassinated, and three other emperors rose and fell within months, Vespasian did become emperor. One of his first acts was to order his soldiers to free Josephus from prison. Henceforth Josephus traveled in Vespasian's entourage as interpreter and mediator. He returned to Jerusalem with Vespasian's son Titus when the young general took over command of the war from his father in order to march against the holy city.

By that time, Josephus says, three factions divided the city: the priestly party working for peace; the revolutionaries from the countryside; and contending against both of these, a second anti-Roman party, led by prominent Jerusalemites, "men of the greatest power," who, according to Josephus, wanted to maintain their power against the radicals from the surrounding countryside. Even before the Roman armies arrived, Josephus says, these "three treacherous factions" were fighting among themselves, while "the people of the city . . . were like a great body torn into pieces."[5] Josephus himself, serving the Roman commander during the siege, stood between two fires: he was bitterly hated by many of his own people as a traitor, and was suspected of treason by the Romans whenever they experienced a setback.

Josephus describes in fine detail the siege of Jerusalem, including the horrors of the famine induced by Roman blockades, in which, he says, "children pulled the very morsels that their fathers were eating out of their mouths, and, what was more pitiable, so did the mothers do to their infants."[6] Even old people and children were tortured for stealing food. Finally, when the Jewish armies could hold out no longer, Roman soldiers entered the city and swarmed over the great Temple. Titus and his staff, apparently curious, entered the Holy of Holies, the sacred room where the ark of the covenant was kept. Roman soldiers looted the treasury, seizing its priceless gold furniture, the golden trumpets, and the massive seven-branched lampstand; then they set the Temple afire and watched it burn.

Later that night they hailed Titus's victory and in triumph desecrated the Temple precincts by sacrificing there to their own gods. Having devastated the Jewish armies, they raped, robbed, and massacred thousands of Jerusalem's inhabitants and left the city in ruins. Josephus, writing from his Roman retirement villa ten to fifteen years later, no doubt hoped not only to express his anguish but also to exonerate himself for collaborating with those who destroyed Jerusalem when he wrote,

> O most wretched city, what misery so great as this did you suffer from the Romans, when they came to purify you from your internecine hatred![7]

Whatever Josephus's motives, his writing conveys a powerful impression of the factions that divided Jerusalem, as well as of the horrifying devastation that the city's inhabitants suffered.

What makes these events important for my purpose in this book is that the first Christian gospel was probably written during the last year of the war, or the year it ended.[8] Where it was written and by whom we do not know; the work is anonymous, although tradition attributes it to Mark, a younger co-worker of the apostle Peter. What we do know is that the author of Mark's gospel was well aware of the war and took sides in the conflicts it aroused, both among Jewish groups and between Jews and Romans.

Mark was writing, after all, about a charismatic Jewish teacher, Jesus of Nazareth, who thirty-five years before had been executed by Pontius Pilate, the Roman governor of Judea, apparently on charges of sedition against Rome. Of all that his followers later claimed to know about him, these charges and his crucifixion are the primary facts on which both Jesus' followers and his enemies agree. None of the surviving accounts of Jesus is contemporaneous with his life, though many people told and retold stories about him and recounted his sayings and parables. Dozens—perhaps even hundreds—of accounts were written about Jesus, including the long-hidden accounts found among the so-called secret gospels discovered at Nag Hammadi in Upper Egypt in 1945.[9] But of these numerous accounts, only four gospels are included in the New Testament. The great majority of those who told and wrote about Jesus did so as his devoted admirers, some even as his worshipers. But others, including Josephus himself, as well as the Roman senator Tacitus, writing c. 115 C.E., mention Jesus and his followers with hostility or contempt.[10] Yet nearly all of these, advocates and adversaries alike, placed Jesus of Nazareth and the movement he started within the context of "the recent troubles in Judea."

According to Mark, Jesus protested at being arrested "like a robber" (Mark 14:48). The author of Luke, writing some ten to twenty years later, says that Jesus was charged, like those crucified along with him, as a robber (Luke 23:40).[11] This Greek term *lēstēs*, literally translated "robber" or "bandit," was in the early first century a catchall term for an undesirable, a troublemaker or criminal. Josephus, however, writing after the Jewish war against Rome, most often uses the term to characterize those Jews who were inciting or participating in anti-Roman activities or in the war against Rome itself.[12] I agree with many other scholars that Jesus himself is unlikely to have been a revolutionary,[13] although each of the four gospels indicates that the Jewish leaders who brought him to Pilate accused him of claiming to be "king of the Jews." According to Mark, Pilate's soldiers, aware of the charge, mocked and abused Jesus as a would-be king of the Jews; apparently the same charge was inscribed over his cross as a warning to others that Rome would similarly dispatch anyone accused of insurrection.

The narratives that we know as the New Testament gospels were written by certain followers of Jesus who lived through the war, and who knew that many of their fellow Jews regarded them as a suspect minority. They wrote their own accounts of some of the momentous events surrounding the war, and the part that Jesus played in events preceding it, hoping to persuade others of their interpretation. We cannot fully understand the New Testament gospels until we recognize that they are, in this sense, wartime literature. As noted before, the gospel we call Mark (although we do not know historically who actually wrote these gospels, I use their traditional attributions) was written either during the war itself, perhaps during a temporary lull in the siege of Jerusalem, or immediately after the defeat, in 70 C.E.[14] Matthew and Luke wrote some ten to twenty years later, each using Mark as his basis and expanding Mark's narrative with further sayings and stories. Most scholars believe that John wrote his gospel, perhaps in Alexandria, about a generation after the war, c. 90–95 C.E.[15]

Only one of Jesus' followers whose writings were later incorporated into the New Testament—Paul of Tarsus—wrote before the war and could, of course, say nothing about Jesus in relation to it. Paul mentions little that concerns Jesus' biography, repeating only a few "sayings of the Lord" (Acts 20:35).[16] What fascinated Paul about Jesus' death was not the crucifixion as an actual event, but what he saw as its profound religious meaning—that, as he says, "Christ died for our sins" (1 Cor. 15:3), that he became an atonement sacrifice, which, Paul believed, transformed the relationship between Israel's God and the whole human race. If he knew the charges made against Jesus—that he was one of many Galileans whom Josephus regards as troublemakers[17] for fomenting rebellion against Rome—Paul apparently regarded these charges as so transparently false or so irrelevant that they needed no rebuttal. Paul died c. 64–65 C.E. in Rome, executed, like Jesus, by order of Roman magistrates.

The catastrophic events of 66–70 permanently changed the world in which Jews lived, not only in Jerusalem, where charred rubble replaced the splendid Temple, but also for Jews throughout the known world. Even those who had never seen Jerusalem knew that the center of their world had been shattered. The hardships and humiliations of defeat exacerbated long-standing divisions within the scattered Jewish communities, some of which had persisted around the eastern Mediterranean for as many as two hundred years, since the time when the armies of the Jewish leader Judas Maccabeus had driven out the Syrian dynasties established by Alexander the Great and had restored the Jewish state. In 65–70 C.E., these divisions were most obvious between those who had advocated war with Rome, and the priestly party, which had worked to keep the fragile peace. In the aftermath of the war against Rome, power relationships among various groups within the Jewish communities scattered around the world from Alexandria and Antioch to Rome shifted to meet the changing situation. In Jerusalem itself, now that the Temple was gone and thousands had been killed or had fled, the priestly class lost much of its influence as other parties jockeyed for position.

The war and its aftermath polarized followers of Jesus, too, in relation to other Jewish communities. Followers of Jesus had refused to fight in the war against the Romans, not because they agreed with Josephus and others that the Romans were invincible, or because they hoped for financial or political advantage. Jesus' followers believed that there was no point in fighting the Romans because the catastrophic events that followed his crucifixion were signs of the end—signs that the whole world was to be shattered and transformed (Mark 13:4–29). Some insisted that what they had seen—the horrors of the war—actually vindicated his call "Repent, for the Kingdom of God is near" (Mark 1:15). Mark shares the conviction, widespread among Jesus' followers, that Jesus himself had predicted these world-shattering events— the destruction of the Temple and its desecration:

> And as he came out of the Temple, one of his disciples said to him, "Look, rabbi, what wonderful stones, and what wonderful buildings!" And Jesus said to him, "Do you see these great buildings? There will not be left here one stone upon another, that will not be thrown down. . . . But when you see the abominable sacrilege set up where it ought not to be (let the

reader understand!), then let those who are in Judea flee to the
mountains (Mark 13:1–14).

This was exactly what had now happened. Others believed—and
some dared to say—that these very catastrophes occurred as an
angry God's punishment upon his own people for the crime of
rejecting their divinely sent Messiah.

In any case, Mark insists that Jesus' followers had no quarrel
with the Romans but with the Jewish leaders—the council of
elders, the Sanhedrin, along with the Jerusalem scribes and
priests—who had rejected God's Messiah. Mark says that these
leaders now have rejected Mark and his fellow believers, calling
them either insane or possessed by demons, the same charges
that they directed against Jesus himself.

Mark takes a conciliatory attitude toward the Romans,
although it was known that the Roman governor, Pontius Pilate,
had sentenced Jesus to death. Nevertheless, the two trial scenes
included in this gospel effectively indict the Jewish leaders for
Jesus' death, while somewhat exonerating the Romans. Mark virtually invents a new Pilate—a well-meaning weakling solicitous
of justice but, as Mark depicts him, intimidated by the chief
priests within his own council chamber and by crowds shouting
outside, so that he executes a man he suspects may be innocent.

Other first-century writers, Jewish and Roman, describe a very
different man. Even Josephus, despite his Roman sympathies,
says that the governor displayed contempt for his Jewish subjects, illegally appropriated funds from the Temple treasury, and
brutally suppressed unruly crowds.[18] Another contemporary
observer, Philo, a respected and influential member of the
Alexandrian Jewish community, describes Pilate as a man of
"ruthless, stubborn and cruel disposition," famous for, among
other things, ordering "frequent executions without trial."[19]

Mark's motives with regard to Pilate are not simple. Insofar as
he addresses his narrative to outsiders, Mark is eager to allay
Roman suspicions by showing that Jesus' followers are no threat
to Roman order, any more than Jesus himself had been. Mark
may also have wanted to convert Gentile readers. Yet Mark is pri-

marily interested in conflicts *within* the Jewish community—especially conflicts between his own group and those who reject its claims about Jesus.

Despite the hostility and suspicion he and his movement aroused among both Jews and Gentiles, including, of course, the Romans, Mark wrote to proclaim the "good news of Jesus of Nazareth, Messiah of Israel" (1:1). Yet Mark knows that to justify such claims about Jesus, he has to answer obvious objections. If Jesus had been sent as God's anointed king, how could the movement he initiated have failed so miserably? How could his followers have abandoned him and gone into hiding, while soldiers captured him like a common criminal? Why did virtually all his own people reject the claims about him—not only the townspeople in Galilee but also the crowds he attracted on his travels throughout Judea and in Jerusalem? And wasn't Jesus, after all, a seditionist himself, tainted in retrospect by association with the failed war, having been arrested and crucified as a rebel? Attempting to answer these questions, Mark places the events surrounding Jesus within the context not simply of the struggle against Rome but of the struggle between good and evil in the universe. The stark events of Jesus' life and death cannot be understood, he suggests, apart from the clash of supernatural forces that Mark sees being played out on earth in Jesus' lifetime. Mark intends to tell the story of Jesus in terms of its hidden, deeper dynamics—to tell it, so to speak, from *God's* point of view.

What happened, Mark says, is this: Jesus of Nazareth, after his baptism, was coming out of the water of the Jordan River when "he saw the heavens torn apart and the spirit descending like a dove on him" and heard a voice speaking to him from heaven (1:10–11). God's power anointed Jesus to challenge the forces of evil that now dominate the world, and drove him into direct conflict with those forces.[20] Mark frames his narrative at its beginning and at its climax with episodes in which Satan and his demonic forces retaliate against God by working to destroy Jesus. Mark begins by describing how the spirit of God descended upon Jesus at his baptism, and "immediately drove him into the wilderness, and he was in the wilderness forty days being tempted by Satan, and was with the animals, and the angels ministered to him" (1:12–13). From that moment on, Mark says, even after Jesus left the wilderness and returned to society, the powers of evil challenged and attacked him at every turn, and he attacked them back, and won. Matthew and Luke, writing some ten to twenty years later, adopted and elaborated this opening scenario. Each turns it into a drama of three temptations, that is, three increasingly intense confrontations between Satan and the spirit of God, acting through Jesus. Luke shows that the devil, defeated in these first attempts to overpower Jesus, withdraws "until an opportune time" (Luke 4:13). Luke then says what Mark and Matthew imply—that the devil returned in person in the form of Judas Iscariot to destroy Jesus, initiating the betrayal that led to his arrest and execution (Luke 22:3). All of the New Testament gospels, with considerable variation, depict Jesus' execution as the culmination of the struggle between good and evil—between God and Satan—that began at his baptism.

Satan, although he seldom appears onstage in these gospel accounts, nevertheless plays a central role in the divine drama, for the gospel writers realize that the story they have to tell would make little sense *without* Satan. How, after all, could anyone claim that a man betrayed by one of his own followers, and brutally executed on charges of treason against Rome, not only *was* but still *is* God's appointed Messiah, *unless* his capture and death were, as the gospels insist, not a final defeat but only a preliminary skirmish in a vast cosmic conflict now enveloping the universe? The final battle has not yet been fought, much less won, but it is imminent. As Jesus warns his interrogator at his trial, soon he will be vindicated when the "Son of man" returns in the clouds of heaven (Mark 14:62); here Mark has Jesus recall one of the prophet Daniel's visions, in which "one like a son of man" (that is, a human being), comes "with the clouds of heaven" and is made ruler of God's Kingdom (Dan. 7:13–14). Many of Mark's contemporaries would have read Daniel's prophecy as predicting the coming of a conqueror who would defeat Israel's foreign rulers.

While at first glance the gospel of Mark may look like historical biography, it is not so simple as this, for Mark does not intend to write history, as Josephus had, primarily to persuade people of the accuracy of his account of recent events and make them comprehensible on a human level. Instead Mark wants to show what these events mean for the future of the world, or, in the scholarly jargon, eschatologically. Mark and his colleagues combine a biographical form with themes of supernatural conflict borrowed from Jewish apocalyptic literature to create a new kind of narrative. These gospels carry their writers' powerful conviction that Jesus' execution, which had seemed to signal the victory of the forces of evil, actually heralds their ultimate annihilation and ensures God's final victory.[21]

Many liberal-minded Christians have preferred to ignore the presence of angels and demons in the gospels. Yet Mark intends their presence to address the anguished question that the events of the previous decades had aroused: How could God allow such death and destruction? For Mark and his fellows, the issue of divine justice involves, above all, the issue of human violence. The gospel writers want to locate and identify the specific ways in which the forces of evil act *through certain people* to effect violent destruction, above all, in Matthew's words, "the righteous blood shed on earth, from the blood of innocent Abel to the blood of Zechariah the son of Barachiah" (23:35)—violence epitomized in the execution of Jesus, which Matthew sees as the culmination of all evils. The subject of cosmic war serves primarily to interpret human relationships—especially all-too-human conflict—in supernatural form. The figure of Satan becomes, among other things, a way of characterizing one's actual enemies as the embodiment of transcendent forces. For many readers of the gospels ever since the first century, the thematic opposition between God's spirit and Satan has vindicated Jesus' followers and demonized their enemies.

But how does the figure of Satan characterize the enemy? What is Satan, and how does he appear on earth? The New Testament gospels almost never identify Satan with the Romans, but they consistently associate him with Jesus' Jewish enemies, primarily Judas Iscariot and the chief priests and scribes. By placing the story of Jesus in the context of cosmic war, the gospel writers expressed, in varying ways, their identification with the embattled minority of Jews who believed in Jesus, and their distress at what they saw as the apostasy of the majority of their fellow Jews in Jesus' time, as well as in their own. As we shall see, Jesus' followers did not *invent* the practice of demonizing enemies within their own group, although Christians (and Muslims after them) carried this practice further than their Jewish predecessors had taken it, and with enormous consequences.

Yet who actually *were* Jesus' enemies? What we know historically suggests that they were the Roman governor and his soldiers. The charge against Jesus and his execution were typically Roman. The Roman authorities, ever watchful for any hint of sedition, were ruthless in suppressing it. The historian Mary Smallwood observes that rounding up and killing troublemakers, especially those who ignited public demonstrations, was a routine measure for Roman forces stationed in Judea.[22] During the first century the Romans arrested and crucified thousands of Jews charged with sedition—often, Philo says, without trial. But as the gospels indicate, Jesus also had enemies among his fellow Jews, especially the Jerusalem priests and their influential allies, who were threatened by his activities.

The crucial point is this: *Had Jesus' followers identified themselves with the majority of Jews rather than with a particular minority, they might have told his story very differently—and with considerably more historical plausibility.* They might have told it, for example, in traditional patriotic style, as the story of an inspired Jewish holy man martyred by Israel's traditional enemies, foreign oppressors of one sort or another. The biblical book of Daniel, for example, which tells the story of the prophet Daniel, who, although threatened with a horrible death—being torn apart by lions—nevertheless defies the king of Babylon in the name of God and of the people of Israel (Dan. 6:1–28). The first book of Maccabees tells the story of the priest Mattathias, who defies Syrian soldiers when they order him to worship idols. Mattathias chooses to die rather than betray his devotion to God.[23]

But unlike the authors of Daniel or 1 Maccabees, the gospel writers chose to *dissociate* themselves from the Jewish majority and to focus instead upon intra-Jewish conflict—specifically upon their own quarrel with those who resisted their claims that Jesus was the Messiah. Within the gospels, as we shall see, the figure of Satan tends to express this dramatic shift of blame from "the nations"—*ha goyim*, in Hebrew—onto members of Jesus' own people. The variation in each gospel as it depicts the activity of the demonic opposition—that is, those perceived as enemies—expresses, I believe, a variety of relationships, often deeply ambivalent, between various groups of Jesus' followers and the specific Jewish groups each writer regards as his primary opponents. I want to avoid oversimplification. Nonetheless it is probably fair to say that in every case the decision to place the story of Jesus within the context of God's struggle against Satan tends to minimize the role of the Romans, and to place increasing blame instead upon Jesus' *Jewish* enemies.

This is not to say that the gospel writers simply intended to exonerate the Romans. Mark surely was aware that during his time, and for some thirty years after the war, the Romans remained wary of renewed sedition. Members of a group loyal to a condemned seditionist were at risk, and Mark probably hoped to persuade those outsiders who might read his account that neither Jesus nor his followers offered any threat to Roman order. But within Mark's account, the Romans, even the few portrayed with some sympathy, remain essentially outsiders. Mark tells the story of Jesus in the context that matters to him most—within the Jewish community. And here, as in most human situations, the more intimate the conflict, the more intense and bitter it becomes.

Mark opens his narrative with the account of John's baptizing Jesus and relates that at the moment of baptism the power of God descended upon Jesus, and "a voice spoke from heaven, saying 'This is my beloved son' " (1:11). At that moment, all human beings disappear from Mark's narrative and, as we have seen, the spirit of God drives Jesus into the wilderness to encounter Satan, wild animals, and angels. Recounting this episode, as James Robinson notes, Mark does not depart from events in the human, historical world but signals that he wants to relate these events to the struggle between good and evil in the universe.[24] Mark's account, then, moves directly from Jesus' solitary struggle with Satan in the desert to his first public appearance in the synagogue at Capernaum, where

> immediately on the Sabbath he entered the synagogue and taught. And they were astonished at his teaching, for he taught as one who had authority, and not as the scribes (1:22).

There Jesus encounters a man possessed by an evil spirit who, sensing Jesus' divine power, challenges him: "What have you to do with us, Jesus of Nazareth? Have you come to destroy us?" (1:24). According to Mark, Jesus has come to heal the world and reclaim it for God; in order to accomplish this, he must overcome the evil powers who have usurped authority over the world, and who now oppress human beings. So, Mark says,

> Jesus rebuked him, saying, "Be silent, and come out of him!" And the unclean spirit, convulsing him and crying with a loud voice, came out of him, and they were all amazed, so that they questioned among themselves, saying, "What is this? New teaching! With authority he commands even the unclean spirits, and they obey him." And at once his fame spread everywhere throughout all the surrounding region of Galilee (1:25–28).

Even in this first episode, the astonished crowds recognize that Jesus possesses a special authority, direct access to God's power. Jesus' power manifests itself especially in action, since Mark does not here record what Jesus taught. Even in this first public challenge to the forces of evil, Mark shows how Jesus' power sets him in contrast—and soon into direct conflict—with the scribes commonly revered as religious authorities. Mark's point is to demonstrate that, as he says, Jesus "taught as one who had authority, and not as the scribes" (1:22).

Throughout this opening chapter, Mark emphasizes that Jesus healed "many who were sick with various diseases" and "drove out many demons" (1:34). He traveled throughout Galilee "preaching in the synagogues and casting out demons," for, as he explains to Simon, Andrew, James, and John, who gather around him, "that is what I came to do" (1:38).

During his next public appearance, as Mark tells it, the scribes immediately took offense at what they considered his usurpation of divine authority. In this episode Jesus speaks to a crowd pressed together so tightly that when four men came carrying a paralyzed man,

> they could not get near him because of the crowd; so they removed the roof above him; and when they had made an opening, they let down the pallet on which the paralytic lay. And when Jesus saw their faith, he said to the paralytic, "My son, your sins are forgiven" (2:4–5).

By pronouncing forgiveness, Jesus claims the right to speak for God—a claim that, Mark says, angers the scribes:

> "Why does this man speak this way? It is blasphemy! Who can forgive sins but God alone?" (2:7).

According to Mark, Jesus, aware of the scribes' reaction, immediately performs a healing in order to *prove* his authority to his critics:

> And immediately Jesus, perceiving in his spirit that they thus questioned within themselves, said, "Why do you question thus in your hearts? . . . *But so that you may know that the Son of man has power on earth to forgive sins*"—he said to the paralytic—"I say to you, *rise, take your pallet, and go home*." And he rose, and immediately picked up his pallet and went out before them all, so that they were all astonished, . . . saying, "We never saw anything like this!" (2:8–12, emphasis added).

When Jesus first appeared proclaiming "Repent: the Kingdom of God is at hand!," he must have sounded to many of his contemporaries like one of the Essenes, who withdrew to the wilderness in protest against ordinary Jewish life. From the desert caves where they lived in monastic seclusion, the Essenes denounced the priestly aristocratic leaders in charge of the Jerusalem Temple—men like Josephus and those he admired—as being hopelessly corrupted by their accommodation to Gentile ways, and by collaboration with the Roman occupiers. The Essenes took the preaching of repentance and God's coming judgment to mean that Jews must separate themselves from such polluting influences and return to strict observance of God's law—especially the Sabbath and kosher laws that marked them off from the Gentiles as God's holy people.[25]

But if Jesus sounded like an Essene, his actions violated the standard of purity that Essenes held sacred. Instead of separating himself from people who polluted themselves by "walking in the ways of the Gentiles" (*Jubilees* 1:9), Jesus chose for one of his disciples a tax collector—a class that other Jews detested as profiteers who collaborated with the hated Romans. Indeed, Mark says, "There were many tax collectors who followed him" (2:15). Instead of fasting, like other devout Jews, Jesus ate and drank freely. And instead of scrupulously observing Sabbath laws, Jesus excused his disciples when they broke them:

> One Sabbath he was going through the grainfields; and as they made their way, his disciples began to pick ears of grain. And the Pharisees said to him, "Look, why are they doing what is not lawful on the Sabbath?" And he said to them, "Have you never read what David did, when he was in need and was hungry, he and those who were with him: how he entered the house of God . . . and ate the sacred bread, . . . and also gave it to those who were with him?" (2:23–26).

Here Jesus dares claim, as precedent for his disciples' apparently casual action, the prerogative of King David himself, who, with his men, broke the sacred food laws during a wartime emergency.

Claiming divine and royal power while simultaneously violating the purity laws, Jesus, at the beginning of his public activity, outrages virtually every party among his contemporaries, from the disciples of John the Baptist to the scribes and Pharisees.

The next time Jesus entered the synagogue on a Sabbath, Mark says,

> a man was there who had a withered hand. And they watched him, to see whether he would heal him on the Sabbath, so that they might accuse him. And he said to the man who had the withered hand, "Come here." And he said to them, "Is it lawful on the Sabbath to do good or to do harm, to save life or to kill?" But they were silent. And he looked around at them with anger, grieved at their hardness of heart, and said to the man, "Stretch out your hand." He stretched it out, and his hand was restored (3:1–5).

Instead of postponing the healing for a day, Jesus had chosen deliberately to defy his critics by performing it on the Sabbath. Seeing this, Mark says:

> The Pharisees went out, and immediately conspired against him with the Herodians [the party of King Herod], how they might kill him (3:6).

For Mark the secret meaning of such conflict is clear. Those who are offended and outraged by Jesus' actions do not know that Jesus is impelled by God's spirit to contend against the forces of evil, whether those forces manifest themselves in the invisible demonic presences who infect and possess people, or in his actual human opponents. When the Pharisees and Herodians conspire to kill Jesus, they themselves, Mark suggests, are acting as agents of evil. As Mark tells the story, Jesus has barely engaged Satan's power before his opponents "conspired . . . how they might kill him" (3:6).

Mark suggests that Jesus recognizes that the leaders who oppose him are energized by unseen forces. Immediately after this powerful coalition has united against him, Jesus retaliates by commissioning a new leadership group, "the twelve," presumably assigning one leader for each of the original twelve tribes of Israel. Jesus orders them to preach and gives them "power to cast out demons" (3:13).

This escalation of spiritual conflict immediately evokes escalating opposition—opposition that begins at home, within Jesus' own family. Mark says that when Jesus "went home . . . his family . . . went out to seize him, for they said, 'He is insane [or: beside himself]' " (3:21).[26] Next "the scribes who came down from Jerusalem" charge that Jesus himself "is possessed by Beelzebub; by the prince of demons he casts out demons" (3:22). Jesus objects:

> "How can Satan cast out Satan? If a kingdom is divided against itself, that kingdom cannot stand. And if a house is divided against itself, that house will not be able to stand. And if Satan has risen up against himself and is divided, he cannot stand, but is coming to an end. But no one can enter a strong man's house and plunder his goods unless he first binds the strong man; then indeed he may plunder his house" (3:23–27).

According to Mark, it is apparently the "house of Israel" that Jesus sees as a divided house, a divided kingdom. Jesus openly contends against Satan, who he believes has overtaken God's own household, which he has come to purify and reclaim: Jesus wants to "bind this enemy" and "plunder his house."

As for the scribes' accusation that Jesus is possessed by the "prince of demons," he throws back upon them the same accusation of demon-possession and warns that in saying this they are sinning so deeply as to seal their own damnation (3:28–30). For, he says, whoever attributes the work of God's spirit to Satan commits the one unforgivable sin:

> "Truly, I say to you, all sins will be forgiven to human beings, and whatever blasphemies they utter; but whoever blasphemes against the holy spirit is never forgiven, but is guilty of an eternal sin"—because they said, "He is possessed by an evil spirit" (3:28–30).

Mark deliberately places these scenes of Jesus' conflict with the scribes between two episodes depicting Jesus' conflict with his own family. Immediately after this, the Greek text of Mark says that members of the family, who had previously declared him insane and had tried to seize him (3:21), now come to the house where he is addressing a large crowd and ask to see him. Jesus repudiates them:

> And his mother and brothers came, and standing outside they sent to him, and called him. And a crowd was sitting about him, and they said to him, "Your mother and your brothers are outside, asking for you." And looking around at those who sat around him, he said, "Here are my mother and brothers! For whoever does the will of God is my brother, and sister, and mother" (3:31–35).

Having formed a new family, and having appointed twelve new leaders for Israel to replace the old ones, Jesus has, Mark suggests, "re-formed God's people." From this point on, Jesus sharply discriminates between those he has chosen, the inner circle, and "those outside." He still draws enormous crowds, but while teaching them, he offers riddling parables, deliberately concealing his full meaning from all but his intimates:

> Again he began to teach beside the sea. And a very large crowd gathered about him . . . and he taught them many things in parables. . . . And when he was alone, those who were around him with the twelve asked him about the parables. And he said to them, "*To you has been given the secret of the Kingdom of God, but for those outside everything is in parables; so that they may indeed see but not perceive; and they may hear but not understand; lest they should turn again, and be forgiven*" (4:1–12, emphasis added).

Although he often criticizes the disciples—in 8:33 he even accuses Peter of playing Satan's role—Jesus shares secrets with them that he hides from outsiders, for the latter, he says, quoting Isaiah, are afflicted with impenetrable spiritual blindness.[27]

Criticized by the Pharisees and the Jerusalem scribes for not living "according to the traditions of the elders" because he and his disciples eat without washing their hands, Jesus, instead of defending his action, attacks his critics as "hypocrites" and charges that they value their own traditions while breaking God's commandments. Then he publicly calls into question the kosher laws themselves—again explaining his meaning to his disciples alone:

> And he called the people to him again, and said to them, "Hear me, all of you, and understand; there is nothing outside a man which by going into him can defile him; but the things which come out of a man are what defile him." And when he had entered the house, and left the people, his disciples asked him about the parable. And he said to them, "Are you, too, without understanding? Do you not see that whatever goes into a man from outside cannot defile him, since it enters not his heart but his stomach, and so passes out of him? What comes out of a man is what defiles him; for from within, from the human heart, come evil thoughts, sexual immorality, theft, murder, . . . envy, pride, foolishness. . . . All these evils come from within" (7:14–23).

Here Mark wants to show that although Jesus discards traditional kosher ("purity") laws, he advocates instead purging the "heart"—that is, impulses, desires, and imagination.

Now that Jesus has alienated not only the scribes, Pharisees, and Herodians, but also his relatives and many of his own townspeople, he travels with his small band of disciples, preaching to the crowds. Anticipating what lies ahead of him in Jerusalem, where he will challenge the priestly party on its own ground, Jesus nevertheless resolutely leads his followers there, walking ahead of them, while "they were astonished, and those who followed were terrified" (10:32). On the way he tells the twelve exactly whom they are to blame for his impending death:

> "The chief priests and scribes . . . will condemn [the Son of man] to death, and hand him over to the nations, and they

will mock him and spit upon him, and scourge him and kill him" (10:33).

Opposition to Jesus intensifies after he enters Jerusalem. Having prepared a formal procession to go into the city, Jesus is openly acclaimed, in defiance of the Romans, as the man who comes to restore Israel's ancient empire: "Blessed is the kingdom of our father David that is coming!" Then, with his followers, he enters the great Temple and makes a shocking public demonstration there:

> He entered the Temple, and began to drive out those who sold and those who bought in the Temple, and he overturned the tables of the money changers and the seats of those who sold pigeons; and he would not allow anyone to carry anything through the Temple (11:15–16).

Now Jesus invokes the words of the prophets Isaiah and Jeremiah, as if to speak for the Lord himself against those who permit financial transactions in the Temple courtyard:

> And he taught, and said to them, "Is it not written, 'My house shall be called a house of prayer for all the nations'? But you have made it a den of robbers." But the chief priests and the scribes heard it, and sought a way to destroy him, for they were afraid of him, because the whole crowd was astonished at his teaching (11:17–18).

When the chief priests and scribes, joined by members of the Jewish council, demand to know by what authority he acts, Jesus refuses to answer. Instead he retells Isaiah's parable of God's wrath against Israel (12:1–12) in a way so transparent that even the chief priests, scribes, and elders recognize that he is telling it "against them" (12:12). The following scenes show Jesus contending first against the Pharisees and Herodians, who fail to trick him into making anti-Roman statements (12:13–15), and then against the scribes (12:35). Finally he warns a great crowd:

> Beware of the scribes, who like to go around in long robes, and
> to have salutations in the marketplaces, and the best seats in
> the synagogues, and the places of honor at feasts, who devour
> widows' houses and for a pretense make long prayers. They
> will receive the greater condemnation (12:38–40).

Then, as Jesus comes out of the Temple, Mark says, he
responds to his disciples' awestruck admiration for the sacred
precincts by predicting the Temple's destruction: "There will not
be left one stone upon another, that will not be thrown down"
(13:2). When Peter, James, John, and Andrew privately ask what
he means, Jesus sits with them on the Mount of Olives opposite
the Temple and explains. He predicts a series of horrifying catastrophes (these are events in which Mark's contemporaries would
recognize their own times, especially the events of the war
between 66 and 70): "wars and rumors of war," famine, public
enthusiasm for false messiahs. Jesus warns in veiled language that
when they see "the desolating sacrilege set up where it ought not
to be"—the pagan desecration of the Temple—they should flee
into the mountains (13:7–14).

Mark intends Jesus' followers, living in terrible times, to take
comfort in knowing that their leader had foreseen how they
would suffer, out of their loyalty to him ("for my sake"),
ostracism and reprisals, hatred and betrayal, even—perhaps especially—from their family members:

> "Take heed to yourselves; for they will deliver you up to coun-
> cils; and you will be beaten in synagogues, and you will stand
> before governors and rulers for my sake . . . and brother will
> deliver up brother to death, and the father his child, and chil-
> dren will rise against parents and have their parents put to
> death; and you will be hated by all for the sake of my name
> (13:9–13).

What is the believer to do, facing betrayal, isolation, and mortal danger? Mark says that Jesus enjoined his followers to
"endure to the end." Now Mark has to tell how Jesus himself

"endured to the end," through arrest, trials in both Jewish and Roman courts, torture, and execution, thus giving his endangered followers an example of how to endure. Two days before Passover, Mark says, "the chief priests and the scribes were seeking how to arrest Jesus secretly and kill him, for they said, 'Not during the festival, lest there be a tumult among the people,' " since so far the people remained on Jesus' side. Shortly afterward, Judas Iscariot, obviously aware of the hostility his master had aroused among influential people, "went to the chief priests in order to betray [Jesus] to them, and when they heard it they were glad, and offered him money" (14:1–11).

At night, Mark says, Judas led "a crowd with swords and clubs from the chief priests and the scribes and Temple officers" to Gethsemane, a garden on the Mount of Olives, to capture Jesus. One of his men fought back with a sword, injuring the high priest's slave, and Jesus protested at being treated "like a robber" (the term that Josephus and others commonly use to characterize an "insurrectionist"). But the rest of his followers abandoned him and fled; Jesus was taken. The armed men "brought him to the high priest," apparently to his residence. Although the Sanhedrin traditionally was not allowed to meet at night, Mark tells us that on the night of Jesus' arrest, "all the chief priests and the elders and the scribes were assembled" at the high priest's residence to try his case in a formal proceeding.

Now Mark presents the first of two trial scenes—the "trial before the Sanhedrin," which he follows with the "trial before Pilate." Most scholars assume that even if these events occurred, Jesus' followers could not have witnessed what went on at either his appearance before the Jewish council or his arraignment by the Romans.[28] But Mark is not concerned with reporting history. By introducing these scenes, Mark wants to show above all that the well-known charge against Jesus—sedition—not only was false but was invented by Jesus' *Jewish* enemies; further, Mark says, the Roman governor himself realized this and tried in vain to save Jesus! According to Mark, the Sanhedrin had already prejudged the case. The trial was only a pretense in order "to put him to death" (14:55). After hearing a series of trumped-up charges and lying witnesses, some accusing Jesus of having threatened to destroy the Temple, the chief priest interrogates Jesus, demanding that he answer the charges against him. Jesus, however, remains silent. Finally the chief priest asks, "Are you the Messiah, the son of the Blessed One?" (14:61). Here, for the first time in Mark's gospel, Jesus publicly admits his divine identity to people other than his disciples, and goes on to warn his accusers that they will soon witness his vindication: "I am; and you will see the Son of man sitting at the right hand of power and coming with the clouds of heaven" (14:62). Then, Mark continues, the high priest, tearing his robe, says, " 'You have heard his blasphemy. What is your decision?' And they all condemned him as deserving death" (14:64).

Many scholars have commented on the historical implausibility of this account.[29] Did the Sanhedrin conduct a trial that violated its own legal practices concerning examining witnesses, self-incrimination, courtroom procedure, and sentencing? Although we know little about Sanhedrin procedures during Jesus' time,[30] did this council actually assemble at night, contrary to what seems to have been its precedent? If so, why does Mark go on to add a *second* version of the council meeting to discuss this case—a meeting that takes place the following morning, as if nothing had happened the night before? For after Mark ends his first, more elaborate account, he lets slip what now becomes a redundancy: that "as soon as it was morning the chief priests, with the elders and scribes, and the whole council, held a consultation, and they bound Jesus, and led him away, and delivered him to Pilate" (15:1).

We cannot, of course, know what actually happened, but Mark's second version, which agrees with Luke's, sounds more likely—that the council convened in the morning, and decided that the prisoner should be kept in custody and turned over to Pilate to face charges.[31] The gospel of John, relying upon a source independent of Mark's, offers another reconstructed account that gives a plausible interpretation of these events.[32] According to John, the chief priests, alarmed by the crowds Jesus attracted, feared that his presence in Jerusalem during Passover might ignite public demonstrations, "and the Romans will come and destroy our holy place and our nation" (11:48). The civil strife that preceded the Jewish war, as John and his contemporaries well knew, had verified the accuracy of such concerns about possible Roman reprisals.

Many New Testament scholars who have analyzed the account of Jesus' appearance before the Sanhedrin agree that Mark (or his predecessors) probably wrote the first version to emphasize his primary point: that Pilate merely ratified a previous Jewish verdict, and carried out a death sentence that he himself neither ordered nor approved—but a sentence unanimously pronounced by the entire leadership of the Jewish people.[33]

This does not mean, however, that Mark is motivated by malice toward the Jewish leaders. Indeed, Mark stops far short of the extent to which Matthew, Luke, and John will go to blame the Jewish leaders for the crucifixion, although the tendency to blame them had already begun before Mark's time and had its effect on his narrative. Nevertheless, Mark and his fellow believers, as followers of a convicted criminal, knew that such allegiance would arouse suspicion and invite reprisals. Roman magistrates had already arrested and executed several prominent members of the movement, including Peter and Paul. It is no wonder, then, that, as one historian says, Mark wanted

> to emphasize the culpability of the Jewish nation for the death of Jesus, particularly of its leaders. . . . [Mark's] tendency was defensive rather than aggressive. He was concerned to avoid mentioning anything that would provoke Roman antagonism towards, or even suspicion of, the ideals for which he stood. . . . The evangelist therefore contrived to conceal that Jesus had been condemned and executed on a charge of sedition.[34]

Mark's account also involves an important positive motive. Mark intends the "trial before the Sanhedrin" to mirror the precarious situation in which he and his fellow believers now stand in relation to leaders of the Jewish communities during and after the war.[35] In this account of Jesus' courage before his judges, Mark offers Jesus' followers a model of how to act when they too are put on trial.

Mark weaves into this account a contrapuntal story—the story of Jesus' chief disciple, Peter, who, in terror, denies Jesus, an example of how *not* to act when on trial. For whereas Jesus stands up to the Sanhedrin and confesses his divine mission, boldly risking—and accepting—the death sentence, Peter claims not to have known Jesus. Having surreptitiously followed Jesus to the scene of the trial, Mark says, Peter stood warming his hands by the fire when one of the household servants said to him, "You, too, were with the Nazarene, Jesus" (14:67). But Peter denies this ("I do not know what you mean; . . . I do not know the man") three times, with increasing vehemence, cursing and swearing, and finally escapes. After recognizing what he has done, Peter "broke down and wept" (14:72).

Mark knows that those who publicly confess their conviction that Jesus is "the Messiah, the Son of God" (14:61) may put themselves in danger of abuse, ridicule, even threats to their lives. The terms *Messiah* and *Son of God* would probably have been anachronistic during the time of Jesus; but many of Mark's contemporaries must have recognized them as the way Christians of their own time confessed their faith. In this dramatic scene, then, Mark again confronts his audience with the question that pervades his entire narrative: Who recognizes the spirit in Jesus as divine, and who does not? Who stands on God's side, and who on Satan's? By contrasting Jesus' courageous confession with Peter's denial, Mark draws a dramatic picture of the choice confronting Jesus' followers: they must take sides in a war that allows no neutral ground.

Having tried to show that the whole affair concerning Jesus was essentially an internal Jewish conflict that got out of hand, Mark now offers his version of Jesus' "trial before Pilate." Many scholars think that all Mark actually knew was that Jesus had been crucified as a would-be king of the Jews during Pilate's administration as governor of Judea. While he takes account of this indisputable fact, Mark intends to minimize its significance.

Consider, then, how Mark tells the story. Pilate, apprised that the prisoner was accused of political insurgency, attempts to interrogate him. "Have you no answer to make? See how many charges they make against you" (15:4). Mark says that when Jesus refused to answer his questions, Pilate, instead of demonstrating anger or even impatience, "was amazed" (15:5). Mark goes further. Claiming to know the governor's private assessment of the case, Mark says that Pilate "recognized that it was out of envy that they had handed him over" (15:10). But instead of making a decision and giving orders, Pilate takes no action. Then, hearing shouts from the crowd outside, he goes out to address them, asking what they want: "Do you want me to release for you the king of the Jews?" But the crowd demands instead the release of Barabbas, whom Mark describes as one of the imprisoned insurrectionists, who "had committed murder in the rebellion" (15:7). Pilate seems uncertain, wanting to refuse but afraid to go against the crowd's demand. As if helpless, he again asks the crowd what to do: "What shall I do with the man whom you call the king of the Jews?" (15:12). When the crowd shouts for Jesus' crucifixion, Pilate in effect pleads with his subjects for justice: "Why, what evil has he done?" (15:14). But the shouting continues, and Pilate, "wishing to satisfy the crowd" (15:15), releases Barabbas and, having ordered Jesus to be flogged, acquiesces to their demand that he be crucified. But according to Mark, Pilate never pronounces sentence, and never actually orders the execution. As Mark tells the story, even inside Pilate's own chamber, the chief priests are in charge: it is they who make accusations and it is they who stir up the crowds, whose vehemence forces Jesus' execution upon a reluctant Pilate.

The Pilate who appears in the gospels, as we have noted, has little to do with the historical Pilate—that is, with the man we know from other first-century historical and political sources, both Jewish and Roman, as a brutal governor. As Raymond Brown notes in his meticulous study of the passion narratives, except in Christian tradition, portraits of Pilate range from bitterly hostile to negative.[36] Philo, an educated, influential member of the Jewish community in Alexandria, the capital of Egypt, was

Pilate's contemporary. In one of his writings, his *Embassy to Gaius,* he describes his experiences as a member of an official delegation sent to Rome to represent the interests of the Alexandrian Jewish community to the Roman emperor, Gaius Caligula. In the course of his narrative, Philo, referring to the situation of the Jewish community in Judea, describes governor Pilate as a man of "inflexible, stubborn, and cruel disposition," and lists as typical features of his administration "greed, violence, robbery, assault, abusive behavior, frequent executions without trial, and endless savage ferocity."[37] Philo writes to persuade Roman rulers to uphold the privileges of Jewish communities, as he claims that the emperor Tiberius had done. In this letter, Philo sees Pilate as the image of all that can go wrong with Roman administration of Jewish provinces.

Philo's testimony is partly corroborated in Josephus's history of the same era. As we have seen, Josephus, like Philo, was a man of considerable political experience; as former Jewish governor of Galilee under the Romans, he writes his history under Roman patronage in a tone sympathetic to Roman interests. Yet Josephus records several episodes that show Pilate's contempt for Jewish religious sensibilities. Pilate's predecessors, for example, recognizing that Jews considered images of the emperor to be idolatrous, had instituted the practice of choosing for the Roman garrison in Jerusalem a military unit whose standards did not carry such images. But when Pilate was appointed governor he deliberately violated this precedent. First he ordered the existing garrison to leave; then he led to Jerusalem a replacement unit whose standards displayed imperial images, timing his arrival to coincide with the Jewish high holy days, the Day of Atonement and the Feast of Tabernacles. Pilate apparently knew that he was committing sacrilege in the eyes of his subjects, for he took care to arrive in Jerusalem at night, having ordered the standards to be covered with cloth during the journey.

When the people of Jerusalem heard that Pilate and his troops had introduced images they regarded as idolatrous into the holy city, they gathered in the streets to protest. A great crowd followed Pilate back to Caesarea and stood outside his residence, pleading with him to remove them. Since the standards always accompanied the military unit, this amounted to a demand that Pilate withdraw the garrison. When Pilate refused, the crowds continued to demonstrate. After five days, Pilate, exasperated but adamant, decided to force an end to the demonstrations. Pretending to offer the demonstrators a formal hearing, he summoned them to appear before him in the stadium. There Pilate had amassed soldiers, ordered them to surround the crowd, and threatened to massacre the demonstrators unless they gave in. To Pilate's surprise, the Jews declared that they would rather die than see their law violated. At this point Pilate capitulated and withdrew the unit. As Mary Smallwood comments:

> The Jews had won a decisive victory in the first round against their new governor, but now they knew what sort of man they were up against, and thereafter anything he did was liable to be suspect. . . . But more was to follow.[38]

Roman authorities also respected Jewish sensitivity by banning images considered idolatrous from coins minted in Judea. Only during Pilate's administration was this practice violated: coins depicting pagan cult symbols have been found dated 29–31 C.E. Did Pilate order the change, as the German scholar E. Stauffer believes, "to force [his] subjects to handle representations of pagan culture"?[39] Raymond Brown suggests that Pilate simply "underestimated Jewish sensitivity" on such matters.[40]

Pilate next decided to build an aqueduct in Jerusalem. But to finance the project, he appropriated money from the Temple treasury, an act of sacrilege even from the Roman point of view, since the Temple funds were, by law, regarded as sacrosanct.[41] This direct assault upon the Temple and its treasury aroused vehement opposition. When Pilate next visited Jerusalem, he was met with larger demonstrations than ever; now the angry crowds became abusive and threatening. Anticipating trouble, Pilate had ordered soldiers to dress in plain clothes, conceal their weapons, and mingle with the people. When the crowd refused to disperse, he signaled to the soldiers to break it up with force. Several people were killed, and others were trampled to death in the stampede that followed.[42] Even the gospel of Luke, which gives an astonishingly benign portrait of Pilate in the trial narrative, elsewhere mentions how people told Jesus about certain Galileans "whose blood Pilate mingled with their sacrifices" (13:1).

Late in Pilate's tenure as governor other provocative incidents prompted Jewish leaders to protest to the emperor Tiberius against Pilate's attacks on their religion. In 31 C.E. Pilate angered his subjects by dedicating golden shields in the Herodian palace in Jerusalem. We cannot be certain what occasioned the protest; the scholar B. C. McGinny suggests that the shields were dedicated to the "divine" emperor, a description that would have incensed many Jews.[43] Again Pilate faced popular protest: a crowd assembled, led by four Herodian princes. When Pilate refused to remove the shields, perhaps claiming he was acting only out of respect for the emperor, Josephus says, they replied, "Do not take [the emperor] Tiberius as your pretext for outraging the nation; he does not wish any of our customs to be overthrown."[44] When Pilate proved adamant, the Jewish princes appealed to the emperor, who rebuked Pilate and ordered him to remove the shields from Jerusalem. One recent commentator remarks that

> the bullying of Pilate by his Jewish adversaries in the case of the shields resembles strongly the bullying of Pilate in [the gospel of] John's account of the passion, including the threat of appeal to the emperor.[45]

Yet characterizing these protests as "bullying" seems strange; what recourse did a subject people have to challenge the governor's decision, except to appeal over his head to a higher authority? Five years later, when a Samaritan leader assembled a large multitude, some of them armed, to gather and wait for a sign from God, Pilate immediately sent troops to monitor the situation. The troops blockaded the crowd, killing some and capturing others, while the rest fled. Pilate ordered the ringleaders executed.[46]

Pilate's rule ended abruptly when the legate of Syria finally responded to repeated protests by stripping Pilate of his commission and dispatching a man from his own staff to serve as governor in his place. Pilate was ordered to return to Rome at once to answer charges against him, and disappeared from the historical record. Philo's account coincides with Mark's on one point: that Pilate, aware of the animosity toward him, was concerned lest the chief priests complain about him to the emperor. Yet Mark, as we have seen, presents a Pilate not only as a man too weak to withstand the shouting of a crowd, but also as one solicitous to ensure justice in the case of a Jewish prisoner whom the Jewish leaders want to destroy.

Mark's benign portrait of Pilate increases the culpability of the Jewish leaders and supports Mark's contention that Jews, not Romans, were the primary force behind Jesus' crucifixion. Throughout the following decades, as bitterness between the Jewish majority and Jesus' followers increased, the gospels came to depict Pilate in an increasingly favorable light. As Paul Winter observes,

> the stern Pilate grows more mellow from gospel to gospel [from Mark to Matthew, from Matthew and Luke to John]. . . . The more removed from history, the more sympathetic a character he becomes.[47]

In depicting Jesus' Jewish enemies, the same process works in reverse. Matthew, writing around ten years later, depicts much greater antagonism between Jesus and the Pharisees than Mark suggests. And while Mark says that the leaders restrained their animosity because the crowds favored Jesus, Matthew's account ends with both leaders *and* crowds unanimously shouting for his execution. Furthermore, what Mark merely implies—that Jesus' opponents are energized by Satan—Luke and John will state explicitly. Both Matthew and Luke, writing ten to twenty years after Mark, adapted the earlier gospel and revised it in various ways, updating it to reflect the situation of Jesus' followers in their own times.

Jesus' followers did not invent the practice of demonizing enemies within their own group. In this respect, as in many others, as
we shall see, they drew upon traditions they shared with other
first-century Jewish sects. The Essenes, for example, had developed and elaborated images of an evil power they called by many
names—Satan, Belial, Beelzebub, Mastema ("hatred")—precisely
to characterize their own struggle against a Jewish majority whom
they, for reasons different from those of Jesus' followers,
denounced as apostate. The Essenes never admitted Gentiles to
their movement. But the followers of Jesus did—cautiously and
provisionally at first, and against the wishes of some members. But
as the Christian movement became increasingly Gentile during
the second century and later, the identification of Satan primarily
with the Jewish enemies of Jesus, borne along in Christian tradition over the centuries, would fuel the fires of anti-Semitism.

The relationship between Jesus' followers and the rest of the
Jewish community, however, especially during the first century, is
anything but simple. Mark himself, like the Essenes, sees his
movement essentially as a conflict within one "house"—as I read
it, the house of Israel. Such religious reformers see their primary
struggle not with foreigners, however ominously Roman power
lurks in the background, but with other Jews who try to define
the "people of God."[48] Yet while Mark sees the Jewish leaders as
doing Satan's work in trying to destroy Jesus, his own account is
by no means anti-Jewish, much less anti-Semitic. After all, virtually everyone who appears in the account is Jewish, including, of
course, the Messiah. Mark does not see himself as separate from
Israel, but depicts Jesus' followers as what Isaiah calls God's
"remnant" *within Israel* (Isaiah 10:22–23). Even the images that
Mark invokes to characterize the majority—images of Satan,
Beelzebub, and the devil—paradoxically express the *intimacy* of
Mark's relationship with the Jewish community as a whole, for,
as we shall see, the figure of Satan, as it emerged over the centuries in Jewish tradition, is not a hostile power assailing Israel
from without, but the source and representation of conflict
within the community.

THE SOCIAL HISTORY OF SATAN:
FROM THE HEBREW BIBLE
TO THE GOSPELS

The conflict between Jesus' followers and their fellow Jews is not, of course, the first sectarian movement that divided the Jewish world, a world whose early history we know primarily from the Hebrew Bible, a collection of authoritative law, prophets, psalms, and other writings assembled centuries before the four gospels and other Christian writings were brought together in the New Testament. Who assembled this collection we do not know, but we may infer from its contents that it was compiled to constitute the religious history of the Jewish people, and so to create the basis for a unified society.[1]

Excluded from the Hebrew Bible were writings of Jewish sectarians, apparently because such authors tended to identify with one group of Jews against another, rather than with Israel as a whole. Christians later came to call the writings of such dissidents from the main group the *apocrypha* (literally, "hidden things") and *pseudepigrapha* ("false writings").[2]

But the writings collected to form the Hebrew Bible encourage identification with Israel itself. According to the foundation story recounted in Genesis 12, Israel first received its identity through election, when "the Lord" suddenly revealed himself to Abraham, ordering him to leave his home country, his family, and his ancestral gods, and promising him, in exchange for exclusive loyalty, a new national heritage, with a new identity:

"I will make you a great nation, and I will make your name
great . . . and whoever blesses you I will bless; and whoever
curses you I will curse" (Gen. 12:3).

So when God promises to make Abraham the father of a new,
great, and blessed nation, he simultaneously defines and constitutes its enemies as inferior and potentially accursed.

From the beginning, then, Israelite tradition defines "us" in
ethnic, political, and religious terms as "the people of Israel," or
"the people of God," as against "them"—the (other) nations (in
Hebrew, *ha goyim*), the alien enemies of Israel, often characterized as inferior, morally depraved, even potentially accursed. In
Genesis 16:12, an angel predicts that Ishmael, although he was
Abraham's son, the progenitor of the Arab people, would be a
"wild ass of a man, with his hand against everyone, and everyone's hand against him; and he shall live at odds with all his kin."
The story implies that his descendants, too, are hostile, no better
than animals. Genesis 19:37–38 adds that the Moabite and
Ammonite nations are descended from Lot's daughters, which
means that they are the illegitimate offspring of a drunken and
incestuous union. The people of Sodom, although they are Abraham's allies, not his enemies, are said to be criminally depraved,
"young and old, down to the last man," collectively guilty of
attempting to commit homosexual rape against a party of angels,
seen by the townspeople as defenseless Hebrew travelers (Gen.
19:4). These accounts do not idealize Abraham or his progeny—
in fact, the biblical narrator twice tells how the self-serving lies of
Abraham and Isaac endangered their allies (Gen. 20:1–18;
26:6–10). Nevertheless, God ensures that everything turns out
well for the Israelites and badly for their enemies.

The second great foundation story is that of Moses and the
Exodus, which also confronts "us" (that is, "Israel") with
"them" (that is, "the nations") as Moses urges Pharaoh to let the
Hebrews leave Egypt. Yet the narrator insists that it was God
himself who increasingly hardened Pharaoh's heart, lest he relent
and relieve the suffering of Moses and his own people—and why?
God, speaking through Moses, threatens Pharaoh with devastat-

ing slaughter and concludes by declaring, "but against any of the Israelites, not a dog shall growl—*so that you may know that the Lord makes a distinction between the Egyptians and Israel.*" (Exod. 11:7; my emphasis).

Many anthropologists have pointed out that the worldview of most peoples consists essentially of two pairs of binary oppositions: human/not human and we/they.[3] Apart from anthropology, we know from experience how people dehumanize enemies, especially in wartime.

That Israel's traditions deprecate the nations, then, is no surprise. What is surprising is that there are exceptions. Hebrew tradition sometimes reveals a sense of universalism where one might least expect it. Even God's election of Abraham and his progeny includes the promise of a blessing to extend through them to all people, for that famous passage concludes with the words, "in you all the families of the earth shall be blessed" (Gen. 12:3). Furthermore, when a stranger appears alone, the Israelites typically accord him protection, precisely because they identify with the solitary and defenseless stranger. Biblical law identifies with the solitary alien: "You shall not wrong or oppress a stranger; for you were strangers in the land of Egypt" (Exod. 22:21). One of the earliest creeds of Israel recalls that Abraham himself, obeying God's command, became a solitary alien: "A wandering Aramean was my father . . ." (Deut. 26:5). Moses, too, was the quintessential alien, having been adopted as an infant by Pharaoh's daughter. Although a Hebrew, he was raised as an Egyptian; the family of his future in-laws, in fact, mistook him for an Egyptian when they first met him. He even named his first son Gershom ("a wanderer there"), saying, "I have been a wanderer in a foreign land" (Exod. 2:16–22).

Nevertheless, the Israelites are often aggressively hostile to the nations. The prophet Isaiah, writing in wartime, predicts that the Lord will drive the nations out "like locusts" before the Israelite armies (Isa. 40:22). This hostility to the alien enemy seems to have prevailed relatively unchallenged as long as Israel's empire was expanding and the Israelites were winning their wars against the nations. Psalms 18 and 41, attributed to King David, builder of Israel's greatest empire, declare, "God gave me vengeance and subdued the nations under me" (Ps. 18:47), and "By this I know that God is pleased with me—in that my enemy has not triumphed over me" (Ps. 41:11).

Yet at certain points in Israel's history, especially in times of crisis, war, and danger, a vociferous minority spoke out, not against the alien tribes and foreign armies ranged against Israel, but to blame Israel's misfortunes upon members of its own people. Such critics, sometimes accusing Israel as a whole, and sometimes accusing certain rulers, claimed that Israel's disobedience to God had brought down divine punishment.

The party that called for Israel's allegiance to "the Lord alone," including such prophets as Amos (c. 750 B.C.E.), Isaiah (c. 730 B.C.E.), and Jeremiah (c. 600 B.C.E.), indicted especially those Israelites who adopted foreign ways, particularly the worship of foreign gods.[4] Such prophets, along with their supporters, thought of Israel as a truly separate people, "holy to the Lord." The more radical prophets denounced those Israelites who tended toward assimilation as if they were as bad as the nations; only a remnant, they said, remained faithful to God.

Certain of these prophets, too, had called forth the monsters of Canaanite mythology to symbolize Israel's enemies.[5] Later (sixth century) material now included in the first part of the book of the prophet Isaiah proclaims that "the Lord is coming *to punish the inhabitants of the earth;* and the earth will disclose the blood shed upon her, and will no more cover the slain" (Isa. 26:21; emphasis added). The same author goes on, apparently in parallel imagery, to warn that "in that day, the Lord with his great hand will *punish the Leviathan, the twisting serpent, and he will slay the dragon that is in the sea*" (Isa. 27:1; emphasis added). The author of the second part of Isaiah also celebrates God's triumph over traditional mythological figures—over Rahab, "the dragon," and "the sea"—as he proclaims God's imminent triumph over Israel's enemies. Thereby, as the biblical scholar Jon Levenson observes, "the enemies cease to be merely earthly powers . . . and become, instead or in addition, cosmic forces of the utmost malignancy."[6]

Certain writers of the sixth century B.C.E. took a bold step further. They used mythological imagery to characterize their struggle against some of their fellow Israelites. But when Israelite
writers excoriated their fellow Jews in mythological terms, the
images they chose were usually not the animalistic or monstrous
ones they regularly applied to their foreign enemies. Instead of
Rahab, Leviathan, or "the dragon," most often they identified
their Jewish enemies with an exalted, if treacherous, member of
the divine court whom they called the *satan*. The *satan* is not an
animal or monster but one of God's angels, a being of superior
intelligence and status; apparently the Israelites saw their intimate enemies not as beasts and monsters but as *superhuman*
beings whose superior qualities and insider status could make
them more dangerous than the alien enemy.

In the Hebrew Bible, as in mainstream Judaism to this day,
Satan never appears as Western Christendom has come to know
him, as the leader of an "evil empire," an army of hostile spirits
who make war on God and humankind alike.[7] As he first appears
in the Hebrew Bible, Satan is not necessarily evil, much less
opposed to God. On the contrary, he appears in the book of
Numbers and in Job as one of God's obedient servants—a messenger, or *angel,* a word that translates the Hebrew term for messenger (*mal'āk*) into Greek (*angelos*). In Hebrew, the angels were
often called "sons of God" (*benē 'elōhīm*), and were envisioned as
the hierarchical ranks of a great army, or the staff of a royal court.

In biblical sources the Hebrew term the *satan* describes an
adversarial role. It is not the name of a particular character.[8]
Although Hebrew storytellers as early as the sixth century B.C.E.
occasionally introduced a supernatural character whom they
called the *satan,* what they meant was any one of the angels sent
by God for the specific purpose of blocking or obstructing
human activity. The root *śṭn* means "one who opposes,
obstructs, or acts as adversary." (The Greek term *diabolos,* later
translated "devil," literally means "one who throws something
across one's path.")

The *satan*'s presence in a story could help account for unexpected obstacles or reversals of fortune. Hebrew storytellers

often attribute misfortunes to human sin. Some, however, also invoke this supernatural character, the *satan,* who, by God's own order or permission, blocks or opposes human plans and desires. But this messenger is not necessarily malevolent. God sends him, like the angel of death, to perform a specific task, although one that human beings may not appreciate; as the literary scholar Neil Forsyth says of the *satan,* "If the path is bad, an obstruction is good."[9] Thus the *satan* may simply have been sent by the Lord to protect a person from worse harm. The story of Balaam in the biblical book of Numbers, for example, tells of a man who decided to go where God had ordered him not to go. Balaam saddled his ass and set off, "but God's anger was kindled because he went; and the angel of the Lord took his stand in the road as his *satan*" [*le-śāṭān-lō*]—that is, as his adversary, or his obstructor. This supernatural messenger remained invisible to Balaam, but the ass saw him and stopped in her tracks:

> And the ass saw the angel of the Lord standing in the road, with a drawn sword in his hand; and the ass turned aside out of the road, and went into the field; and Balaam struck the ass, to turn her onto the road. Then the angel of the Lord stood in a narrow path between the vineyards, with a wall on each side. And when the ass saw the angel of the Lord, she pushed against the wall, so he struck her again (22:23–25).

The third time the ass saw the obstructing angel, she stopped and lay down under Balaam, "and Balaam's anger was kindled, and he struck the ass with his staff." Then, the story continues,

> the Lord opened the mouth of the ass, and she said to Balaam, "What have I done to you, that you have struck me three times?" And Balaam said to the ass, "Because you have made a fool of me. I wish I had a sword in my hand, for then I would kill you." And the ass said to Balaam, "Am I not your asṣ, that you have ridden all your life to this very day? Did I ever do such things to you?" And he said, "No" (22:28–30).

Then "the Lord opened the eyes of Balaam, and he saw the angel of the Lord standing in the way, with his drawn sword in his hand, and he bowed his head, and fell on his face." Then the *satan* rebukes Balaam, and speaks for his master, the Lord:

> "Why have you struck your ass three times? Behold, I came here to oppose you, because your way is evil in my eyes; and the ass saw me. . . . If she had not turned away from me, I would surely have killed you right then, and let her live" (22:31–33).

Chastened by this terrifying vision, Balaam agrees to do what God, speaking through his *satan*, commands.

The book of Job, too, describes the *satan* as a supernatural messenger, a member of God's royal court.[10] But while Balaam's *satan* protects him from harm, Job's *satan* takes a more adversarial role. Here the Lord himself admits that the *satan* incited him to act *against* Job (2:3). The story begins when the *satan* appears as an angel, a "son of God" (*ben 'elōhīm*), a term that, in Hebrew idiom, often means "one of the divine beings." Here this angel, the *satan,* comes with the rest of the heavenly host on the day appointed for them to "present themselves before the Lord." When the Lord asks whence he comes, the *satan* answers, "From roaming on the earth, and walking up and down on it." Here the storyteller plays on the similarity between the sound of the Hebrew *satan* and *shût,* the Hebrew word "to roam," suggesting that the *satan*'s special role in the heavenly court is that of a kind of roving intelligence agent, like those whom many Jews of the time would have known—and detested—from the king of Persia's elaborate system of secret police and intelligence officers. Known as "the king's eye" or "the king's ear," these agents roamed the empire looking for signs of disloyalty among the people.[11]

God boasts to the *satan* about one of his most loyal subjects: "Have you considered my servant Job, that there is no one like him on earth, a blessed and upright man, who fears God and turns away from evil?" The *satan* then challenges the Lord to put Job to the test:

"Does Job fear God for nothing? . . . You have blessed the work of his hands, and his possessions have increased. But put forth your hand now, and touch all that he has, and he will curse you to your face" (1:9–11).

The Lord agrees to test Job, authorizing the *satan* to afflict Job with devastating loss, but defining precisely how far he may go: "Behold, all that belongs to him is in your power; only do not touch the man himself." Job withstands the first deadly onslaught, the sudden loss of his sons and daughters in a single accident, the slaughter of his cattle, sheep, and camels, and the loss of all his wealth and property. When the *satan* appears again among the sons of God on the appointed day, the Lord points out that "Job still holds fast to his integrity, although you incited me against him, to harm him without cause." Then the *satan* asks that he increase the pressure:

"Skin for skin. All that a man has he will give for his life. But put forth your hand now, and touch his flesh and his bone, and he will curse you to your face." And the Lord said to the *satan,* "Behold, he is in your power; only spare his life" (2:4–6).

According to the folktale, Job withstands the test, the *satan* retreats, and "the Lord restored the fortunes of Job . . . and he gave him twice as much as he had before" (42:10). Here the *satan* terrifies and harms a person but, like the angel of death, remains an angel, a member of the heavenly court, God's obedient servant.

Around the time Job was written (c. 550 B.C.E.), however, other biblical writers invoked the *satan* to account for division within Israel.[12] One court historian slips the *satan* into an account concerning the origin of census taking, which King David introduced into Israel c. 1000 B.C.E. for the purpose of instituting taxation. David's introduction of taxation aroused vehement and immediate opposition—opposition that began among the very army commanders ordered to carry it out. Joab, David's chief officer, objected, and warned the king that what he was proposing to do was evil. The other army commanders at first refused to obey, nearly precipitating a revolt; but finding the king adamant, the officers finally obeyed and "numbered the people."

Why had David committed what one chronicler who recalls the story regards as an evil, aggressive act "against Israel"? Unable to deny that the offending order came from the king himself, but intent on condemning David's action without condemning the king directly, the author of 1 Chronicles suggests that a supernatural adversary within the divine court had managed to infiltrate the royal house and lead the king himself into sin: "The *satan* stood up against Israel, and incited David to number the people" (1 Chron. 21:1). But although an angelic power incited David to commit this otherwise inexplicable act, the chronicler insists that the king was nevertheless personally responsible—and guilty. "God was displeased with this thing, and he smote Israel." Even after David abased himself and confessed his sin, the angry Lord punished him by sending an avenging angel to destroy seventy thousand Israelites with a plague; and the Lord was barely restrained from destroying the city of Jerusalem itself.

Here the *satan* is invoked to account for the division and destruction that King David's order aroused within Israel.[13] Not long before the chronicler wrote, the prophet Zechariah had depicted the *satan* inciting factions among the people. Zechariah's account reflects conflicts that arose within Israel after thousands of Jews—many of them influential and educated—whom the Babylonians had captured in war (c. 687 B.C.E.) and exiled to Babylon, returned to Palestine from exile. Cyrus, king of Persia, having recently conquered Babylon, not only allowed these Jewish exiles to go home but intended to make them his allies. Thus he offered them funds to reconstruct Jerusalem's defensive city walls, and to rebuild the great Temple, which the Babylonians had destroyed. Those returning were eager to reestablish the worship of "the Lord alone" in their land, and they naturally expected to reestablish themselves as rulers of their people.

They were not warmly welcomed by those whom they had left behind. Many of those who had remained saw the former exiles not only as agents of the Persian king but as determined to retrieve the power and land they had been forced to relinquish when they were deported. Many resented the returnees' plan to take charge of the priestly offices and to "purify" the Lord's worship.

As the biblical scholar Paul Hanson notes, the line that had once divided the Israelites from their enemies had separated them from foreigners. Now the line separated two groups *within Israel:*

> Now, according to the people who remained, their beloved land was controlled by the enemy, and although that enemy in fact comprised fellow Israelites, yet they regarded these brethren as essentially no different from Canaanites.[14]

The prophet Zechariah sides with the returning exiles in this heated conflict and recounts a vision in which the *satan* speaks for the rural inhabitants who accuse the returning high priest of being a worthless candidate:

> The Lord showed me Joshua, the high priest, standing before the angel of the Lord, and the *satan* standing at his right hand to accuse him. The Lord said to the *satan,* "The Lord rebuke you, O *satan*! The Lord who has chosen Jerusalem rebuke you" (Zech. 3:1–2).

Here the *satan* speaks for a disaffected—and unsuccessful—party against another party of fellow Israelites. In Zechariah's account of factions within Israel, the *satan* takes on a sinister quality, as he had done in the story of David's census, and his role begins to change from that of God's agent to that of his opponent. Although these biblical stories reflect divisions within Israel, they are not yet sectarian, for their authors still identify with Israel as a whole.

Some four centuries later in 168 B.C.E., when Jews regained their independence from their Seleucid rulers, descendents of Alexander the Great, internal conflicts became even more acute.[15] For centuries, Jews had been pressured to assimilate to the ways of the foreign nations that successively had ruled their land—the Babylonians, then the Persians, and, after 323 B.C.E., the Hellenistic dynasty established by Alexander. As the first book of Maccabees tells the story, these pressures reached a breaking point in 168 B.C.E., when the Seleucid ruler, the Syrian king Antiochus Epiphanes, suspecting resistance to his rule, decided to eradicate every trace of the Jews' peculiar and "barbaric" culture. First he outlawed circumcision, along with study and observance of Torah. Then he stormed the Jerusalem Temple and desecrated it by rededicating it to the Greek god Olympian Zeus. To enforce submission to his new regime, the king built and garrisoned a massive new fortress overlooking the Jerusalem Temple itself.

Jewish resistance to these harsh decrees soon flared into a widespread revolt, which began, according to tradition, when a company of the king's troops descended upon the village of Modein to force the inhabitants to bow down to foreign gods. The old village priest Mattathias rose up and killed a Jew who was about to obey the Syrian king's command. Then he killed the king's commissioner and fled with his sons to the hills—an act of defiance that precipitated the revolt led by Mattathias's son Judas Maccabeus.[16]

As told in 1 Maccabees, this famous story shows how those Israelites determined to resist the foreign king's orders and retain their ancestral traditions battled on two fronts at once—not only against the foreign occupiers, but against those Jews who inclined toward accommodation with the foreigners, and toward assimilation. Recently the historian Victor Tcherikover and others have told a more complex version of that history. According to Tcherikover, many Jews, especially among the upper classes, actually favored Antiochus's "reform" and wanted to participate fully in the privileges of Hellenistic society available only to Greek citizens.[17] By giving up their tribal ways and gaining for Jerusalem the prerogatives of a Greek city, they would win the right to govern the city themselves, to strike their own coins, and to increase commerce with a worldwide network of other Greek cities. They could participate in such cultural projects as the Olympic games with allied cities and gain the advantages of mutual defense treaties. Many wanted their sons to have a Greek education. Besides reading Greek literature, from the *Iliad* and the *Odyssey* to Sophocles, Plato, and Aristotle, and participating in public athletic competitions, as Greeks did, they could advance themselves in the wider cosmopolitan world.

But many other Jews, perhaps the majority of the population of Jerusalem and the countryside—tradespeople, artisans, and farmers—detested these "Hellenizing Jews" as traitors to God and Israel alike. The revolt ignited by old Mattathias encouraged people to resist Antiochus's orders, even at the risk of death, and oust the foreign rulers. After intense fighting, the Jewish armies finally won a decisive victory. They celebrated by purifying and rededicating the Temple in a ceremony commemorated, ever since, at the annual festival of Hanukkah.

Jews resumed control of the Temple, the priesthood, and the government; but after the foreigners had retreated, internal conflicts remained, especially over who would control these institutions. These divisions now intensified, as the more rigorously separatist party dominated by the Maccabees opposed the Hellenizing party. The former, having won the war, had the upper hand.

Ten to twenty years after the revolt began, the influential Hasmonean family gained control of the high priesthood in what was now essentially a theocratic state. Although originally identified with their Maccabean ancestors, successive generations of the family abandoned the austere habits of their predecessors. Two generations after the Maccabean victory, the party of Pharisees, advocating increased religious rigor, challenged the Hasmoneans. According to Tcherikover's analysis, the Pharisees, backed by tradespeople and farmers, despised the Hasmoneans as having become essentially secular rulers who had abandoned Israel's ancestral ways. The Pharisees demanded that the Hasmoneans relinquish the high priesthood to those who deserved it—people like themselves, who strove to live according to religious law.[18]

During the following decades, other, more radical dissident groups joined the Pharisees in denouncing the great high priestly family and its allies. Such groups were anything but uniform: they were fractious and diverse, and with the passage of time included various groups of Essenes, the monastic community at Kirbet Qûmran, as well as their allies in the towns, and the followers of Jesus of Nazareth. What these groups shared was their opposition to the high priest and his allies and to the Temple, which they controlled.

The majority of Jews, including the Pharisees, still defined themselves in traditional terms, as "Israel against 'the nations.' " But those who joined marginal or more extreme groups like the Essenes, bent on separating Israel radically from foreign influence, came to treat that traditional identification as a matter of secondary importance. What mattered primarily, these rigorists claimed, was not whether one was Jewish—this they took for granted—but rather "which of us [Jews] really are on God's side" and which had "walked in the ways of the nations," that is, adopted foreign cultural and commercial practices. The separatists found ammunition in biblical passages that invoke terrifying curses upon people who violate God's covenant, and in prophetic passages that warn that only a "righteous remnant" in Israel will remain faithful to God.

More radical than their predecessors, these dissidents began increasingly to invoke the *satan* to characterize their Jewish opponents; in the process they turned this rather unpleasant angel into a far grander—and far more malevolent—figure. No longer one of God's faithful servants, he begins to become what he is for Mark and for later Christianity—God's antagonist, his enemy, even his rival.[19] Such sectarians, contending less against "the nations" than against other Jews, denounce their opponents as apostate and accuse them of having been seduced by the power of evil, whom they call by many names—Satan, Beelzebub, Semihazah, Azazel, Belial, Prince of Darkness. These dissidents also borrowed stories, and wrote their own, telling how such angelic powers, swollen with lust or arrogance, fell from heaven into sin. Those who first elaborated such stories, as we shall see, most often used them to characterize what they charged was the "fall into sin" of human beings—which usually meant the dominant majority of their Jewish contemporaries.

As Satan became an increasingly important and personified figure, stories about his origin proliferated. One group tells how one of the angels, himself high in the heavenly hierarchy, proved insubordinate to his commander in chief and so was thrown out of heaven, demoted, and disgraced, an echo of Isaiah's account of the fall of a great prince:

> How are you fallen from heaven, day star, son of the dawn! How are you fallen to earth, conqueror of the nations! You said in your heart, "I will ascend to heaven, above the stars of God; I will set my throne on high . . . I will ascend upon the high clouds. . . ." But you are brought down to darkness [or: the underworld, *sheol*], to the depths of the pit (Isa. 14:12–15).

Nearly two and a half thousand years after Isaiah wrote, this luminous falling star, his name translated into Latin as Lucifer ("light-bearer") was transformed by Milton into the protagonist of *Paradise Lost*.

Far more influential in first-century Jewish and Christian circles, however, was a second group of apocryphal and pseudepigraphic stories, which tell how lust drew the angelic "sons of God" down to earth. These stories derive from a cryptic account in Genesis 6, which says:

> When men began to multiply on the earth, and daughters were born to them, the sons of God saw the daughters of men, that they were fair.

Some of these angels, transgressing the boundaries that the Lord had established between heaven and earth, mated with human women, and produced offspring who were half angel, half human. According to Genesis, these hybrids became "giants in the earth . . . the mighty men of renown" (Gen. 6:4). Other storytellers, probably writing later,[20] as we shall see, say that these monstrous offspring became demons, who took over the earth and polluted it.

Finally, an apocryphal version of the life of Adam and Eve gives a third account of angelic rebellion. In the beginning, God, having created Adam, called the angels together to admire his work and ordered them to bow down to their younger human sibling. Michael obeyed, but Satan refused, saying,

> "Why do you press me? I will not worship one who is younger than I am, and inferior. I am older than he is; he ought to worship me!" (*Vita Adae et Evae* 14:3).

Thus the problem of evil begins in sibling rivalry.[21]

At first glance these stories of Satan may seem to have little in common. Yet they all agree on one thing: that this greatest and most dangerous enemy did not originate, as one might expect, as an outsider, an alien, or a stranger. Satan is not the distant enemy but the intimate enemy—one's trusted colleague, close associate, brother. He is the kind of person on whose loyalty and goodwill the well-being of family and society depend—but one who turns unexpectedly jealous and hostile. Whichever version of his origin one chooses, then, and there are many, all depict Satan as an *intimate* enemy—the attribute that qualifies him so well to express conflict among Jewish groups. Those who asked, "How could God's own angel become his enemy?" were thus asking, in effect, "How could one of *us* become one of *them*?" Stories of Satan and other fallen angels proliferated in these troubled times, especially within those radical groups that had turned against the rest of the Jewish community and, consequently, concluded that others had turned against them—or (as they put it) against *God*.

One anonymous author who collected and elaborated stories about fallen angels during the Maccabean war was troubled by wartime divisions among Jewish communities. He addressed this divisiveness indirectly in the *Book of the Watchers*, one of the apocryphal books that would become famous and influential, especially among Christians, by introducing the idea of a division in heaven. The *Book of the Watchers,* a collection of visionary stories, is set, in turn, into a larger collection called the *First Book of Enoch.* It tells how the "watcher" angels, whom God appointed to supervise ("watch over") the universe, fell from heaven. Starting from the story of Genesis 6, in which the "sons of God" lusted for human women, this author combines two different accounts of how the watchers lost their heavenly glory.[22] The first describes how Semihazah, leader of the watchers, coerced two hundred other angels to join him in a pact to violate divine order by mating with human women. These mismatches produced "a race of bastards, the giants known as the nephilim ["fallen ones"], from whom there were to proceed demonic spirits," who brought violence upon earth and devoured its people. Interwoven with this story is an alternate version, which tells how the archangel Azazel sinned by disclosing to human beings the secrets of metallurgy, a pernicious revelation that inspired men to make weapons and women to adorn themselves with gold, silver, and cosmetics. Thus the fallen angels and their demon offspring incited in both sexes violence, greed, and lust.

Because these stories involve sociopolitical satire laced with religious polemic, some historians have recently asked to what specific historical situations they refer. Are Jews who thus embellish the story of angels that mate with human beings covertly ridiculing the pretensions of their Hellenistic rulers? George Nickelsburg points out that from the time of Alexander the Great, Greek kings had claimed to be descended from gods as well as from human women; the Greeks called such hybrid beings heroes. But their Jewish subjects, with their derisive tale of Semihazah, may have turned such claims of divine descent against the foreign usurpers.[23] The *Book of the Watchers* says pointedly that these greedy monsters "consumed the produce of all the people until the people hated feeding them"; the monsters then turned directly to "devour the people."

Or does the story express instead a pious people's contempt for a specific group of Jewish enemies—namely, certain members of the Jerusalem priesthood? David Suter suggests that the story aims instead at certain priests who, like the "sons of God" in the story, violate their divinely given status and responsibility by allowing lust to draw them into impurity—especially marriages with outsiders, Gentile women.[24]

Either interpretation is possible. As John Collins points out, the author of the *Book of the Watchers,* by choosing to tell the story of the watchers instead of that of the actual Greek rulers or corrupt priests, offers "a paradigm which is not restricted to one historical situation, but which can be applied whenever an analogous situation arises."[25] The same is true of all apocalyptic literature, and accounts for much of its power. Even today, readers puzzle over books that claim the authority of angelic revelation, from the biblical book of Daniel to the New Testament book of Revelation, finding in their own circumstances new applications for these evocative, enigmatic texts.

The primary apocalyptic question is this: Who are God's people?[26] To most readers of the *Book of the Watchers,* the answer would have been obvious—Israel. But the author of *Watchers,* without discarding ethnic identity, insists on moral identity. It is not enough to be a Jew. One must also be a Jew who acts morally. Here we see evidence of a historical shift—one that Christians will adopt and extend and which, ever after, will divide them from other Jewish groups.

The author of the *Book of the Watchers* intended nothing so radical as the followers of Jesus undertook when they finally abandoned Israel to form their own distinct religious tradition. He takes for granted Israel's priority over the rest of the nations, always mentioning Israel first. But this author takes a decisive step by separating ethnic from moral identity and suggesting a contrast between them. He takes his beginning from the opening chapters of Genesis, choosing as his spokesman the holy man Enoch, who far antedates Abraham and Israel's election and, according to Genesis, belongs not to Israel but to the primordial history of the human race. This author omits any mention of the law given to Moses at Sinai, and praises instead the universal law that God wrote into the fabric of the universe and gave to all humankind alike—the law that governs the seas, the earth, and the stars. Addressing his message to "the elect and the righteous" among all humankind, he demonstrates not only, as George Nickelsburg observes, an "unusual openness to the Gentiles," but also an unusually negative view of Israel, or, more precisely, many—perhaps a majority—of Israel's people.[27]

The *Book of the Watchers* tells the stories of Semihazah and Azazel as a moral warning: if even archangels, "sons of heaven," can sin and be cast down, how much more susceptible to sin and damnation are mere human beings, even those who belong to God's chosen people. In the *Book of the Watchers*, when Enoch, moved with compassion for the fallen watchers, tries to intervene with God on their behalf, one of God's angels orders him instead to deliver to them God's judgment: "You used to be holy, spirits possessing eternal life; but now you have defiled yourselves." Such passages suggest that the *Book of the Watchers* articulates the judgment of certain Jews upon others, and specifically upon some who hold positions that ordinarily convey great authority.

In 160 B.C.E., after the Maccabees' victory, a group who regarded themselves as moderates regained control of the Temple priesthood and temporarily ousted the Maccabean party. Recalling this event, one of the Maccabeans adds to the collection called the *First Book of Enoch* another version of the story of the watcher angels, a version aimed against those who had usurped control of the Temple. This author says that the watchers, falling like stars from heaven, themselves spawned Israel's foreign enemies, depicted as bloody predators—lions, leopards, wolves, and snakes intent on destroying Israel, here depicted as a herd of sheep. But, he continues, God's chosen nation is itself divided; some are "blind sheep," and others have their eyes open. When the day of judgment comes, he warns, God will destroy the errant Jews, these "blind sheep," along with Israel's traditional enemies. Furthermore, God will finally gather into his eternal home not only Israel's righteous but also the righteous from the nations (although these will remain forever secondary to Israel).

A third anonymous writer whose work is included in the *First Book of Enoch* is so preoccupied with internal division that he virtually ignores Israel's alien enemies. This author has Enoch predict the rise of "a perverse generation," warning that "all its deeds shall be apostate" (*1 Enoch* 93:9). Castigating many of his contemporaries, this author, as George Nickelsburg points out, like several biblical prophets, speaks for the poor, and denounces the rich and powerful, predicting their destruction.[28] He even insists that slavery, along with other social and economic inequities, is not divinely ordained, as others argue, but "arose from oppression" (*1 Enoch* 98:5b)—that is, human sin.[29]

The story of the watchers, then, in some of its many transformations, suggested a change in the traditional lines separating Jew from Gentile. The latest section of the *First Book of Enoch,* the "Similitudes," written about the time of Jesus, simply contrasts those who are righteous, who stand on the side of the angels, with those, both Jews and Gentiles, seduced by the *satan*s. Accounts like this would open the way for Christians eventually to leave ethnic identity aside, and to redefine the human community instead in terms of the moral quality, or membership in the elect community, of each individual.

Another devout patriot, writing around 160 B.C.E., also siding with the early Maccabean party, wrote an extraordinary apocryphal book called *Jubilees* to urge his people to maintain their separateness from Gentile ways. What troubles this author is this: How can so many Israelites, God's own people, have become apostates? How can so many Jews be "walking in the ways of the Gentiles" (*Jub.* 1:9)? While the author takes for granted the traditional antithesis between the Israelites and "their enemies, the Gentiles" (*Jub.* 1:19), here again this conflict recedes into the background. The author of *Jubilees* is concerned instead with the conflicts over assimilation that divide Jewish communities internally, and he attributes these conflicts to that most intimate of enemies, whom he calls by many names, but most often calls Mastema ("hatred"), Satan, or Belial.

The story of the angels' fall in *Jubilees,* like that in the *First Book of Enoch,* gives a moral warning: if even angels, when they sin, bring God's wrath and destruction upon themselves, how can mere human beings expect to be spared? *Jubilees* insists that every creature, whether angel or human, Israelite or Gentile, shall be judged according to deeds, that is, ethically.

According to *Jubilees,* the angels' fall spawned the giants, who sow violence and evil, and evil spirits, "who are cruel, and created to destroy" (*Jub.* 10:6). Ever since, their presence has dominated this world like a dark shadow, and suggests the moral ambivalence and vulnerability of every human being. Like certain of the prophets, this author warns that election offers no safety, certainly no immunity; Israel's destiny depends not simply on election but on moral action or, failing this, on repentance and divine forgiveness.

Yet Jews and Gentiles do not confront demonic malevolence on equal footing. *Jubilees* says that God assigned to each of the nations a ruling angel or spirit "so that they might lead them astray" (*Jub.* 15:31); hence the nations worship demons (whom *Jubilees* identifies with foreign gods).[30] But God himself rules over Israel, together with a phalanx of angels and spirits assigned to guard and bless them.

What, then, does God's election of his people mean? The author of *Jubilees,* echoing the warnings of Isaiah and other prophets, suggests that belonging to the people of Israel does not guarantee deliverance from evil. It conveys a legacy of moral struggle, but ensures divine help in that struggle.

Jubilees depicts Mastema testing Abraham himself to the breaking point. For according to this revisionist writer, it is Mastema—not the Lord—who commands Abraham to kill his son, Isaac. Later Abraham expresses anxiety lest he be enslaved by evil spirits, "who have dominion over the thoughts of human hearts"; he pleads with God, "Deliver me from the hands of evil spirits, and do not let them lead me astray from my God" (*Jub.* 12:20). Moses, too, knows that he and his people are vulnerable. When he prays that God deliver Israel from their external enemies, "the Gentiles" (*Jub.* 1:19), he also prays that God may deliver them from the intimate enemy that threatens to take over his people internally and destroy them: "Do not let the spirit of Belial rule over them" (*Jub.* 1:20). This sense of ominous and omnipresent danger in *Jubilees* shows the extent to which the author regards his people as corruptible and, to a considerable extent, already corrupted. Like the *Book of the Watchers, Jubilees* warns that those who neglect God's covenant are being seduced by the powers of evil, fallen angels.

Despite these warnings, the majority of Jews, from the second century B.C.E. to the present, reject sectarianism, as well as the universalism that, among most Christians, would finally supersede ethnic distinction. The Jewish majority, including those who sided with the Maccabees against the assimilationists, has always identified with Israel as a whole.

The author of the biblical book of Daniel, for example, who wrote during the crisis surrounding the Maccabean war, also sides with the Maccabees, and wants Jews to shun contamination incurred by eating with Gentiles, marrying them, or worshiping their gods. To encourage Jews to maintain their loyalty to Israel, the book opens with the famous story of the prophet Daniel, sentenced to death by the Babylonian king for faithfully praying to his God. Thrown into a den of lions to be torn apart, Daniel is divinely delivered; "the Lord sent an angel to shut the lions' mouths," so that the courageous prophet emerges unharmed.

Like the authors of *Jubilees* and *Watchers*, the author of Daniel, too, sees moral division within Israel, and warns that some people "violate the covenant; but the people who know their God shall stand firm and take action" (Dan. 11:32). Though concerned with moral issues, he never forgets ethnic identity: what concerns him above all is Israel's moral destiny as a whole. Unlike the writers of the *Book of the Watchers* and *Jubilees,* the author of Daniel envisions no sectarian enemy, either human or divine. Grieved as he is at Israel's sins, he never condemns many, much less the majority, of his people as apostate; consequently, he never speaks of Satan, Semihazah, Azazel, Mastema, Belial, or fallen angels of any kind.

Although there are no devils in Daniel's world, there *are* angels, and there are enemies. The author presents the alien enemies, rulers of the Persian, Medean, and Hellenistic empires, in traditional visionary imagery, as monstrous beasts. In one vision, the first beast is "like a lion with eagles' wings"; the second "like a bear," ferociously devouring its prey; the third like a leopard "with four wings of a bird on its back and four heads"; and "a fourth beast [is] terrible and dreadful and exceedingly strong; and it had great iron teeth: it devoured and broke in pieces, and stamped the residue with its feet." In another vision, Daniel sees a horned ram that the angel Gabriel explains to him "is the king of Greece." Throughout the visions of Daniel, such monstrous animals represent foreign rulers and nations who threaten Israel. When Daniel, trembling with awe and terror, prays for his people, he is rewarded with divine assurance that all Israelites who remain true to God will survive (12:1–3). Thus the book of Daniel powerfully reaffirms the integrity of Israel's moral and ethnic identity. It is for this reason, I suggest, that Daniel, unlike such other apocalyptic books as the *Book of the Watchers* and *Jubilees,* is included in the canonical collection that we call the Hebrew Bible and not relegated to the apocrypha.

The majority of Jews, at any rate those who assembled and drew upon the Hebrew Bible, apparently endorsed Daniel's reaffirmation of Israel's traditional identity, while those who valued such books as *1 Enoch* and *Jubilees* probably included a significant minority more inclined to identify with one group of Jews against another, as Daniel had refused to do. Most of those who *did* take sides within the community stopped far short of proclaiming an all-out civil war between one Jewish group and another, but there were notable exceptions. Starting at the time of the Maccabean war, the more radical sectarian groups we have mentioned—above all, those called Essenes—placed this cosmic battle between angels and demons, God and Satan, at the very center of their cosmology and their politics. In so doing, they expressed the importance to their lives of the conflict between themselves and the majority of their fellow Jews, whom the Essenes consigned to damnation.

Many scholars believe that the Essenes are known to us from such first-century contemporaries as Josephus, Philo, and the Roman geographer and naturalist Pliny the Elder, as well as from the discovery in 1947 of the ruins of their community, including its sacred library, the Dead Sea Scrolls. Josephus, at the age of sixteen, was fascinated by this austere and secretive community: he says that they "practiced great holiness" within an extraordinarily close-knit group ("they love one another very much").[31] Josephus and Philo both note, with some astonishment, that these sectarians practiced strict celibacy, probably because they chose to live according to the biblical rules for holy war, which prohibit sexual intercourse during wartime. But the war in which they saw themselves engaged was God's war against the power of evil—a cosmic war that they expected would result in God's vindication of their fidelity. The Essenes also turned over all their money and property to their leaders in order to live "without money," as Pliny says, in a monastic community.[32]

These devout and passionate sectarians saw the foreign occupation of Palestine—and the accommodation of the majority of Jews to that occupation—as evidence that the forces of evil had taken over the world and—in the form of Satan, Mastema, or the Prince of Darkness—infiltrated and taken over God's own people, turning most of them into allies of the Evil One.

Arising from controversies over purity and assimilation that followed the Maccabean war, the Essene movement grew during the Roman occupation of the first century to include over four thousand men. Women, never mentioned in the community rule, apparently were not eligible for admission. Although the remains of a few women and children have been found among the hundreds of men buried in the outer cemetery at Qûmran, they probably were not community members.[33] (Since the whole cemetery has not yet been excavated, these conclusions remain inconclusive.) Many adjunct members of the sect, apparently including many who were married, lived in towns all over Palestine, pursuing ordinary occupations while striving to devote themselves to God; but the most dedicated withdrew in protest from ordinary Jewish life to form their own "new Israel," the monastic community in desert caves overlooking the Dead Sea.[34] There, following the rigorous community rule, they dressed only in white and regulated every detail of their lives according to strict interpretations of the law set forth by their priestly leaders.

In their sacred books, such as the great *Scroll of the War of the Sons of Light Against the Sons of Darkness,* the brethren could read how God had given them the Prince of Light as their supernatural ally to help them contend against Satan, and against his human allies.

> The Prince of Light thou has appointed to come to our support: but Satan, the angel Mastema, thou hast created for the pit; he rules in darkness, and his purpose is to bring about evil and sin (1 QM 19:10–12).

The Essenes called themselves the "sons of light" and indicted the majority as "sons of darkness," the "congregation of traitors," as people who "depart from the way, having transgressed the law, and violated the precept" (CD 1:13–20). The Essenes retell the whole history of Israel in terms of this cosmic war. Even in earliest times, they say, "the Prince of Light raised up Moses" (CD 5:18), but the Evil One, here called Beliar, aroused opposition to Moses among his own people. Ever since then, and especially now, Beliar has set traps in which he intends to "catch Israel," for God himself has "unleashed Beliar against Israel" (CD 4:13). Now the "sons of light" eagerly await the day of judgment, when they expect God will come with all the armies of heaven to annihilate the corrupt majority along with Israel's foreign enemies.

Had Satan not already existed in Jewish tradition, the Essenes would have invented him. In the *Book of the Watchers* fallen angels incite the activities of those who violate God's covenant, but the Essenes go much further and place at the center of their religious understanding the cosmic war between God and his allies, both angelic and human, against Satan, or Beliar, along with his demonic and human allies. The Essenes place themselves at the very center of this battle between heaven and hell. While they detest Israel's traditional enemies, whom they call the *kittim* (probably a coded epithet for the Romans),[35] they struggle far more bitterly against their fellow Israelites, who belong to the "congregation of Beliar." David Sperling, scholar of the ancient Near East, suggests that substitution of Beliar for earlier Belial may be a pun on *belî 'ôr*, "without light."[36] They invoke Satan—or Beliar—to characterize the irreconcilable opposition between themselves and the "sons of darkness" in the war taking place simultaneously in heaven and on earth. They expect that soon God will come in power, with his holy angels, and finally overthrow the forces of evil and inaugurate the Kingdom of God.

The Essenes agree with *Jubilees* that being Jewish is no longer enough to ensure God's blessing. But they are much more radical: the sins of the people have virtually canceled God's covenant with Abraham, on which Israel's election depends. Now, they insist, whoever wants to belong to the true Israel must join in a *new* covenant—the covenant of their own congregation.[37] Whoever applies to enter the desert community must first confess himself guilty of sin—guilty, apparently, of participating in Israel's collective apostasy against God. Then the candidate begins several years of probation, during which he turns over his property to the community leaders and swears to practice sexual abstinence, along with ritual purity in everything he eats, drinks, utters, or touches. During the probationary period he must not touch the pots, plates, or utensils in which the members prepare the community's food. Swearing can earn him instant expulsion, and so can complaining against the group's leaders; spitting or talking out of turn incurs strict penalties.

A candidate who finally does gain admission is required, at his initiation ritual, to join together with the whole community to bless all who belong to the new covenant and ritually curse all who are not initiates, who belong to the "men of Beliar." The leaders now reveal to the initiate the secrets of angelology, and according to Josephus, he must solemnly swear to "keep secret the names of the angels" (*War* 2.8). Through practices of purity, prayer, and worship, the initiate strives to unite himself with the company of the angels. As the historian Carol Newsome has shown, Essene community worship—like the Christian liturgy to this day—reaches its climax as the community on earth joins with angels in singing the hymn of praise that the angels sing in heaven ("Holy, holy, holy, Lord God of hosts; heaven and earth are filled with thy glory").[38] Sacred Essene texts like the *Scroll of the War of the Sons of Light Against the Sons of Darkness* reveal secrets of angelology, which the sectarians regarded as valuable and necessary information, for recognizing and understanding the interrelationship of supernatural forces, both good and evil, is essential for their sense of their own identity—and the way they identify others.[39]

The Essenes, then, offer the closest parallel to Mark's account of Jesus' followers, as they invoke images of cosmic war to divide the universe at large—and the Jewish community in particular—between God's people and Satan's. Yet the two movements differ significantly, especially in relation to outsiders. The Essene covenant, as we have seen, was extremely exclusive, restricted not only to Jews, who must be freeborn and male, but to those devout few who willingly joined the "new covenant." Although Mark and Matthew saw the beginning of Jesus' movement primarily within the context of the Jewish community, its future would increasingly involve the Gentile world outside.

Nonetheless, the Essenes, though rigorously exclusive, were led by their objections to the assimilationist tendencies of their fellow Jews to move, paradoxically, in the universalist direction indicated by the *Book of the Watchers* and *Jubilees*. (The Essenes treasured both of these writings in their monastic library; *Jubilees*, wrote an anonymous Essene, is a book that reveals divine secrets "to which Israel has turned a blind eye" [CD 16.2].) The Essenes outdid their predecessors in setting ethnic identity aside, not as wrong, but as inadequate, and emphasized moral over ethnic identification. When they depict the struggle of the Prince of Light against the Prince of Darkness, they do not identify the Prince of Light with the archangel Michael, the angelic patron of Israel.[40] Instead, they envision the Prince of Light as a universal energy contending against an opposing cosmic force, the Prince of Darkness. For the Essenes these two energies represent not only their own conflicts with their opponents but a conflict within every person, within the human heart itself:

> The spirits of truth and falsehood struggle within the human heart. . . . According to his share in truth and right, thus a man

hates lies; and according to his share in the lot of deceit, thus he hates truth (1 QS 4:12–14).

The Essenes, of course, took their own identification with Israel for granted. Since they required every initiate to their covenant to be Jewish, male, and freeborn, "every person" meant in practice only Jews who met these qualifications. But certain followers of Jesus, especially after 100 C.E., having met with disappointing responses to their message within the Jewish communities, would draw upon such universalist themes as they moved to open their movement to Gentiles.

As we saw in the previous chapter, Jesus' followers, according to Mark, also invoke images of cosmic war to divide the universe at large—and the Jewish community in particular—between God's people and Satan's. Mark, like the Essenes, sees this struggle essentially in terms of intra-Jewish conflict. So does the follower of Jesus we call Matthew, who, as we shall see in the next chapter, took up and revised Mark's gospel some ten to twenty years later. Taking Mark's basic framework, Matthew embellished it and in effect updated it, placing the story of Jesus in a context more relevant to the Jewish world of Matthew's own time, Palestine c. 80–90 C.E. By the time Matthew was writing, Jesus' followers were a marginal group opposed by the ruling party of Pharisees, which had gained ascendancy in Jerusalem in the decades following the Roman war. In the central part of Matthew's version of the gospel, the "intimate enemies" had become primarily Pharisees.

About the same time, another follower of Jesus, whom tradition calls Luke, also took up Mark's account and extended it to fit his own perspective—apparently that of a Gentile convert. Yet Luke, as fervently as any Essene, depicts his own sect as representing Israel at its best; according to Luke, as we shall see, Jesus' followers are virtually the only true Israelites left.

Near the end of the century, c. 90–100 C.E., the writer called John offers a bold interpretation of these events. Many scholars agree that the gospel of John presents the viewpoint of a radically sectarian group alienated from the Jewish community because they have been turned out of their home synagogues for claiming that Jesus is the Messiah. Like the Essenes, John speaks eloquently of the love among those who belong to God (John 10:14); and yet John's fierce polemic against those he sometimes calls simply "the Jews" at times matches in bitterness that of the Essenes.

Let us investigate, then, how each of these New Testament gospel writers reshaped Mark's message as the Christian movement changed throughout the first century.

III

MATTHEW'S CAMPAIGN AGAINST THE PHARISEES: DEPLOYING THE DEVIL

Jesus' followers succeeded, far more than many of them expected—or perhaps even hoped—in attracting Gentiles (from the Latin term for "nations," *gentes*) but, to their disappointment, largely failed to attract Jews. Between 70 and 100 C.E., this movement, which began, as George Nickelsburg says, as "a relative latecomer among the sects and groups in post-exilic Judaism,"[1] grew rapidly. Although many of Jesus' followers were Jewish, they tended increasingly to separate from other Jews, often meeting for worship in the homes of fellow members, rather than in synagogues. This situation distressed many of them, who insisted that they didn't want to depart from traditional ways but had been forced into it, having been rejected by Jewish leaders, sometimes even expelled from their home synagogues.

As the Jesus movement spread throughout the Roman world, various adherents began to drop distinctively Jewish practices, most notably circumcision, and then also dietary and Sabbath laws. By 100 C.E., in regions that include Greece, Asia Minor, Italy, and Egypt, many Christian churches had become predominantly Gentile. They still insisted, nonetheless, that they alone were the true embodiment of Israel. George Nickelsburg points out the irony of their situation:

> A young, upstart group, whose membership had rapidly and radically changed, was asserting that it was more authentic

than its parent group; and this attitude of superiority and exclusion was derived, in part, from ideas and attitudes already present in the parent body.[2]

As the historian and New Testament scholar Wayne Meeks notes, the path to separation was by no means simple or uniform.[3] We have already seen that Jewish communities scattered throughout Palestine and the provincial cities of the Roman empire not only were internally diverse but were also undergoing complex postwar changes. The various groups of converts to Christianity were, if anything, even more diverse internally, since they often included Gentiles along with Jews. These groups of Jesus' followers struggled to find a place to stand in relation to the Jewish communities whose Scriptures and traditions they largely appropriated.

Not all Christians abandoned Jewish practices at the same time. In the decades after Jesus' death, many of his followers may not have meant to abandon them at all. The group centered in Jerusalem around Jesus' brother James, for example, remained observant of the law, like James himself (hence his nickname, "James the Just," or "the Righteous"). Other groups, like those who followed teachings associated with Peter, modified observance of dietary and sexual laws. Groups that identified with Paul, the converted Pharisee, largely adopted his conviction that "Christ is the end of the law to everyone who believes," whether Jew or Gentile.[4] Most believers took Paul to mean that practicing circumcision and observing kosher laws and Jewish festivals were antithetical to embracing the gospel, and his preaching attracted many converts among the Gentiles who associated themselves with Jewish synagogue congregations.

When we look at the three other gospels included with Mark in the New Testament, all written between 70 and 100 C.E., we can see three representative communities, each in the process of separating from particular Jewish groups and attempting to forge a new and distinctively Christian pattern of community identity. New Testament scholar Krister Stendahl characterizes Matthew's gospel as a kind of "community rule," considerably more liberal than that of the Essenes.[5] The gospel of Luke, probably written by the only Gentile author in the New Testament for a predominantly Gentile community, insists that his group has inherited Israel's legacy as God's people. The author of John, probably Jewish himself, describes a close-knit group of "Jesus' own"—insiders who follow Jesus' command to "love one another" (15:12) while regarding their Jewish opponents as offspring of Satan.

That such patterns of group identity are found in these gospels—patterns that have shaped Christian churches ever since—is certainly no accident. The four gospels collected in the New Testament were canonized around 200 C.E., apparently by a consensus of churches ranging from those in provincial Gaul to the church in the capital city of Rome; they were chosen not necessarily because they were the earliest or the most accurate accounts of Jesus' life and teaching but precisely because they could form the basis for church communities.

The canonical gospels were not by any means the only accounts of Jesus' life and teaching. During the years following his death, stories about him and his disciples were told and retold, not only in Palestine, but throughout Asia Minor, Greece, Egypt, Africa, Gaul, and Spain. Some twenty years after Jesus' crucifixion, when Paul traveled to synagogues in Antioch, the capital of Syria, and in Greece and Rome to proclaim "the gospel of Jesus Christ," there were as yet no written gospels. According to Paul, "the gospel" consisted of what he preached, which he summarized as follows: "that Christ died for our sins, according to the scriptures; that he was buried; and that he was raised on the third day" (1 Cor. 15:3–4). Although Paul preached in synagogues, he found his audience largely among Gentiles, most often among Gentiles attracted to Jewish congregations. Many were people who had moved from their native towns to sprawling, heterogeneous cities like Syrian Antioch, Asian Ephesus, and Greek Corinth. Proclaiming that Jews and Gentiles, slaves and free people, men and women, could now become "one in Christ" (Gal. 3:28), Paul formed from those he baptized the close-knit groups that Wayne Meeks calls "the first urban Christians"—ethnically diverse communities where tradespeople, slaves, and the groups' wealthy patrons mingled together, now bound to help and support one another as they awaited the time when Christ would return in glory.[6] Writing to various congregations as he traveled, Paul sometimes invoked a "saying of the Lord." Once he invoked Jesus' authority to prohibit divorce (1 Cor. 7:10); another time he explained how Jesus had told his followers to ritually eat bread and drink wine "in order to manifest the Lord's death, until he comes" (1 Cor. 11:26).

Paul had no interest in Jesus' earthly life, however, and none in collecting his sayings. But other Christians did begin to collect Jesus' sayings and write them down.[7] The *Secret Book of James,* one of the many traditions that circulated after Jesus' death, gives a stylized description of this process:

> The twelve disciples were all sitting together at one time and remembering what the savior said to each one of them, whether secretly or openly, and putting it into books (NHC I.27.15).

In fact, many people, not just "the twelve" enshrined in Christian tradition, gathered Jesus' sayings into various collections. Most scholars agree that a collection of Jesus' sayings, translated from the Aramaic he spoke into Greek, circulated widely during the first century, although we do not have an actual copy of that source. If each of the gospel writers had individually translated Jesus' sayings, we would expect to see some variation in the way each presented his words. But gospels as diverse as Matthew and Luke, as well as the suppressed *Gospel of Thomas,* all quote sayings of Jesus in identical translation. This suggests that they relied on the common source, which scholars call Q (for *Quelle,* the German word for "source").[8] To this source we owe many familiar sayings, including the Beatitudes ("Blessed are you poor; for yours is the kingdom of heaven . . .") and what we know from Matthew's gospel as the Sermon on the Mount (which becomes, in Luke's gospel, the Sermon on the Plain). Still other sayings are known to us from scraps of papyrus that have been found preserved in dry climates like that of Upper Egypt. From the late 1800s through this century, archaeologists working in Egypt have found papyrus leaves that contain glimpses of Jesus tradition—for example, a story of Jesus healing a leper, or another of Jesus raising a dead young man to life.[9] Other papyrus fragments yield enigmatic sayings otherwise unknown:

> Jesus said, "I am the light which is above them all. It is I who am the all. From me did all come forth and to me the all extends. Split a piece of wood, and I am there. Lift up the stone, and you will find me there" (NHC II.46.23–38).

As stories, sayings, and anecdotes proliferated, various interpretations of Jesus' life and teaching circulated among diverse Christian groups throughout the Roman world. What Jesus actually taught often became a matter of bitter dispute, as we can see from the *Gospel of Mary Magdalene,* another early source, discovered in 1896 on papyrus fragments in Egypt. This remarkable text, like other noncanonical texts, depicts Mary Magdalene among the disciples—indeed, as one of Jesus' most beloved disciples, to whom he entrusted secret teaching.[10] In the following passage (17:18–18:15), Peter first addresses Mary with a request.

> "Sister, we know that the savior loved you more than the rest of women. Tell us the words of the savior which you remember, which . . . we do not [know] and have not heard."

After Mary answers, revealing to Peter secret teaching on the soul's spiritual journey, Andrew objects:

> "Say what you want about what she has said. I, at least, do not believe that the savior said this. For certainly these teachings are strange ideas."

Peter joins in, challenging Mary's veracity:

> "Did he really speak with a woman without our knowledge, and in secret? Are we all to turn around and listen to her? Did he love her more than us?"

Mary protests:

> "My brother Peter, what do you think? Do you think I made
> this up in my heart? Do you think I am lying about the Lord?"

Then Levi breaks in to mediate the dispute, saying that "the Savior knew her very well, and made her worthy" to receive such teachings. The *Gospel of Mary* concludes as the disciples agree to accept what they learn from Mary, and they all prepare to go out to preach. But most Christian groups, including the one in Rome identified with Peter, who was often depicted as Mary's antagonist, rejected such claims of revelation given through Mary, since she was not one of the twelve, and rejected many other widely circulating "gospels" as well. By the late second century, certain church leaders began to denounce such teachings as heresy.

In 1945, the extraordinary discovery of a hidden library of early Christian writings at Nag Hammadi greatly extended our understanding of the early Christian movement.[11] This is not the place to describe that discovery, discussed in my book *The Gnostic Gospels;* but when we glance at one of the gospels discovered there, one that most church leaders who knew it rejected, we can see more clearly their reasons for preferring the gospels of the New Testament. The *Gospel of Thomas* begins with these words: "These are the secret words which the Living Jesus spoke, and which the twin, Judas Thomas, wrote down." Did Jesus have a twin brother, as this text implies? Could this be an authentic record of Jesus' sayings? According to its title, the text contained the gospel according to Thomas. Yet unlike the gospels of the New Testament, this text identified itself as a *secret* gospel. It contained many sayings that parallel those in the New Testament, particularly sayings from the Q source; yet others were strikingly different—sayings as strange and compelling as Zen koans:

> Jesus said, "If you bring forth what is within you, what you
> bring forth will save you. If you do not bring forth what is
> within you, what you do not bring forth will destroy you"
> (NHC II.45.29–33).

Although the complete text of *Thomas*, written in Coptic, probably dates to the third or fourth century C.E., the original probably was written in Greek, perhaps much earlier.[12] New Testament scholar Helmut Koester has argued that the *Gospel of Thomas* contains a collection of sayings that *predates* the gospels of the New Testament.[13] If the earliest of the New Testament gospels, the gospel of Mark, dates from about 70 C.E., the *Gospel of Thomas*, he argues, may date back a generation earlier. Although many scholars dispute Koester's dating of *Thomas*, this gospel, discovered less than fifty years ago, does in some ways resemble the kind of source that the authors of Matthew and Luke used when they composed their own gospels.

Why was this gospel suppressed, along with many others that have remained virtually unknown for nearly two thousand years? Originally part of the sacred library of the oldest monastery in Egypt, these books were buried, apparently, around 370 C.E., after the archbishop of Alexandria ordered Christians all over Egypt to ban such books as heresy and demanded their destruction. Two hundred years earlier, such works had already been attacked by another zealously orthodox bishop, Irenaeus of Lyons. Irenaeus was the first, so far as we know, to identify the four gospels of the New Testament as canonical, and to exclude all the rest. Distressed that dozens of gospels were circulating among Christians throughout the world, including his own Greek-speaking immigrant congregation living in Gaul, Irenaeus denounced as heretics those who "boast that they have more gospels than there really are . . . but really, they have no gospels that are not full of blasphemy."[14] Only the four gospels of the New Testament, Irenaeus insisted, are *authentic*. What was his reasoning? Irenaeus declared that just as there are only four principal winds, and four corners of the universe, and four pillars holding up the sky, so there can be only four gospels. Besides, he added, only the New Testament gospels were written by Jesus' own disciples (Matthew and John) or their followers (Mark, disciple of Peter, and Luke, disciple of Paul).

Few New Testament scholars today agree with Irenaeus. Although the gospels of the New Testament—like those discovered at Nag Hammadi—are *attributed* to Jesus' followers, no one knows who actually wrote any of them; furthermore, what we know about their dating makes the traditional assumptions, in all cases, extremely unlikely. Yet Irenaeus's statements remind us that the collection of books we call the New Testament was formed as late as 180–200 C.E. Before that time, many gospels circulated throughout the Christian communities scattered from Asia Minor to Greece, Rome, Gaul, Spain, and Africa. Yet by the late second century, bishops of the church who called themselves orthodox rejected all but the four canonical gospels, denouncing all the rest, in Irenaeus's words, as "an abyss of madness, and blasphemy against Christ."[15] Irenaeus wanted to consolidate Christian groups threatened by persecution throughout the world. The gospels he endorsed helped institutionalize the Christian movement. Those he denounced as heresy did not serve the purposes of institutionalization. Some, on the contrary, urged people to seek direct access to God, unmediated by church or clergy.

The *Gospel of Thomas,* as noted above, claims to offer secret teaching—teaching quite different from that of Mark, Matthew, Luke, and John. According to Mark, for example, Jesus first appears proclaiming that "the time is at hand; the Kingdom of God is drawing near. Repent, and believe in the gospel" (1:15). According to Mark, the world is about to undergo cataclysmic transformation: Jesus predicts strife, war, conflict, and suffering, followed by a world-shattering event—the coming of the Kingdom of God (13:1–37).

But in the *Gospel of Thomas* the "kingdom of God" is not an event expected to happen in history, nor is it a "place." The author of *Thomas* seems to ridicule such views:

> Jesus said, "If those who lead you say to you, 'Lord, the kingdom is in the sky,' then the birds of the sky will precede you. If they say to you, 'It is in the sea,' then the fish will precede you" (NHC II.32.19–24).

Here the kingdom represents a state of self-discovery:

"Rather, the kingdom is inside of you, and it is outside of you. When you come to know yourselves, then you will become known, and you will realize that it is you who are the sons of the living Father" (NHC II.32.25–33.5).

But the disciples, mistaking that kingdom for a future event, persist in naïve questioning:

"When will . . . the new world come?" Jesus said to them, "What you look forward to has already come, but you do not recognize it" (NHC II.42.10–12).

According to the *Gospel of Thomas*, then, the kingdom of God symbolizes a state of transformed consciousness. One enters that kingdom when one attains self-knowledge. The *Gospel of Thomas* teaches that when one comes to know oneself, at the deepest level, one simultaneously comes to know God as the source of one's being.

If we then ask, "Who is Jesus?," the *Gospel of Thomas* gives an answer different from that in the gospels of the New Testament. Mark, for example, depicts Jesus as an utterly unique being—the Messiah, God's appointed king. According to Mark, it was Peter who discovered the secret of Jesus' identity:

And Jesus went on with his disciples to the villages of Caesarea Philippi; and on the way he asked his disciples, "Who do men say that I am?" And they told him "John the Baptist; and others say, Elijah; and others, one of the prophets." And he asked them, "But who do you say that I am?" Peter answered him, "You are the Messiah" (8:27–29).

But the *Gospel of Thomas* tells the same story differently:

Jesus said to his disciples, "Compare me to someone, and tell me whom I am like." Simon Peter said to him, "You are like a righteous messenger." Matthew said to him, "You are like a wise philosopher." Thomas said to him, "Master, my mouth is wholly incapable of saying whom you are like" (NHC II.34.30–35.3).

The author of *Thomas* here interprets, for Greek-speaking readers, Matthew's claim that Jesus was a rabbinic teacher ("wise philosopher"), and Peter's conviction that Jesus was the Messiah ("righteous messenger"). Jesus does not deny these roles, at least in relation to Matthew and Peter. But according to Thomas, here they—and their answers—represent an inferior level of understanding. Thomas, who recognizes that he himself cannot assign a specific role to Jesus, transcends at that moment the relation of disciple to master. Jesus declares that Thomas has become like himself:

> "I am not your Master, for you have drunk, and become drunk from the bubbling stream I measured out. . . . Whoever drinks from my mouth will become as I am, and I myself will become that person, and things that are hidden will be revealed to him" (NHC II.35.4–7; 50:27–30).

The New Testament gospel of John emphasizes Jesus' uniqueness even more strongly than Mark does. According to John, Jesus is not a mere human being but the divine and eternal Word of God, God's "only begotten son," who descends to earth in human form to rescue the human race from eternal damnation:

> God so loved the world that He gave his only begotten Son, that whosoever believes in him should not perish, but have eternal life. . . . Whoever believes in him is not condemned, but whoever does not believe in him is condemned already because he has not believed in the name of the only begotten Son of God (3:16–18).

But, as we have seen, *Thomas* offers a very different message. Far from regarding himself as the only begotten son of God, Jesus says to his disciples, "When you come to know yourselves" (and discover the divine within you), then "you will recognize that it is *you* who are the sons of the living Father"—just like Jesus. The *Gospel of Philip* makes the same point more succinctly: one is to "become not a Christian, but a Christ." This, I believe, is the symbolic meaning of attributing the *Gospel of Thomas* to Jesus' "twin brother." In effect, "You, the reader, are the twin brother of Christ" when you recognize the divine within you. Then you will see, as Thomas does, that you and Jesus are, so to speak, identical twins.

One who seeks to "become not a Christian, but a Christ" no longer looks only to Jesus—and later to his church and its leaders—as most believers do, as the source of all truth. So, while the Jesus of the gospel of John declares, "I am the door; whoever enters through me shall be saved," the *Teaching of Silvanus* points in a different direction:

> Knock upon yourself as upon a door, and walk upon yourself as on a straight road. For if you walk upon that road, it is impossible for you to go astray. . . . Open the door for yourself, that you may know what is. . . . Whatever you open for yourself, you will open (NHC VII.106.30–35; 117.5–20).

Why did the majority of early Christian churches reject such writings as *Thomas* and accept other, possibly later accounts—for example, Matthew, Luke, and John? *Thomas* appeals to people engaged in spiritual transformation, but it does not answer the practical questions of many potential converts who lived in or near Jewish communities scattered throughout the cities of Palestine and the imperial provinces. Potential converts asked questions like these: Do you want us to fast? How shall we pray? Shall we give alms? What diet should we observe? In short, are believers to follow traditional Jewish practices, or not? According to the *Gospel of Thomas*, when the disciples ask "the living Jesus" these very questions, he refuses to give them specific directions, answering only,

> "Do not tell lies, and do not do what you hate: for all things are manifest in the sight of heaven" (NHC II.33.18–21).

This enigmatic answer leaves each person to his or her own conscience; for who else knows when one is lying, and who else knows what one hates? Profound as such an answer may be, it offers no programmatic guidelines for group instruction, much less for the formation of a religious institution. The gospels included in the New Testament, by contrast, do offer such guidelines. According to Matthew and Luke, for example, Jesus answers each one of these questions authoritatively and specifically:

> "When you pray, say, 'Our Father, who art in heaven . . .'
> When you fast, wash your face. . . . When you give alms, do so
> in secret" (6:2–12).

As for the kosher laws, Mark says that Jesus "proclaimed all foods clean."

Furthermore, while *Thomas* says that finding the kingdom of God requires undergoing a solitary process of self-discovery, the gospels of the New Testament offer a far simpler message: one attains to God not by spiritual self-knowledge, but by believing in Jesus the Messiah. Now that God has sent salvation through Christ, repent; accept baptism and forgiveness of sins; join God's people and receive salvation.

Finally, while *Thomas* blesses "the solitary and the chosen" (*Thomas* 34:29) and addresses the solitary seeker, or at most a select inner circle, Mark and his successors combine many elements of earlier Jesus tradition—miracle stories, teachings, and controversy stories, along with an account of Jesus' passion—to show Jesus and his disciples in a social context, contending at various times with Jewish leaders, with crowds, both friendly and hostile, and with ruling authorities, Jewish and Roman. In the process, Mark and his successors offer social models by which Jesus' followers identify themselves as a group—often a deficient and threatened group, as they describe it, but one that claims to be God's own people, continuing Jesus' work of healing, casting out demons, and proclaiming the coming of God's kingdom.

The author of Mark, then, offers a rudimentary model for Christian community life. The gospels that the majority of Christians adopted in common all follow, to some extent, Mark's example. Successive generations found in the New Testament gospels what they did not find in many other elements of early Jesus tradition—a practical design for Christian communities.

The writer whom tradition calls Matthew updates Mark to address the circumstances he confronts in the immediate postwar decades. Many scholars think that Matthew lived outside of Palestine, perhaps in Antioch, the capital of Syria; he wrote as if he had been part of that thriving Jewish community, which, like all Jewish communities, had experienced intense upheaval following the war.[16]

In Jerusalem the Temple lay in ruins, and Vespasian had stationed a permanent Roman garrison there. Roman troops and civilians had built a settlement that included pagan shrines along with Roman baths, shops, and other amenities of Roman life. Vespasian also penalized Jews throughout the empire for the war by appropriating for the Roman treasury the tax that Jews had previously paid to support their own Temple. With the Temple's destruction the high priest, formerly the chief spokesman for the Jewish people, lost his position, along with all his priestly allies. The Sanhedrin, formerly the supreme Jewish council, also lost its power.

The war permanently changed the nature of Jewish leadership in Jerusalem and in Jewish communities everywhere. Yet even during the war, some Jews and Romans had already begun preparing alternative leadership to replace the priests and the Sanhedrin after the war. When the Romans besieged the Temple in March, 68 C.E., the Jewish teacher Johanan ben Zakkai fled Jerusalem and took refuge in a Roman camp. There, anticipating the Roman victory, he asked Vespasian for permission to found an academy for Jewish teachers in Jamnia, a town the Romans had already recovered. Vespasian and his advisers, apparently expecting that Jews would resume internal self-government after the war, granted permission to Johanan to establish this school as a legitimate Jewish authority. According to the historian Mary Smallwood,

> Rabbi Johanan's escape, technically an act of treachery, was the Jews' spiritual salvation when the rabbinic school which he founded took the place of the Sanhedrin . . . and its president,

the Nasi, or patriarch, replaced the high priest as the Jews' leader and spokesman, both religious and political.[17]

The high-priestly dynasty and its aristocratic allies in the San-hedrin, along with the Sadducean scribes associated with the former Temple, were now swept aside. A growing group of teachers, mostly Pharisees, many of them self-supporting tradesmen (like Paul, a tentmaker, who had been a Pharisee), now took over leadership roles, expanding their authority throughout Judea, and eventually in Jewish communities throughout the world. Thus began the rabbinic movement, which would become increasingly dominant in Jewish commu-nity life.[18]

Matthew, proclaiming the message of Jesus the Messiah c. 80 C.E., found himself in competition primarily with these Pharisaic teachers and rabbis, who were successfully establishing themselves throughout the Jewish world as authoritative inter-preters of the Torah. The Pharisees wanted to place the Torah at the center of Jewish life as a replacement for the ruined Temple. Their aim was to teach a practical interpretation of Jewish law that would preserve Jewish groups throughout the world as a separate and holy people. Matthew saw the Pharisees as the chief rivals to his own teachings about Jesus[19] and decided to present Jesus and his message in terms comprehensible to the Pharisees and their large following—not only as God's Messiah, but also as the one whose teaching embodies and fulfills the true righteous-ness previously taught in "the law and the prophets."

As we shall see, Matthew insists that Jesus offers a universaliz-ing interpretation of Torah ("Love God and your neighbor"; "Do unto others what you would have them do unto you") without giving up "a jot or a tittle" of divine law. But because Matthew's Jesus interprets the Torah so that Gentiles can fulfill it as well as Jews, Matthew in effect encourages people to abandon traditional ethnic identification with Israel. This was a radical position that most Jews found—and declared—anathema. In Matthew, Jesus repeatedly attacks the Pharisees as "hypocrites" obsessed with petty regulations while ignoring "justice and mercy and faith"—attacks that caricature the rabbis' concern to preserve Israel's integrity through observant behavior. Thus Matthew takes part in a bitter controversy central to Jewish—and what will become Christian—identity.[20]

In writing his gospel, Matthew was concerned to refute damaging rumors about Jesus—for example, that his birth was illegitimate, which would disgrace and disqualify him as a suitable candidate for Israel's Messiah. Furthermore, Jesus was known to have come from Nazareth in Galilee, and from a common family—not from the royal, Davidic dynasty established in Bethlehem, as would befit a king of Israel. Even more serious, perhaps, was the charge that Jesus, according to Mark, neglected or even violated observance of Sabbath and kosher laws.

Matthew, like his predecessors in the Christian movement, was troubled by such criticisms. But as he searched through the Scriptures, he was repeatedly struck by biblical passages, especially among the prophets' writings and among the psalms, that he believed illuminated the events surrounding Jesus' life. For example, in opposition to the rumor that Jesus was born illegitimate, Matthew and his predecessors found vindication for their faith in Jesus in Isaiah 7:14. There the Lord promises to give Israel a "sign" of the coming of God's salvation. Apparently Matthew knew the Hebrew Bible in its Greek translation, where he would have read the following:

> "The Lord himself shall give you a sign: Behold, a virgin shall conceive and bear a son; and shall call his name Immanuel—God with us" (Isaiah 7:14).

In the original Hebrew, the passage had read "young woman" (*almah*), apparently describing an ordinary birth. But the translation of *almah* into the Greek *parthenos* ("virgin"), as many of Jesus' followers read the passage, confirmed their conviction that Jesus' birth, which unbelievers derided as sordid, actually was a miraculous "sign."[21] Thus Matthew revises Mark's story by saying that the spirit descended upon Jesus not at his baptism but at the moment of his conception. So, Matthew says, Jesus' mother "was discovered to have a child in her womb through the holy spirit" (1:18); and God's angel explains to Joseph that the child "was conceived through the holy spirit." Jesus' birth was no scandal, Matthew says, but a miracle—one that precisely fulfills Isaiah's ancient prophecy.

To prove that Jesus, despite his humble birth, possessed messianic credentials, Matthew works out a royal genealogy for Jesus, tracing his ancestry back to Abraham by way of King David (Luke does the same, apparently working independently, since Luke's genealogy differs from Matthew's; compare Matthew 1:1–17 with Luke 3:23–38).

Matthew tells an elaborate story to explain why Jesus, the descendant of kings, was thought to belong to an obscure family in the town of Nazareth in Galilee, and not to a royal dynasty based in Bethlehem. Matthew insists that Jesus' miraculous birth shook Jerusalem's ruling powers, both secular and religious. When King Herod, whom the Romans supported as a client king of the Jews, heard that a new star had appeared, which portends a royal birth, Matthew says, "he was troubled, and all Jerusalem with him" (2:3). Frustrated in his first attempt to find and destroy Jesus, Herod "was in a furious rage, and he sent and killed all the male children in Bethlehem, and in all that region who were two years old and under" (2:16). Jesus' father, warned by an angel, took the child and his mother and fled into Egypt. After Herod's death they returned, Matthew says, but Jesus' father, knowing that Herod's son still ruled Judea, chose to protect Jesus by taking his family to live incognito in the village of Nazareth. Thus Matthew explains how Jesus came to be associated with this obscure Galilean town, instead of with Bethlehem, which was his actual birthplace, according to Matthew.

Since no historical record mentions a mass slaughter of infants among Herod's crimes, many New Testament scholars regard the story of the "slaughter of the innocents," like the "flight into Egypt," as reflecting Matthew's programmatic conviction that Jesus' life must recapitulate the whole history of Israel. According to these scholars, Matthew is less concerned to give biographical information than to show a connection between Jesus,

Moses, and Israel's exodus from Egypt. Like Moses, who, as a newborn, escaped the furious wrath of the Egyptian Pharaoh, who had ordered a mass slaughter of Hebrew male infants, so Jesus, Matthew says, escaped the wrath of King Herod. And as God once delivered Israel from Egypt, so now, Matthew claims, he has delivered Jesus. Matthew does here what he does throughout his gospel; he takes words from the prophetic writings (here words from the prophet Hosea), generally understood to apply to the nation of Israel ("Out of Egypt I have called my son"), and applies them to Jesus of Nazareth, whom he sees as the culmination of Israel's history.[22]

Many scholars have noted these parallels between Jesus, Moses, and Israel. But no one, so far as I know, has observed that Matthew *reverses* the traditional roles, casting the Jewish king, Herod, in the villain's role traditionally reserved for Pharaoh. Through this device he turns the alien enemies of Israel's antiquity into the intimate enemies, as Matthew perceives them. Matthew includes among Jesus' enemies the chief priests and scribes as well as all the other inhabitants of Jerusalem, for Matthew says that not only was Herod "troubled" to hear of Jesus' birth, but so was "all Jerusalem with him" (2:3). Matthew intends, no doubt, to contrast Herod, Idumean by background, and so from a suspect dynasty, with Jesus, whose legitimately Davidic (and so royal) lineage Matthew proclaims. Now it is Herod, not Pharaoh, who ruthlessly orders the mass slaughter of Jewish male infants. According to Matthew, no sooner was Jesus born than the "chief priests and the scribes of the people" assembled, apparently united behind Herod's attempt to "search for the child and kill him" (2:13). Matthew's account of Jesus' birth is no Christmas-card idyll, but foreshadows the terrible events of the crucifixion.

While assigning to Herod Pharaoh's traditional role, Matthew simultaneously reverses Israel's symbolic geography. Egypt, traditionally the land of slavery, now becomes a sanctuary for Jesus and his family—a place of refuge and deliverance from the slaughter ordered by the *Jewish* king. This reversal of imagery is nearly as shocking as that in the book of Revelation, which refers to Jerusalem as the place "allegorically called Sodom and Egypt, where our Lord was crucified" (11:8). Later Matthew will have Jesus favorably compare Tyre and Sidon, and even Sodom, with the local towns of Bethsaida, Chorazin, and Capernaum (11:20–24).

Throughout his gospel, Matthew sustains this reversal of alien and intimate enemies. Directly following his Sermon on the Mount, Jesus heals a leper outcast from Israel, and then performs a healing for a Roman centurion who recognizes Jesus' divine power and appeals to him to use it on his behalf. Astonished to hear a Roman officer express faith "greater than any" he has found in Israel, Jesus immediately declares, "I tell you, many shall come from east and west and sit down with Abraham and Isaac and Jacob in the Kingdom of God, while the sons of the kingdom shall be cast out into outer darkness; there people will weep and gnash their teeth" (8:11–12).

From the beginning of his gospel to its end, Matthew indicts Israel's present leaders while he campaigns in favor of Jesus— Israel's Messiah—and those the new King himself appoints. Not only was Herod an Idumean, his family lived in a notoriously Gentile way, despite their religious professions. John the Baptist had been beheaded for proclaiming openly that Herod had married his former sister-in-law and so lived in open violation of Jewish law. Matthew wants to show not only that Jesus was Israel's legitimate king, rather than such unworthy usurpers as Herod, but also that he was God's designated teacher of righteousness, destined, so Matthew claims, to replace the Pharisees, who held that role in the eyes of many of his contemporaries. Matthew, who, along with his fellow Christians, opposes the rival party of Pharisees, casts his gospel primarily as a polemic between Jesus and the Pharisees, in which the two antagonistic parties are not equally matched. The Pharisees are widely respected and honored, accepted by the people as religious authorities; Jesus' followers are a suspect minority, maligned and persecuted.

In Mark, Jesus contests wordlessly against Satan in the wilderness. But Matthew borrows sayings from the Q source and shows Satan appearing three times to "test" Jesus, as Pharisees and other opponents will test him. Here the Q source turns Satan into a caricature of a scribe, a debater skilled in verbal challenge and adept in quoting the Scriptures for diabolic purposes, who repeatedly questions Jesus' divine authority ("If you are the son of God . . ."). Having twice failed to induce Jesus to perform a miracle to prove his divine power and authority, Satan finally offers him "all the kingdoms of this world and their glory," which Satan claims as his own. Thus Matthew, following Mark's lead, implies that political success and power (such as the Pharisees enjoy under Roman patronage) may evince a pact with the devil—and not, as many of Matthew's contemporaries would have assumed, marks of divine favor.

Matthew next assails the Pharisees on the question that concerns them most, the interpretation of Torah. To correct the impression that Jesus simply ignored traditional Jewish concern with righteous obedience to Torah—an impression any reader could get from Mark—Matthew makes Jesus embody all that is best and truest in Jewish tradition. Mark begins his gospel with descriptions of healings and exorcisms, but Matthew begins by showing Jesus proclaiming a new interpretation of divine law. Like Moses, who ascended Mount Sinai to receive and promulgate God's law, Jesus goes up on a mountain, where he proclaims what we know as the Sermon on the Mount. Taking aim at the Pharisees and those impressed by their interpretation of Torah, Matthew insists that Jesus does not reject the Torah. Instead, Matthew says, Jesus proclaims its essential meaning:

"Do not think that I came to abolish the law and the prophets;
I came not to abolish but to fulfill them" (5:17).

Jesus then warns that "unless your righteousness exceeds that of the scribes and the Pharisees, you will never enter the Kingdom of heaven" (5:20). Thus Matthew defends Jesus against charges of laxity in Sabbath and kosher observance by insisting that he practices a *greater* righteousness, not a lesser one. According to Matthew 5 and 6, Jesus demands an enormous *increase* in religious scrupulosity: the traditional Torah is not half strict enough for him! Where Moses' law prohibits murder, Jesus' "new Torah" prohibits anger, insults, and name calling; where Moses' law prohibits adultery, Jesus' prohibits lust. Much of the Mosaic law was couched in negative terms ("You shall not . . ."). Jesus reinterprets it positively:

> "Whatever you would have people do to you, do the same to them; for this is the law and the prophets" (7:12).

Simultaneously Matthew insists that Jesus' critics, "the scribes and the Pharisees," use mere hypocritical "observance" as a cover for violating what Jesus here proclaims to be the Torah's central commands of love for God and neighbor (6:1–18).

As we have seen, Matthew diverges from Mark in making the Pharisees Jesus' primary antagonists.[23] For Mark it was the Jerusalem scribes who were angered by Jesus' powerful effect on the crowd and charged him with demon possession; but Matthew changes the story to say that the Pharisees accused Jesus of "casting out demons by the prince of demons" (12:24). While Mark says that the Pharisees and the Herodians first plotted to kill Jesus, Matthew says that only the Pharisees "went and took counsel, how to destroy him" (12:14). Matthew even has the Pharisees repeat the charge that Jesus is "possessed by Beelzebub" (12:24); Jesus adamantly denies the charge and warns: "If it is by the spirit of God that I cast out demons, then the kingdom of God has come upon you" (12:28). Matthew's Jesus declares that this supernatural conflict has now split God's people into two separate—and opposing—communities: "Whoever is not with me is against me, and whoever does not gather with me scatters" (12:30).

Distressed that the people of Israel are "harassed and helpless, like sheep without a shepherd," lacking true leadership, Jesus now designates the twelve, and gives them "authority over unclean spirits, to cast them out" (10:1). Warning them that the people "will deliver you up to sanhedrins, and beat you in their synagogues" (10:17), Jesus tells them to anticipate murderous hatred within their own households (10:21), as well as from "everyone" (10:22); for, as he says, "if they have called the master of the house Beelzebub, how much more will they malign those members of his household?" (10:25). As the narrative proceeds, the antagonism between Jesus and his enemies becomes—as in the literature of the Essene sectarians—a contest between those whom Matthew's Jesus calls "sons of the kingdom" and the "sons of the evil one" (13:38). Jesus repeats John the Baptist's denunciation of the Pharisees: "You brood of vipers! How can you say good things, when you are evil?" (12:34). Then Jesus predicts that foreigners shall "arise at the judgment of this generation and condemn it" (12:41). Finally, he implicitly accuses those who oppose him of being possessed by demons, telling the parable of a man who, having been exorcised, experiences a new invasion of "seven other spirits more evil" than the first, "so that the last state of that man becomes worse than the first. So shall it be also with this evil generation" (12:45).

Later, Jesus explains privately to his followers that the generation he addresses—except for the elect—*already* has been judged and condemned; his opponents' refusal to receive his preaching, he says, reveals Satan's power over them. In the parable of the sower, Jesus identifies the "evil one" as the enemy who has "snatched away" the seeds he has planted and so prevented his preaching from bearing fruit among his own people (13:19). Immediately thereafter Jesus tells the parable of the weeds, explicitly identifying his opponents as the offspring of Satan: "the weeds are the sons of the evil one, and the enemy who sowed them is the devil" (13:38–39).

Jesus, finally recognized by his disciples as Messiah, tells them that now, by the authority of God's spirit, he is establishing his *own* assembly, which shall triumph over all the forces of evil, as if to say that God has replaced Israel with a new community. Many scholars agree with George Nickelsburg that Matthew's Jesus claims in chapter 16 that what previously was the "congregation of Israel" has become "his church."[24]

Jesus' conflict with the Pharisees reaches a climax in Matthew 23. Throughout this chapter, Matthew takes sayings attributed to Jesus and turns them into stories of conflict that pit Jesus against those he denounces seven times as "scribes and Pharisees, hypocrites," and even "children of hell" (23:15). Matthew has Jesus call down divine wrath upon "this generation" (23:36),

> "that upon you may come all the righteous blood shed on earth, from the blood of the innocent Abel to that of Zechariah, son of Barachiah, whom you murdered between the sanctuary and the altar" (23:35).

Many scholars have noted and commented on the bitter hostility expressed in this chapter.[25] Biblical scholar Luke Johnson shows that philosophic groups in antiquity often attacked their rivals in strong terms.[26] But philosophers did not engage, as Matthew does here, in *demonic* vilification of their opponents. Within the ancient world, so far as I know, it is only Essenes and Christians who actually escalate conflict with their opponents to the level of cosmic war.

Matthew's Jesus acknowledges that the Pharisees say much that is valid ("Practice and observe whatever they tell you, but do not do what they do"), but he charges that they are more concerned with maintaining their authority than anything else. Moreover, he says, they neglect essential moral concerns, preoccupying themselves with legal haggling:

> "Woe to you, scribes and Pharisees, hypocrites! for you tithe mint and dill and cummin, and have neglected the weightier matters of the law, justice and mercy and faith; these you ought to have done, without neglecting the others. You blind guides, straining out a gnat, and swallowing a camel!" (23:23–24)

Scholars know that many Jewish teachers at the time of Jesus—teachers like Hillel and Shammai, Jesus' contemporaries—engaged in moral interpretation of the law. One famous story tells how Hillel answered a student who asked him to teach the whole of the Torah while standing on one foot. Hillel replied, "Whatever you do not want others to do to you, do not do to them. That is the whole of the Torah." Yet even a liberal like Hillel would have opposed a movement that claimed to reinterpret the Torah morally but put aside the ritual precepts that define Jewish identity. Many Jews of the first century saw such tendencies in the Christian movement. Many Pharisees, concerned to keep Israel holy and separate through Torah observance, may well have regarded Jesus' followers as threatening Israel's integrity—even its existence.

Matthew wants to say, as we have seen, that Jesus never deviated from total loyalty to the Torah, but Matthew means by this that Jesus fulfilled the deeper meaning of the law, which, Matthew insists, has nothing essential to do with ethnic identity. In Matthew, Jesus twice summarizes "the law and the prophets," both times in ways that depend solely on moral action. First, what Hillel stated negatively, Jesus states positively: "Whatever you want people to do to you, do the same to them; on this depends the whole of the law and the prophets" (7:12). Second, he summarizes the Torah in the dual command, "Love the Lord your God with all your heart, soul, and mind, and your neighbor as yourself" (22:37). Finally Matthew's Jesus offers a parable depicting the coming of God's judgment. On that day, Jesus says, the divine king will gather *all the nations,* inviting some to enter into God's eternal kingdom, and consigning others to what Jesus calls "the eternal fire prepared for the devil and his angels." What is the criterion of divine judgment? According to Matthew, Jesus says that the king will say to those on his right hand,

" 'Come, O blessed of my Father, inherit the kingdom prepared for you from the foundation of the world. For I was hungry and you gave me food; I was thirsty and you gave me drink; I was a stranger and you welcomed me; I was sick and you visited me; I was in prison and you came to me.' Then the righteous will answer him, 'Lord, when did we see thee a stranger and welcome thee or naked and clothe thee? And when did we see thee sick or in prison and visit thee?' And the king will answer them, 'Truly, I say to you, as you did it to one of the least of my brethren, you did it to me.' Then he will say to those at his left hand, 'Depart from me, you cursed ones, into the eternal fire prepared for the devil and his angels; for I was hungry and you gave me no food, I was thirsty and you gave me no drink, I was a stranger and you did not welcome me, naked and you did not clothe me, sick and in prison and you did not visit me.' Then they also will answer, 'Lord, when did we see thee hungry or thirsty or a stranger or sick or in prison, and did not minister to thee?' Then he will answer them, 'Truly I say to you, as you did it not to one of the least of these, you did it not to me.' And they will go away into eternal punishment, but the righteous into eternal life" (25:34–46).

Inclusion in God's kingdom depends, then, not on membership in Israel but on justice combined with generosity and compassion. Ethnicity as a criterion has vanished. Gentiles as well as Jews could embrace this reinterpretation of divine law—and in Matthew's community many did.

According to Matthew, Jesus and the movement he began articulate the true meaning of God's law. Jesus denounces the Pharisees not only as false interpreters but deadly opponents to truth—those who "kill and crucify" God's prophets (23:34). From this final denunciation of the Pharisees, Matthew turns immediately to the story of Jesus' crucifixion. Closely following Mark's account, Matthew describes the involvement of the chief priest, scribes, and elders, but does not mention the Pharisees again until after Jesus' death.

But Matthew does add episodes that highlight the greater guilt of Jesus' Jewish enemies. Only Matthew says that even Judas Iscariot bitterly regretted betraying Jesus, "and throwing down the pieces of silver in the Temple, he departed, and went and hanged himself" (27:3–5). Matthew adds, too, the story of Pilate's wife:

> While Pilate was sitting on the judgment seat, his wife sent word to him, "Have nothing to do with that righteous man, for I have suffered much over him today in a dream" (27:19).

As in Mark, here Pilate offers to release Jesus, and protests to the crowds shouting for Jesus' crucifixion, "Why, what evil has he done?" But Matthew also supplies a pragmatic reason for Pilate's acquiescence to the crowd: Pilate "saw that he was gaining nothing, but rather that a riot was starting" (27:24). At that point, Matthew claims, in a most unlikely scene, Pilate performed a ritual that derives from Jewish law, described in the book of Deuteronomy. He washed his hands to indicate his innocence of bloodshed, and said, "I am innocent of this man's blood; see to it yourselves" (27:24). At that moment, according to Matthew alone, the Jewish leaders as well as "the whole nation" acknowledged collective responsibility and invoked what turned out to be a curse upon themselves and their progeny: "His blood be upon us and upon our children!" (27:25).

Matthew also adds the story that following the crucifixion, "the chief priests and Pharisees" solicited Pilate to secure Jesus' tomb with a guard, lest his followers steal his body to fake a resurrection. To account for the common rumor that Jesus' disciples had stolen his body, Matthew says that the Jewish authorities bribed the Roman soldiers to start this rumor. "So," Matthew concludes, "they took the money and did as they were told; and this story has been spread among the Jews to this day" (28:15).

As the gospel moves toward its conclusion, Matthew dissociates Jesus' followers from those he calls "the Jews," and tries to account for the hostility and disbelief that he and his fellow Christians apparently encounter from the Jewish majority. Matthew takes this to mean that the majority, who reject the gospel, have forfeited their legacy. The former insiders have now become outsiders. According to Matthew, Jesus tells an ominous parable: A great king invited his people to attend his son's wedding. (Here Matthew evokes a prophetic metaphor to imply that the wedding symbolizes the intended union between the Lord himself and Israel, his bride; see Jeremiah 2:1–3:20; Isaiah 50:1; Hosea 1:2–3:5.) But when those who are invited refuse to attend, and even beat, abuse, and kill the king's messengers, Jesus says, the king declares that "the invited guests were not worthy," and proceeds to invite others in their place. Then, Matthew's Jesus continues, "the king was angry, and sent his troops and destroyed those murderers, and burned their city"

(22:7). Thus Matthew goes so far as to suggest that God himself brought on the Roman massacre and destruction of Jerusalem in 70 C.E. to punish the Jews for rejecting "his son."

Most scholars agree that although Matthew's own group probably included both Jewish and Gentile believers, its members were finding more receptive audiences among Gentiles than among Jews. Thus Matthew ends with a scene in which the resurrected Jesus, having received "all authority on heaven and on earth," orders his followers to "go and make disciples of all nations" (28:19). Matthew, himself rooted in the Jewish community, looks at it with enormous ambivalence—ambivalence that will influence Christian communities for centuries, even millennia. Matthew's contemporary and fellow Christian Luke, who also adapts Mark and revises it, takes a different line. This Gentile convert relegates Israel's greatness to the past, and confidently claims its present legacy for his own—predominantly Gentile—community. In both Luke and John, as we see next, Jesus himself identifies his Jewish opponents with Satan.

IV

LUKE AND JOHN CLAIM
ISRAEL'S LEGACY:
THE SPLIT WIDENS

Luke, the only Gentile author among the gospel writers, speaks for those Gentile converts to Christianity who consider themselves the true heirs of Israel. Luke goes beyond Matthew in radically revising Mark's account of Jesus' life. Matthew had said that the Jewish majority had lost their claim on God's covenant by refusing to acknowledge his Messiah; consequently, God had offered his covenant to the Gentiles in their place. Luke goes further, however, and agrees with Paul that God had always intended to offer salvation to everyone. Luke's vision of universal salvation invited Greeks, Asians, Africans, Syrians, and Egyptians to identify themselves, as confidently as any Essene, as members of the "true Israel." Christians everywhere still rely on Luke's message every day in their prayers, hymns, and liturgies. Luke also goes further than Mark and Matthew in making explicit what Mark and Matthew imply—the connection between Jesus' Jewish enemies and the "evil one," the devil. In Luke, Jesus himself, at the moment of his arrest, suggests that the arresting party of "chief priests and scribes and elders" is allied with the evil one, whom Jesus here calls "the power of darkness."

Luke, like Matthew, refutes common allegations against Jesus—that he was illegitimate and lacked the dynastic credentials to be Israel's Messiah. Like Matthew, Luke begins his story before Jesus' conception, to show that God's spirit enacted this miraculous event. According to Luke, it was the spirit, or its agents, the angels, who initiated the marvelous events surrounding Jesus' birth and infancy.

But Luke, unlike Matthew, reports no animosity on the part of Herod or the people of Jerusalem toward the infant Jesus. As in Mark, however, the moment Jesus appears as a grown man, baptized and "full of the holy spirit," the devil immediately challenges him. The devil is thrice defeated, and Luke says that "the devil departed from him *until an opportune time* [*achri kairou*]" (emphasis added). Frustrated in his initial attempt to overpower Jesus, the devil finds his opportunity only at the end of the story, when the chief priests and scribes "sought to kill Jesus." At that point, Luke says, "Satan entered into Judas Iscariot," who "went and conferred with the chief priest how he might betray him; and they were glad, and agreed to give him money." From that time, Luke says, Judas "sought an opportunity [*eukairan*] to betray him."

After his first engagement with Jesus, Satan did not withdraw from the contest but bided his time; throughout Jesus' public career the devil worked underground—or, more accurately, *on* the ground—through human agents. Immediately after his solitary contest with Satan in the desert, Jesus' first episode of public teaching begins with a favorable reception from the crowd but suddenly turns into a scene of brutal, nearly lethal, violence. Luke says that Jesus, after his baptism, enters the synagogue as usual in his hometown of Nazareth and reads for the congregation a prophetic passage from Isaiah. Then he announces, " 'Today this Scripture has been fulfilled in your hearing.' And they all spoke well of him, and marveled at the gracious words that came from his mouth" (4:21–22). Jesus now predicts that his townspeople will reject him, and declares that God intends to bring salvation to the Gentiles, even at the cost of bypassing Israel, saying:

> "There were many widows in Israel in the days of Elijah . . . and Elijah was sent to none of them, but only to Zarephath, in the land of Sidon, to a woman who was a widow. There were many lepers in Israel in the time of the prophet Elisha and none of them was cleansed, but only Naaman the Syrian" (4:25–27).

Hearing this, Luke continues,

> all those in the synagogue were filled with rage, and they rose
> up to throw him out of the city, and led him to the edge of the
> hill on which the city was built, in order to throw him down
> headlong (4:28–29).

But Jesus quickly departs, and so escapes this first attempt on his
life.

Now the "the scribes and the Pharisees" begin to plot against
Jesus, eyeing him suspiciously, looking for an opportunity "to
make an accusation against him" (6:7). When they see him heal
on the Sabbath, they "were filled with fury and discussed with
one another what they might do to Jesus" (6:11).

But Luke's Pharisees, unlike Matthew's, are not unanimously
hostile to Jesus.[1] Some express interest in him and invite him to
dinner, some even warn him of danger, but others willingly play
Satan's role, plotting to kill him. Luke sometimes calls the Pharisees "lovers of money" (16:14) and self-righteous (18:9–14),
qualities he castigates in others as well; and he shows the special
empathy between Jesus and those who are despised—the destitute,
the sick, women, and Samaritans. Jesus' followers include many tax
collectors and prostitutes; Luke believes that these too are God's
people. From the opening scenes in the Temple involving Jesus'
infancy and adolescence to the gospel's close, which describes how
the disciples "went to Jerusalem, and were continually in the Temple praising God," the followers of Jesus are deeply loyal to the
Temple—perhaps the only genuine Israelites left in Jerusalem.
Luke certainly intends to show that they are closer to God than the
Pharisees or any other Jewish religious leaders.

Spiritual warfare between God and Satan—which is reflected
in conflict between Jesus and his followers and the Jewish leaders—intensifies throughout the gospel.[2] As people divide against
him, Jesus says,

> "Do not think that I have come to bring peace on earth, no,
> rather division; from now on in one house there shall be five

divided, three against two and two against three; they will be
divided, father against son and son against father, mother
against daughter and daughter against her mother" (12:51–55).

As the chief priests and their allies harden their opposition, certain Pharisees warn Jesus, in an episode unique to Luke, about
the Jewish king: "Herod wants to kill you." Jesus' reply suggests
that what angers Herod is that Jesus has challenged Satan, the
power that rules this world: "Go and tell that fox, 'Today and
tomorrow I cast out demons and heal, and the third day I finish
my course' " (13:32). After Jesus sends out seventy apostles to
heal and proclaim the message of the kingdom, they return "with
joy," astonished and triumphant, saying, "Lord, even the
demons are subject to us in your name." Jesus exults, foreseeing
Satan's impending defeat:

> "I saw Satan fall like lightning from heaven: Behold, I have
> given you power to tread on snakes and scorpions, and upon
> every power of the enemy" (10:18–19).

Immediately before Satan enters into Judas and initiates the
betrayal, Jesus warns, in parable, that he himself will return as
king to see his enemies annihilated. As soon as he begins his
final journey to Jerusalem, where he will enter the city publicly
acclaimed as king by his disciples but will be rejected by the
majority of Jerusalemites, Jesus tells the story of "a certain
nobleman" who travels to a distant land "in order to claim his
kingly power and return" (19:12). When the nobleman succeeds and returns in triumph, his first act is to demand that his
enemies be killed: "*As for those enemies of mine, who did not want
me to rule over them, bring them here and slaughter them before
me*" (19:27; emphasis added). Luke makes the parallel unmis-
takable: "While saying these words, Jesus traveled before [the
disciples], going up to Jerusalem." When he arrives, he immediately orders his disciples to prepare for his royal entry into the
city (cf. Zech. 9:9). But Luke alone, among the synoptic gospels,
inserts the words "the king," taken from Psalm 118, into the
acclamation the disciples shouted at Jesus' arrival in Jerusalem:

"Blessed is the one, the king, who comes in the name of the Lord!" (Ps. 118:26; Luke 19:38). When some Pharisees in the crowd, apparently shocked by this open proclamation of Jesus as king, admonished Jesus, "Rabbi, rebuke your disciples," Luke says, he answered, "I tell you, if these were silent, the very stones would cry out."

Then, Luke says, as that fateful Passover drew near, "the chief priests and the scribes were seeking how to put him to death." This was the opportunity for which Satan had been waiting: "Then Satan entered into Judas Iscariot," who immediately conferred with the chief priests and the Temple officers, to arrange the betrayal. But here, as in Mark, Jesus himself declares that neither Satan's role nor God's preordained plan absolves Judas's guilt: "The Son of man goes as it has been determined; but woe to that man by whom he is betrayed" (22:22; cf. Mark 14:21).

John mentions armed Roman soldiers among the arresting party, but Luke mentions only Jews, and omits a saying common to Mark and Matthew, that "the Son of man is betrayed *into the hands of sinners*" (that is, Gentiles). Instead, when the armed party arrives in Gethsemane, Luke's Jesus turns directly to "the chief priests and temple officers and elders who had come out against him," and identifies them as Satan incarnate: "Have you come out as against a robber, with swords and clubs? When I was with you in the temple every day, you did not lay hands upon me. But this is *your* [plural] *hour,* and *the power of darkness*" (22:52–53; emphasis added).

Like Mark, Luke says that the arresting party "seized Jesus and led him away, bringing him to the high priest's house," while Peter followed surreptitiously into the high priest's courtyard. But at this point Luke diverges from Mark, omitting Mark's elaborate scene of a trial before the Sanhedrin in which, as we have seen, the whole Sanhedrin gathered at night to hear a parade of witnesses and to witness the high priest's interrogation of Jesus, which culminated in the unanimously pronounced death sentence for blasphemy. Mark—and Matthew following him—depicts members of the Sanhedrin spitting on Jesus, beating him, and mocking him before the guards join them in beating him (Mark 14:65; Matt. 26:67–68).

Luke tells a starker and simpler story: After his arrest, Jesus is held and guarded all night in the courtyard of the high priest's house to await a morning session of the Sanhedrin. Luke says it is not members of the aristocratic Sanhedrin but "the men holding Jesus" who entertained themselves during the long night by beating and mocking the prisoner (22:63–65). In the morning, the guards lead Jesus to the council chamber near the Temple for interrogation by the assembled Sanhedrin. Instead of a formal trial, this seems to be a kind of court hearing—an interrogation with no witnesses and no formal sentence. Nevertheless, the Sanhedrin decides to take Jesus to Pilate to present formal—and capital—charges against him.

Did Luke have access to independent—perhaps earlier—accounts of what led to the crucifixion? Many scholars, prominently including the British scholar David Catchpole, believe that he did.[3] Luke reconstructs a scene in which the Sanhedrin members interrogate Jesus:

> "If you are the Messiah, tell us." But he said to them, "If I tell you, you will not believe; and if I ask you, you will not answer. But from now on the Son of man will be seated at the right hand of the power of God." And they said to him, "Are you the Son of God, then?" And he said to them, "You say that I am" (22:67–70).

Luke's account, like Matthew's and John's, contradicts Mark's claim that Jesus resoundingly and publicly affirmed his divine appointment at his trial (Mark 14:62). In Luke, Jesus answers only evasively. Given the lack of supporting evidence, no one can say what actually happened, though hundreds of scholars, Jewish and Christian, have attempted an answer. One has only to glance at Catchpole's meticulous monograph *The Trial of Jesus* to see that every act in every episode has become the subject of intense debate.

Despite these uncertainties, everyone who interprets the texts has to sort out the tradition to some extent, and to reconstruct, however provisionally, what may have happened, and correspondingly, what each evangelist added, and for what reasons.

Catchpole himself argues that Luke's account of the Sanhedrin trial is more "historically reliable" than any other.[4] This would mean that the Sanhedrin members accused Jesus of claiming to be Messiah and Son of God. Raymond Brown disagrees, and sides with those who are convinced that the titles Messiah and Son of God emerged later, from Christian communities (in this case, from Luke's community) and not from the Jewish Sanhedrin. In any case, Luke's account suggests that Jesus had received public acclaim as king (19:38) and, as we noted, even when the Pharisees warned him to silence those who were shouting these acclamations, Jesus refused to do so (19:39–40). Whether he made these same claims for himself, as Mark alone insists (14:61), or merely accepted what others said of him, as Matthew, Luke, and John say, apparently mattered less to the Sanhedrin than the effect that such claims could have upon the restless crowds gathered for Passover. Consequently, Luke says, Jesus' enemies decided to bring him to Pilate, accusing him of three charges calculated to arouse the governor's concern: "We found this man guilty of perverting our nation [apparently, of teaching in opposition to the designated religious leaders], forbidding us to pay tribute to Caesar, and saying that he himself is Messiah, a king" (23:2).

Mark and Matthew said that Pilate was skeptical of the charges, but Luke's Pilate pronounces Jesus innocent no less than three times. At first Pilate says, "I find no crime in this man." Then, after the chief priests and the crowds object and insist that Jesus is guilty of disturbing the peace, Pilate tries to rid himself of responsibility by sending Jesus to King Herod. While Mark and Matthew show Pilate's soldiers mocking and beating Jesus, Luke further exonerates Pilate by showing that it was Herod and his officers (like the Jewish officers involved in the arrest) who abused and mocked Jesus as a would-be king (23:11).

Jesus is then returned to Pilate, who formally assembles "the chief priests and the rulers and the people." These three groups, which had previously divided between the leaders, who hated Jesus, and the people, whose presence had protected him, now present a united front against him. To all those assembled before him Pilate declares again:

"You brought me this man as one who was misleading the people, and after examining him before you, behold, I did not find this man guilty of any of your charges against him; neither did Herod, for he sent him back to us. Behold, nothing deserving death has been done by him; I will therefore chastise him and release him."

But Luke says that the Jewish leaders and people, hearing Pilate's decision, unanimously protested: "They *all* cried out *together,* 'Away with this man' " (23:18; emphasis added). According to Luke, Pilate still refused to give in, and "addressed them once more, desiring to release Jesus, but they shouted out, 'Crucify him, crucify him!' " Luke apparently thinks he cannot emphasize this too much, for he now repeats Pilate's verdict a third time: "What evil has he done? I found in him no crime deserving death; therefore I will chastise him and release him." But the onlookers, Luke says,

demanded with loud cries that Jesus should be crucified, and their voices prevailed; and Pilate ordered that their demand be granted, and . . . he gave Jesus over *to their will* (emphasis added).

In earlier passages, nevertheless, Luke had followed Mark in saying that Jesus' enemies delivered him "to the Gentiles" (18:32); later, Luke, like Mark, will mention a Roman centurion present at the crucifixion. These clues, along with Luke's acknowledgment that the written accusation was that Jesus had claimed to be "king of the Jews," and the charge was sedition (23:38), indicate that Luke knew that the Romans had actually pronounced sentence and carried out the execution. Yet as Luke tells the story, he allows, and perhaps even wants, the reader— especially one unfamiliar with other accounts—to infer that after Jews had arrested Jesus and a Jewish court had sentenced him to death, it was Jewish soldiers who actually crucified him.

Luke changes many details of the death scene to emphasize Jesus' innocence, and to give a more uplifting account than

Mark's of how God's faithful should die. When Jesus is crucified between two robbers (that is, as we have seen, between two *lēstai,* men perhaps also charged with sedition), he prays for his tormentors: "Father, forgive them; for they do not know what they are doing."[5] Mark had shown the extreme humiliation to which Jesus was subjected, saying that even the other condemned criminals joined in ridiculing Jesus, but Luke offers a different version of the story:

> One of the criminals who were hung there kept mocking him, and saying, "Aren't you the Messiah? Save yourself and us!" But the other rebuked him, saying, "Do you not fear God, since you are under the same sentence? And we are justly condemned, since we are getting what we deserve for what we did. But this man has done nothing wrong." Then he said, "Jesus, remember me when you come into your kingdom." He replied, "Truly, I tell you, today you shall be with me in Paradise."

Thus Luke again emphasizes Jesus' innocence—innocence recognized even by a condemned criminal—and shows that even the dying Jesus has power to forgive, to redeem, and to save the lost. Luke omits Jesus' anguished cry ("My God, my God, why have you forsaken me?" Psalm 22:1), along with Jesus' last, inarticulate scream, and replaces them instead with a prayer of faith taken from Psalm 31:5: "Then Jesus, crying with a loud voice, said, 'Father, into your hands I commit my spirit.' Having said this, he breathed his last." Thus Luke banishes the scene of agony and replaces it with trusting submission to God. Finally, Luke goes so far as to say that many of the bystanders, seeing all this, repented what they had done: "When all the crowds who had gathered there for the spectacle saw what had taken place, they returned home, beating their breasts" (23:48). He also changes Mark's account to say that the Roman centurion who saw Jesus die "praised God," and echoed Pilate's verdict: "Certainly this man was innocent!"

In the early chapters of the Acts of the Apostles Luke again emphasizes the role of the Jews rather than of the Romans in

Jesus' crucifixion. Peter specifically addresses the "men of Israel," charging that they "crucified and killed" the righteous one whom God had sent to Israel. Shortly after, Peter again addresses the "men of Israel," preaching of Jesus,

> "whom you delivered up and denied in the presence of Pilate, when Pilate had decided to release him ... you denied the holy and righteous one, and you asked instead for a murderer to be granted to you."

Luke provides many details that have contributed to later Christians' perceptions that Pilate was a well-meaning weakling and that the Jewish people—that is, those he regarded as the apostate majority—were responsible for Jesus' death and for the deaths of many of his followers. The well-known French commentator Alfred Loisy says that according to Luke, "The Jews are the authors of all evil."[6] Loisy's comment oversimplifies, yet as we have seen, Luke wants to show that those who reject Jesus accomplish Satan's work on earth.

Writing independently of Luke and probably a decade later, the author of the gospel of John, who most scholars think was a Jewish convert to the movement, speaks with startlingly similar bitterness of the Jewish majority.[7] In one explosive scene, Jesus accuses the Jews of trying to kill him, saying, "You are of your father, the devil!" and "the Jews" retaliate by accusing Jesus of being a Samaritan—that is, not a real Jew—and himself "demon-possessed," or insane.

Most scholars agree that Jesus probably did not make these accusations, but that such strong words reflected bitter conflict between a group of Jesus' followers to which John belonged (c. 90–100 C.E.) and the Jewish majority in their city, especially the synagogue leaders. Writing from within a Jewish community, perhaps in Palestine, John is anguished that after a series of clashes with Jewish leaders, he and his fellow Christians have been forcibly expelled from the synagogues, and denied participation in common worship. We do not know for certain what happened; John says only, "The Jews had already agreed that anyone who confessed Jesus to be the Messiah would be put out of the synagogue"—literally, would become *aposynagoge,* expelled from one's home synagogue. New Testament scholar Louis Martyn has shown that whatever it meant in particular, this traumatic separation defined how John's group saw itself—as a tiny minority of God's people "hated by the world," a group that urged its members to reject in turn the whole social and religious world into which they had been born.[8]

Martyn suggests, too, that the crisis in John's community occurred when a group of Jewish scholars, led by the rabbi Gamalial II (80–115 C.E.), introduced into synagogue worship the so-called *birkat ha-minim* (literally, "benediction of the heretics"), a prayer that invoked a curse upon "heretics," including Christians, here specifically identified as "Nazarenes." This might have enabled synagogue leaders to ask anyone suspected of being a secret "Nazarene" to "stand before the ark" and lead the congregation in the benediction, so that anyone guilty of being a Christian would be calling a curse upon himself and his fellow believers. The historian Reuven Kimelman disagrees, and argues that this ritual curse entered synagogue services considerably later and so could not have precipitated a first-century crisis. The author of John speaks, however, as if synagogue leaders had taken measures more drastic than the *birkat ha-minim,* suggesting that they actually excluded Jesus' followers to prevent them from worshiping alongside other Jews.

Whatever the actual circumstances, John chooses to tell the story of Jesus as a story of cosmic conflict—conflict between divine light and primordial darkness, between the close-knit group of Jesus' followers and the implacable, sinful opposition they encountered from "the world." Ever since the first century, John's version of the gospel has consoled and inspired groups of believers who have found themselves an oppressed minority—but a minority that they believe embodies divine light in the world. Whereas Mark begins his narrative with Jesus' baptism, and Luke and Matthew go beyond Jesus' birth to his conception, John goes back to the very origin of the universe. John begins his gospel with the opening words of Genesis, which tell how "in the beginning" God separated light from darkness. Echoing the grand cosmology of Genesis 1, John's prologue identifies the *logos,* God's energy acting in creation, with life (*zoē*) and light (*phōs*), that is, the "light of human beings." Anticipating the message of his entire gospel, John declares that "the light shines in the darkness, and the darkness has not overcome it." According to John, "the light of humankind" finally came to shine in and through Jesus of Nazareth, who is revealed to be the Son of God.

Thus John takes the primordial elements separated in creation—light and darkness—and casts them in a human drama, interpreting them simultaneously in religious, ethical, and social terms. According to John, this divine "light" not only "became human, and dwelt among us," but also is the spiritual progenitor of those who "become the children of God" (1:12), the "sons of light" (12:35). The crisis of Jesus' appearance reveals others as the "sons of darkness"; thus Jesus explains to the Jewish ruler Nicodemus that

> "this is the judgment [literally, *crisis*]: that the light came into the world and people loved darkness rather than light, because their deeds were evil. . . . But whoever does the truth comes to the light." (3:19–21).

By the end of the gospel, Jesus' epiphany will have accomplished in human society what God accomplished cosmologically in creation: the separation of light from darkness—that is, of the "sons of light" from the offspring of darkness and the devil. Having first placed the story of Jesus within this grand cosmological frame, John then sets it entirely within the dynamics of the world of human interaction, so that "the story of Jesus in the gospel is all played out on earth."[9] The frame, nevertheless, informs the reader that both Jesus' coming and *all* his human relationships are elements played out in a supernatural drama between the forces of good and evil.

Casting the struggle between good and evil as that between light and darkness, John never pictures Satan, as the other gospels do, appearing as a disembodied being. At first glance, then, the image of Satan seems to have receded; the German scholar Gustave Hoennecke goes so far as to claim that "in John,

the idea of the devil is completely absent."[10] More accurate, however, is Raymond Brown's observation that John, like the other
gospels, tells the whole story of Jesus as a struggle with Satan
that culminates in the crucifixion.[11] Although John never depicts
Satan as a character on his own, acting independently of human
beings, in John's gospel it is *people* who play the tempter's role.

All of the three "temptation scenes" in Luke and Matthew
occur in John, but Satan does not appear directly. Instead, as
Raymond Brown has shown, Satan's role is taken first by "the
people," members of Jesus' audience, and finally by his own
brothers.[12] For example, Matthew and Luke show Satan challenging Jesus to claim earthly power (Matt. 4:8–9; Luke 4:5–6);
but according to John, this challenge occurs when "the people
were about to come and take him by force to make him king"
(6:15). Here, as in the other gospels, Jesus resists the temptation,
eludes the crowd, and escapes. In another temptation, Matthew
and Luke, following Q, relate that the devil challenged Jesus to
prove his divine authority by making "these stones into bread."
But John says that those who witnessed Jesus' miracles—and in
particular his multiplication of five loaves into many—then challenged him to perform *another* miracle as further proof of his
messianic identity. Like the devil who quotes the Scriptures in
Luke and Matthew, "the people" in John quote them as they
urge Jesus to produce bread miraculously:

> So they said to him, "What sign do you do, that we may see
> and believe you? What work do you perform? Our fathers ate
> manna in the wilderness; as it is written, 'He gave them bread
> from heaven to eat' " (6:30–31).

Jesus resists this temptation as well, and just as Matthew's Jesus
had answered the devil with a response about spiritual nourish-
ment ("Man does not live by bread alone, but by every word
which proceeds from the mouth of God"), so, in John, Jesus
speaks of the "true bread from heaven" (6:32). The temptation
in which the devil asks Jesus to display his divine powers in public (Matt. 4:5–6; Luke 4:9–12) is echoed in John when Jesus'

own brothers, who, John says, did not believe in him, challenge Jesus to "go to Judea," to "show yourself to the world" in Jerusalem where, as he and they are well aware, his enemies want to kill him (7:1–5). This temptation, too, Jesus rejects.

According to John, it is Jesus himself who reveals the identity of the evil one. When Jesus hears Peter declare that "we [disciples] believe that you are the Messiah, the Son of God," he answers brusquely:

> "Have I not chosen you twelve, and one of you is a devil?" He spoke of Judas Iscariot, the son of Simon, for it was he that would betray him, being one of the twelve (6:70–71).

Anticipating his betrayal, Jesus again identifies his betrayer, Judas, along with the accompanying posse of Roman and Jewish soldiers, as his supernatural enemy appearing in human form. According to Matthew, Jesus signals Judas's arrival in Gethsemane with the words, "Rise; let us be going; my betrayer is coming" (26:46); but in John, Jesus announces instead that "the ruler of this world [that is, the "evil one"] is coming. . . . Rise, let us be going" (14:30–31). Shortly before, Jesus had accused "the Jews who had believed in him" of plotting his murder: twice he charged that "you seek to kill me." When they find his words incomprehensible, Jesus proceeds to identify "the Jews" who had previously believed in him as Satan's own: "You are of your father, the devil; and you want to accomplish your father's desires. He was a murderer from the beginning" (8:44). Raymond Brown comments that in these passages,

> for the first time the fact that the devil is Jesus' real antagonist comes to the fore. This motif will grow louder and louder as the "hour" of Jesus['s death] approaches, until the passion is presented as a struggle to the death between Jesus and Satan.[13]

This is true, but Brown is concerned only with theological observations. What do these passages mean in terms of human conflict? Many commentators, along with countless Christian readers, have agreed with the blunt assessment of the influential German New Testament scholar Rudolph Bultmann: "There can be no doubt about the main point of the passage, which is to show that *the Jews' unbelief,* with its hostility to truth and life, *stems from their being children of the devil*" (emphasis added).[14] Bultmann adds that John, like Matthew and Luke, in effect charges the Jews with "intentional murder."[15] (Elsewhere, as we shall see, Bultmann makes statements bearing different implications.) In recent decades these passages from John have elicited a flurry of discussion, often from Christian commentators insisting that these words do not—or morally *cannot*—mean what most Christians for nearly two millennia have taken them to mean.

Many scholars have observed that the term "Jews" occurs much more frequently in John than in the other gospels, and that its usage indicates that John's author and his fellow believers stand even further from the Jewish majority than do the other evangelists. Dozens, even hundreds, of articles propose different solutions to the question of how John uses the Greek term *Ioudaios,* usually translated "Jew."[16] Sometimes, of course, John's usage coincides with general contemporary usage in passages that simply describe people who are Jewish and not Gentile: twice, in John, outsiders, first a Samaritan woman and later the Roman governor, Pontius Pilate, identify Jesus himself as "a Jew" (John 4:9; 18:34). In other passages, the term apparently designates Judeans—that is, people who live in or around Jerusalem—as distinct from Galileans and Samaritans. In still other passages, the term "the Jews" clearly serves as a synonym for the Jewish leaders. But in certain passages that may overlap with these, John uses "the Jews" to designate people alien to Jesus and hostile to him; he repeatedly says, for example, that "the Jews sought to kill [him]," and that Jesus at times avoided travel to Jerusalem "for fear of the Jews."

In chapter 8, when Jesus engages in a hostile dialogue with "the Jews who had believed in him," and finally denounces "the Jews" as Satan's offspring, he is obviously not making a simple ethnic distinction, since, of course, in that scene Jesus and all his disciples are Jews as well as their opponents. Here, just as Jesus embodies the divine light of God's presence, "the Jews" represent "the world" that rejected that light. As John had declared in his prologue:

> The true light that enlightens everyone was coming into the world; he was in the world, and the world was made through him; yet the world did not recognize him. He came unto his own; and his own people did not receive him.

Later, as Bultmann points out, "the Jews" become synonymous with that rejecting, unbelieving "world."[17] The German New Testament scholar Heinrich Schneider expresses a view commonly held by Christian scholars when he says:

> From a general non-acceptance of Jesus by people in the early chapters [of John], the opposition becomes more and more identified with a [specific] group . . . , the Jews. Ultimately the group stands for the forces opposed to Jesus, which are the forces of darkness. *It is obvious that we are not dealing with an ethnic group, but with a dramatic theological symbol. . . . We would miss the full significance of this symbol if we considered the Jew in John only as an historical figure. . . . "The Jews" are an ever-present reality and threat to any worship of God in spirit and in truth* (emphasis added).[18]

Yet other commentators, including Samuel Sandmel, do not find it obvious that "we are not dealing with an ethnic group." Sandmel insists that such interpreters want "to exculpate the gospel from its manifest anti-Semitism." Sandmel points out that John does not charge "humanity" or "the world" in general for actively seeking Jesus's execution, but specifically singles out "the Jews."[19]

Anyone who reads the gospel of John can see that "the Jews" have become for John what Bultmann sees as a symbol of human evil.[20] But those who agree with Rudolph Bultmann and Heinrich Schneider that the use of the term is merely symbolic and thus has no social or political implications seem to be engaging in apologetic evasions. John's decision to make an actual, identifiable group—among Jesus' contemporaries and his own—into a symbol of "all evil" obviously bears religious, social, and political implications. Would anyone doubt this if an influential author today made women, or for that matter Muslims or homosexuals, the "symbol of all evil"? Having cast "the Jews" in that role, John's gospel can arouse and even legitimate hostility toward Judaism, a potential that New Testament scholar Reginald Fuller says "has been abundantly and tragically actualized in the course of Christian history."[21]

It is not my purpose here to describe in detail, as others have done, the complex historical situation that gave rise to the Johannine passion narrative. Let us assume, first, that it is historically likely that certain Jewish leaders may have collaborated with the Roman authorities in Jesus' arrest and execution. Let us assume as valid, too, the point well explicated by Louis Martyn and others, that the author of John reads into his story conflicts he has himself experienced between his own group and those he calls "the Jews," by whom the author probably means primarily the leaders of Jewish communities known to him (c. 90–100 C.E.), together with their followers. My purpose here is not to define precisely John's use of the term "Jew." Instead, it is much simpler: to show how the gospel of John, like the other gospels, associates the mythological figure of Satan with specific human opposition, first implicating Judas Iscariot, then the Jewish authorities, and finally "the Jews" collectively.

From the beginning of the gospel, then, as we have seen, the author of John, like his predecessors at Qûmran, draws the battle lines between the "sons of light" and the "sons of darkness," although in this case the "light" is specifically represented by Jesus. After "the Jews" attempt to stone Jesus for speaking words they take as blasphemy—claiming in effect, the divine name (8:58)—Jesus declares:

> "I must do the work of him who sent me, while it is day; the night is coming, when no one may work. As long as I am in the world, I am the light of the world" (9:4–5).

Moving quickly toward the passion narrative, which here constitutes half of the entire gospel, John, like Luke, makes explicit the charge implicit in Mark and Matthew—that Satan himself initiated Judas' treachery:

> During supper, the devil had already put it into the heart of Judas Iscariot, the son of Simon, to betray him. . . . Then after the morsel, Satan entered into him. Jesus said to him, "What you are going to do, do quickly." . . . So after receiving the morsel, [Judas] immediately went out; and it was night" (13:2, 27–30).

Because John insists that Jesus, fully aware of the future course of events, remains in complete control of them, he writes that Jesus himself gives Judas the morsel that precedes Satan's entry (thus fulfilling the prophecy of Psalm 41:9). Jesus then directs Judas's subsequent action ("What you are going to do, do quickly"). At that fateful moment, which initiates Jesus' betrayal, John, like Luke, depicts the "power of darkness" (cf. Luke 22:53) eclipsing the "light of the world": hence his stark final phrase, *en de nux* (*"it was night"*).

Here the passion narrative is more than a story; in the words of John's Jesus, it is a *judgment,* or *crisis* (to translate literally the Greek term *krisis*). When Jesus predicts his crucifixion, he declares that instead of showing a judgment against *him,* it shows God's judgment against "this world"; instead of destroying Jesus, it will destroy the diabolic "ruler of the world":

> "Now is the judgment [*krisis*] of this world; now the ruler of this world shall be cast out; and I, when I am lifted up from the earth, will draw all people to myself." He said this to show by what death he would die (John 12:31–32; see also 14:30).

John's readers are thus warned that the events he describes—and, for that matter, John's account of them—also serve to judge and condemn as "sons of darkness" those who have participated in Jesus' destruction. John, like Luke, suppresses all traces of Roman initiative in Jesus' execution. In nearly every episode, John displays what one scholar calls "bizarre exaggeration" to insist that the blame for initiating, ordering, and carrying out the crucifixion falls upon Jesus' *intimate* enemies, his fellow Jews.

Apparently using an early source independent of the other gospels, John reports that before Jesus' arrest

> the chief priests and the Pharisees gathered the Sanhedrin together and said, "What shall we do? This man performs many signs. . . . If we let him go on like this, the Romans will come and destroy our holy place and our nation" (11:47–48).

I agree with those, including the British classical scholar Fergus Millar, who regard this part of John's account as perhaps closer to the actual events than the other gospel accounts.[22] Unlike the elaborate trial that Mark and Matthew present, John shows the council members concerned about the disturbances Jesus arouses among the people, a plausible motive for their judgment, for they want to protect their own constituency from the risk of Roman reprisals, even at the risk of a wrongful execution. After "Judas, procuring a band of [presumably Roman] soldiers, and some officers from the chief priests of the Pharisees" (18:8), betrayed Jesus, the arresting party seized and bound him and led him to Annas, "father-in-law of the high priest," who, after interrogating him, "sent him bound to Caiaphas the high priest." Rosemary Reuther observes that John here intends to suppress political charges against Jesus—that he had claimed to be king—in favor of a religious one, that he threatened the Temple.[23]

Although John reports no other trial by a Jewish tribunal, he leaves no doubt that the chief priests want Jesus killed. John depicts the priests as evasive and self-righteous when Pilate inquires about the charge: "If this man were not a malefactor, we would not have brought him to you" (18:30). When Pilate, still having heard no charge, answers, with indifference or contempt, "Take him yourselves and judge him by your own law," the "Jews" answer, "It is not lawful for us to put anyone to death" (18:31).

Some scholars insist that this last statement is wrong. Richard Husband claims that under first-century Roman law the Jewish

Sanhedrin retained its traditional right to execute people for certain crimes defined as religious, such as violating the Temple precincts, transgressing the law, and adultery.[24] Husband and other scholars point out that only about five years after Jesus' death, in 36 C.E., Jews stoned to death his follower Stephen for "speaking against the law." But was this a lynch mob, or a crowd carrying out a Sanhedrin sentence?

Josephus writes that in 62 C.E. the high priest Ananus II assembled the Sanhedrin and condemned Jesus' brother James to death by stoning, along with several others, on charges of transgressing the law. These executions apparently cost Ananus II his position as high priest after some Jerusalemites complained to the Jewish king, Agrippa II, and to the Roman procurator, Albinus, that Ananus had executed James and others without notifying the procurator, much less gaining his permission. Josephus describes a later case—one that suggests that Jewish leaders had become more cautious about executing without Roman permission. A man named Jesus bar Ananias, who had loudly predicted the downfall of Jerusalem and its Temple, was arrested and beaten by prominent Jewish leaders. When they brought him before Albinus, the same Roman prefect, apparently hoping to secure the death penalty,

> Jesus refused to answer the prefect's questions, and so Albinus let him go as a maniac. Thus, despite their anger, the Jewish leaders, who could arrest and flog, did not dare execute this Jesus as they had executed James (*War* 6.2).

By the sixties, then, Roman permission to execute seems to have been a necessary, or at least an expedient, measure. For lack of definitive evidence, intense scholarly investigation and debate have not solved the issue. In the case of Jesus of Nazareth, however, Christian sources seldom suggest that the Jews actually executed Jesus, whether or not this act was ratified by the Romans. Although the gospels do not describe Pilate actually sentencing Jesus to death, the historical evidence and the gospel accounts indicate that the governor must have ordered his soldiers to execute Jesus on grounds of sedition. As for what took place between

Jewish authorities and the governor, our only evidence comes from the gospels themselves and from later Christian and Jewish reinterpretations of these events, charged as they are with mutual accusation and polemic. Whatever the legal situation of the Sanhedrin in regard to capital punishment, the point John wants to make is clear enough: that although Romans were known to have carried out Jesus' execution by their own peculiar method (see 19:32), they did so only because "the Jews" forced them to.[25]

When Pilate asks Jesus, "Are you a king?," Jesus parries the question, and Pilate retorts, "*Am I a Jew? Your own nation and the chief priests have handed you over to me:* what have you done?" (18:35; emphasis added). Were his kingdom an earthly one, Jesus says, "my servants would fight so that I might not be handed over to the Jews" (18:36)—an ironic Johannine reversal of the charges in Mark, Luke, and Matthew, which repeatedly describe the Jews "handing Jesus over" to "the nations."

In John as in Luke, Pilate three times proclaims Jesus innocent, and proposes three times to release him; but each time the chief priests and those John calls "the Jews" cry out, demanding instead that Pilate "crucify him" (18:38–40; 19:5–7; 19:14–15). John "explains," too, that Pilate allowed his soldiers to scourge and torture Jesus only in order to arouse the crowd's compassion (19:1–4), and so to placate what British scholar Dennis Nineham calls "the insatiable fury of the Jews."[26] John adds that when they protest that Jesus has violated their religious law, and therefore "deserves to die," Pilate is "more terrified" (19:8). Returning to Jesus as if he still hoped to find a way to acquit him, Pilate instead receives from the prisoner relative exoneration of his *own* guilt: speaking as if he were Pilate's judge (as John believes he is), Jesus declares to the governor that "the one who delivered me to you has the greater sin." When the crowd threatens to charge Pilate with treason against Rome (19:12), Pilate makes one more futile attempt to release Jesus—"Shall I crucify your king?"—to which the chief priests answer, "We have no king but Caesar," and at last Pilate gives in to the shouting. At this point, John says, Pilate, having neither sentenced Jesus nor ordered his execution, "handed [Jesus] over to them to be crucified" (19:16). In this scene, as C. H. Dodd has commented, "the priests exert unrelenting pressure, while the governor turns and doubles like a hunted hare."[27] Immediately after Pilate hands Jesus over to the Jews, the narrator goes on to say, "they took Jesus . . . to the place called in Hebrew Golgotha. There they crucified him, and with him two others" (19:17–18).

After John's account of the crucifixion, in which he shows how Jesus' ignominious death fulfills prophecy in every detail, he adds that Joseph of Arimathea, "a disciple of Jesus, though a secret one for fear of the Jews" (19:38), petitions Pilate to allow him to recover Jesus' body and to bury it. The story implies that Jesus' enemies are so vindictive that Joseph and another secret disciple, Nicodemus, are afraid even to offer him a decent burial. Many scholars have discussed John's motives for thus depicting Pilate as wishing to free the innocent Jesus, while presenting the Jews as not only the "villains, but the ultimate in villainy."[28]

Instead of completely exonerating Pilate, however, John's Jesus, playing judge to his judge, as we saw, pronounces Pilate guilty of sin, although "less" sin than the Jews. Nevertheless, as Paul Winter observes:

> The stern Pilate grows more mellow from gospel to gospel [from Mark to Matthew, from Matthew to Luke and then to John]. The more removed from history, the more sympathetic a character he becomes.[29]

With regard to the Jews, Jesus' "intimate enemy," a parallel process occurs, but in reverse; the Jews become increasingly antagonistic. In the opening scene of Mark, Jesus boldly challenges not his fellow Jews but the powers of evil. Then he comes into increasingly intense conflict, first with "the scribes" and then with the Pharisees and Herodians, until crowds of his own people, in a conflict Mark depicts as essentially intra-Jewish, persuade reluctant Roman forces to execute him. Matthew, as we saw, writing some twenty years after Mark, depicts a far more bitter and aggressive antagonism between Jesus and the majority of his Jewish contemporaries, even casting King Herod in the role of the hated tyrant Pharaoh. Indeed, no sooner was Jesus born than Herod and "all Jerusalem with him," specifically including "all the chief priests and scribes of the people," were troubled, and Herod decided to kill him. Matthew describes the Pharisees, religious leaders of his time, as "sons of hell," destined, along with all who reject Jesus' teaching, for eternal punishment in the "fire reserved for the devil and all his angels." Yet I agree with recent analysis by Andrew Overman that even Matthew intends to show, in effect, a battle between rival reform groups of Jews, each insisting upon its own superior righteousness, and each calling the other demon-possessed.[30]

Luke, as we have seen, goes considerably further. No sooner has the devil appeared to tempt and destroy Jesus than all Jesus' townspeople, hearing his first public address in their synagogue, are aroused to fury, and attempt to throw him down a cliff. Only at the climax of Luke's account does Satan return in person, so to speak, to enter into Judas and so to direct the operation that ends with the crucifixion.

Writing c. 100 C.E., John dismisses the device of the devil as an independent supernatural character (if, indeed, he knew of it, as I suspect he did). Instead, as John tells the story, Satan, like God himself, appears incarnate, first in Judas Iscariot, then in the Jewish authorities as they mount opposition to Jesus, and finally in those John calls "the Jews"—a group he sometimes characterizes as Satan's allies, now as separate from Jesus and his followers as darkness is from light, or the forces of hell from the armies of heaven.

The evangelists' various depictions of the devil correlate with the "social history of Satan"—that is, with the history of increasing conflict between groups representing Jesus' followers and their opposition. By presenting Jesus' life and message in these polemical terms, the evangelists no doubt intended to strengthen group solidarity. In the process, they shaped, in ways that were to become incalculably consequential, the self-understanding of Christians in relation to Jews for two millennia.

SATAN'S EARTHLY KINGDOM:
CHRISTIANS AGAINST PAGANS

Between 70 and 100 C.E.—the interval between the writing of the gospel of Mark and of the gospel of John—the Christian movement became largely Gentile. Many converts found that having become Christians placed their lives in danger, and that they were threatened not by Jews but by pagans—Roman officers and city mobs who hated Christians for their "atheism," which pagans feared could bring the wrath of the gods upon whole communities. Only two generations after Mark and Matthew, Gentile converts, many of them former pagans from Roman provinces—Asia Minor, Syria, Egypt, Africa, and Greece—adapted the gospel vocabulary to face a new enemy. As earlier generations of Christians had claimed to see Satan among their fellow Jews, now converts facing Roman persecution claimed to see Satan and his demonic allies at work among *other Gentiles.*

The pressures of state persecution complicated such characterizations of Gentiles as we found in Matthew and Luke; those writers, hoping for a favorable hearing among Gentile audiences, had depicted Romans and other Gentiles in generally favorable ways, as we have seen.[1] So long as Christians remained a minority movement within Jewish communities, they tended to regard other Jews as potential enemies, and Gentiles as potential converts. Although the apostle Paul, writing c. 55 C.E., complained that he had faced danger at every turn—"danger from robbers, danger from my own people, danger from Gentiles, even danger from false brethren" (2 Cor. 11:26)—he mentions actual persecution only from his fellow Jews: "Five times I received at the hands of the Jews forty lashes save one; three times I have been beaten with rods; once I was stoned" (2 Cor. 11:24). According to Luke's account in Acts, Paul regarded Roman magistrates as his protectors against Jewish hostility; and Paul himself, writing to Christians in Rome, orders them to "obey the higher powers; for there is no authority except from God, and the powers that exist are instituted by God," even in their God-given right to "bear the sword" and "execute God's wrath" (Rom. 13:1).

But Paul himself was executed, probably by order of a Roman magistrate; and about ten years later, when many Romans blamed the emperor Nero for starting a fire that devastated much of Rome, the emperor ordered the arrest of a group of Christians, charged them with arson, and had them hung up in his garden and burned alive as human torches.[2]

One follower of Paul, aware of the circumstances of his teacher's death and of the various dangers Christians faced, warned in a letter attributed to Paul, called the Letter to the Ephesians, that Christians are not contending against mere human beings:

> Our contest is not against flesh and blood [human beings] but against powers, against principalities, against the world rulers of this present darkness, against the spiritual forces of evil in heavenly places (6:12).

This Pauline author articulates the sense of spiritual warfare experienced by many Christians, especially by those who face persecution. The author of Revelation, claiming to have suffered exile "on account of the word of God and the testimony of Jesus" (Rev. 1:9), and aware of others suffering imprisonment, torture, and death at the hands of Roman magistrates, describes horrific and ecstatic visions that invoke traditional prophetic images of animals and monsters to characterize the powers of Rome, which he identifies with "the devil and Satan" (20:2; passim). Despite the gospels' generally conciliatory attitude toward the Romans, the crucifixion account nevertheless invites Christians to see demonic forces working through Roman officials as well as through Jewish leaders; Luke goes so far as to suggest that Jesus' crucifixion forged an unholy alliance between Pilate and Herod, so that the Roman and Jewish authorities became friends "that day" (23:12).

Gentile converts who were hated by other Gentiles—often members of their own families, their townspeople, and their city magistrates—believed that worshipers of the pagan gods were driven by Satan to menace God's people. As Christian preachers increasingly appealed to Gentiles, many found that what had offended most Jews about Christianity offended pagans even more: "Christians severed the traditional bonds between religion and a nation or people," and, as the historian Robert Wilken points out, "Ancient people took for granted that religion was indissolubly linked to a particular city, nation or people."[3] Jews identified their religion with the Jewish people as a whole, united by tradition, however dispersed throughout the world; for pagans, *pietas* consisted precisely in respecting ancient customs and honoring traditional mores. The Christian movement, however, encouraged people to abandon ancestral customs and break the sacred bonds of family, society, and nation.

The movement that began as a sect within Judaism and was rejected by the majority of Jews, whom it repudiated in turn, now appealed to people of every nation and tribe to join the new "Christian society" and to break all former bonds of kinship and affiliation. "In Christ," the apostle Paul had declared, "there is no longer Jew nor Greek . . . slave nor free, male nor female" (Gal. 3:28); for those "born again" in baptism (John 3:5–8), the world consists of only two kinds of people—those who belong to God's kingdom, whose citizenship is in heaven (Heb. 12:22–24; 13:14), and those still ruled by the evil one, subjects of Satan.

Despite official Roman censure and popular pagan hostility, the movement grew. The North African convert Tertullian boasts in an appeal to the Roman emperors:

Those who once hated Christianity . . . now begin to hate what they formerly were, and to profess what they formerly hated. . . . The outcry is that the State is filled with Christians—that they are in the fields, in the cities, in the islands; many people lament, as if for some calamity, that both men and women, every age and condition, even people of high rank, are passing over to professing the Christian faith.[4]

What would impel pagans to "profess what they formerly hated"—even at the cost of endangering their lives? Tertullian and a few others—Justin, from the coast of Asia Minor, his student Tatian, from Syria, and Origen, an Egyptian—have left us some clues.

Justin, a young man who had come to Rome from Asia Minor about 140 C.E. to pursue his study of philosophy, went one day with friends to the amphitheater to see the spectacular gladiatorial fights held there to celebrate imperial birthdays. The spectators cheered the men who recklessly courted death, and thrilled to the moment of the death blow. The crowd would go wild when a defeated gladiator defiantly thrust out his neck to meet his antagonist's sword; and they jeered and hooted when a loser bolted in panic.[5]

Justin was startled to see in the midst of this violent entertainment a group of criminals being led out to be torn apart by wild beasts. The serene courage with which they met their brutal public execution astonished him, especially when he learned that these were illiterate people, Christians, whom the Roman senator Tacitus had called "a class of people hated for their superstitions," whose founder, Christos, had himself "suffered the extreme penalty under Pontius Pilate" about a hundred years before.[6] Justin was profoundly shaken, for he saw a group of uneducated people actually accomplishing what Plato and Zeno regarded as the greatest achievement of a philosopher—accepting death with equanimity, an accomplishment which the gladiators' bravado merely parodied. As he watched, Justin realized that he was witnessing something quite beyond nature, a miracle; somehow these people had tapped into a great, unknown source of power.

Justin would have been even more startled had he known that these Christians saw themselves not as philosophers but as combatants in a cosmic struggle, God's warriors against Satan.[7] As Justin learned later, their amazing confidence derived from the conviction that their own agony and death actually were hastening God's victory over the forces of evil, forces embodied in the Roman magistrate who had sentenced them, and, for that matter, in spectators like Justin himself.

Sometime later, while taking a solitary walk in a field near the sea, Justin unexpectedly met an old man who turned out to be a member of this group.[8] At first the old man questioned Justin about his pursuit of philosophy; but instead of being impressed, as Justin expected, the old man challenged him and said he could never find illumination in philosophy.

What Justin sought in philosophy was not simply intellectual understanding but self-realization: How shall I live in order to be happy? What are the steps toward transformation?[9] At an earlier stage of his philosophical search, Justin says, he had "surrendered himself" to a Stoic teacher, hoping to transcend his ordinary, "human" point of view. Stoic teachers promised that by studying physics—literally, "nature"—one could learn to place each event, obstacle, or circumstance in one's life within a universal perspective, and to participate in the divine, which is synonymous with nature. Justin says he became frustrated because his teacher seldom spoke about the divine and discouraged questions on the subject; so Justin left, and began to study with a peripatetic philosopher. After a few days, when his new teacher demanded a tuition fee, Justin quit in disgust, deciding that the man "was no philosopher at all." Justin did not give up; next he tried a Pythagorean master, who offered to teach physical and mental discipline to attune the soul to the divine. Told that he would have to master astronomy, mathematics, and music before he could even begin to understand "what makes for a happy life," Justin left this teacher as well.

Defeated and helpless, Justin finally discovered in the teachings of a brilliant expositor of Plato what he believed was the true path. He says he had already made great progress toward enlightenment and expected soon to be able to raise his mind to apprehend the divine. But the old Christian he met walking by the sea challenged his basic philosophic premise: "Is there, then, such a great power in our mind? Will the human mind ever see God through its own capacity?" The old man voiced Justin's worst fear—that he was wasting his time; that the human mind, however one educates and increases its capacity, is intrinsically incapable of reaching that goal; the mind cannot understand God through its own efforts.

When the old man first challenged him, Justin vehemently objected, repeating Platonic clichés. Later, retelling the story, Justin acknowledged the irony of his earlier naïveté: he found himself repeating the phrase "Plato says . . . and I believe him." Feeling increasingly foolish, Justin realized that his objections to the old man's arguments derived simply from his blind acceptance of Plato's authority—not from any conviction or experience of his own.

As Justin and the old man talked, he saw for the first time that he had stumbled into a process much deeper than the intellect could fathom. Justin had assumed that he possessed a mind free to think rationally about everything, including the divine. Now he heard the opposite: that the mind itself is infested with demonic powers that distort and confuse our thinking. Before he—or anyone else—could achieve understanding, the old man said, Justin would have to receive the divine spirit—a power far greater than our comprehension, a power that "illuminates the mind."[10] But first Justin would need to undergo exorcism, a ritual in which the celebrant, himself filled with the divine spirit, would invoke that spirit to drive out the demonic powers inhabiting the candidate's mind and body and holding him, like all the unbaptized, captive to confusion and ignorance.

After heated argument with the old man and considerable internal struggle, Justin became convinced that Christians had discovered access to great power—divine power, which was always there, waiting to break through the clouds, and which was brought to earth by the Christians' powerful rituals, beginning with baptism.[11]

Before the old man left him, Justin says, he admonished the young man to

> "pray that, above all things, the gates of light may be opened to you; for these things cannot be perceived or understood by everyone, but only by the person to whom God and his Christ have given wisdom."[12]

After he left, Justin says,

> immediately a flame was kindled in my soul, and a love . . . of those people who are friends of Christ possessed me; and, while turning his words over and over in my mind, I found this philosophy alone to be safe and profitable.[13]

Seeking out other "friends of Christ," Justin asked to become a candidate for the rite of baptism. He does not tell us the story of his own baptism, but other sources suggest the following: Having fasted and prayed to prepare himself, Justin would await, probably on the night before Easter, the rite that would expel the indwelling demonic powers and charge him with new, divine life. First the celebrant would demand to know whether Justin was willing to "renounce the devil, and all his pomp, and his angels"; Justin would ritually declare three times, "I renounce them." Then Justin would descend naked into a river, immersing himself to signify the death of the old self and the washing away of sins. Once the divine name was pronounced and the celebrant had invoked the spirit to descend on him, he would emerge reborn, to be clothed with new white garments at the shore and offered a mixture of milk and honey—babies' food, suitable for a newborn.[14]

Justin said that he had received in baptism what he had sought in vain in philosophy: "this washing we call illumination; because those who learn these things become illuminated in their understanding."[15] He later explained to other potential converts, "Since at our birth we were born without consciousness or choice, by our parents' intercourse, and were brought up in bad habits and evil customs," we are baptized "so that we may no longer be children of necessity and ignorance, but become the children of choice and knowledge."[16] His ritual rebirth to new parents—God and the holy spirit—enabled Justin to renounce not only his natural family but the "habits and evil customs" they had taught him from childhood—above all, traditional piety toward the gods, whom he now saw as evil spirits. Having entered the stark and polarized Christian world, Justin joined those brave, illiterate Christians whose bloody death he had witnessed in the Roman amphitheater. Now Justin, like them, saw the entire universe as a battleground where cosmic forces clash.

Justin believed that his eyes had suddenly been opened to the truth behind the most apparently innocuous appearances: the marble statues of the goddesses Fortuna and Roma that he saw every day in the marketplace, the image of Hercules that presided over the public baths, and those of Dionysus and Apollo at the theater. Behind those familiar chiseled faces Justin now recognized "spiritual forces of evil in heavenly places." Justin suddenly understood, as Paul had, that the forces that play upon a helpless humanity are neither human nor divine, as pagans imagined, but demonic.

Justin's pagan parents had brought him up in traditional piety, revering the forces of nature as divine. For pious pagans, as the classicist A. H. Armstrong says,

> the old gods have the beauty and goodness of the sun, the sea, the wind, the mountains, great wild animals; splendid, powerful, and dangerous realities that do not come within the sphere of morality, and are in no way concerned about the human race.[17]

Pagan worship mingled awe with terror of the vast forces that threaten our fragile species. The oracle at Delphi warned worshipers, "Know yourself," not as an invitation to lofty contemplation or introspection, but as a blunt reminder that they were mortal, *ephemeral*, literally, "creatures of a day," propelled toward living and dying by the interplay of cosmic forces far beyond their comprehension.

From the sixth century B.C.E. onward, philosophers reflected upon those cosmic forces in various ways. Plato spoke of "necessity," others of the powers of "destiny" or "fate" that govern the universe. Later Stoic philosophers "demythologized" the old myths and reinterpreted the gods themselves—Zeus, Hera, Aphrodite—as representing elements of the natural universe. Some suggested, for example, that Hera represents the air, Zeus the lightning and thunder, Eros and Aphrodite the erotic energies that drive us into copulation, and Ares the aggressive energy that impels us into war.[18] Many classical philosophers agreed that these gods were neither bad nor good in themselves; although the gods might appear to be capricious—sometimes benevolent, sometimes hostile—most pagan thinkers agreed that such judgments had nothing to do with the gods themselves, but only with human reactions to specific events.

For Justin, conversion changed all this. Every god and spirit he had ever known, including Apollo, Aphrodite, and Zeus, whom he had worshiped since childhood, he now perceived as allies of Satan—despite the brilliant panoply of their public processions, their thousands of temples and glittering priesthoods, despite the fact that they were worshiped by the emperor himself, who served in person as their *pontifex maximus* ("greatest priest"). Born again, Justin saw the universe of spiritual energies, which pious pagan philosophers called *daimones,* as, in his words, "*foul* daimones."[19] By the time the Christian movement had swept across the Western world, our language would reflect that reversed perception, and the Greek term *daimones,* "spirit energies," would become, in English, *demons.*[20] So, Justin says,

> we, who out of every race of people, once worshiped Dionysus the son of Semele, and Apollo the son of Leto, who in their passion for human beings did things which it is shameful even to mention; who worshiped Persephone and Aphrodite . . . or Asklepius, or some other of those who are called gods, now, through Jesus Christ, despise them, even at the cost of death. . . . We pity those who believe such things, for which we know that the *daimones* are responsible.[21]

Philosophers who say that "whatever happens, happens according to fatal necessity" are proved wrong, Justin says, by the evidence of those "born again to God"; for in them we see "the same person making transition to opposite things."[22] Justin says that he found that "the words of Christ" have a "terrible power in them that can inspire those who turn away from the right path"[23]; now he and his fellow Christians, once driven, like most others by passion, greed, and hatred,

> stand apart from demons and follow God; . . . we, who once took pleasure in fornication, now embrace self-control; we, who . . . valued the acquisition of wealth and possessions above everything else, now put what we have into a common fund, and share with everyone in need; we, who hated and killed one another, and would not share our lives with certain people because of their ethnic differences from us, now live intimately with them.[24]

Justin sees in his own life and the lives of Christians all around him evidence of divine power that enables them to live "beyond nature." Just as those Christians he watched die in the amphitheater overcame with their inspired courage the instinct to survive, so, he says, may others have overcome the tyranny of instinctual drives:

> Many among us, both men and women, who have been Christians since childhood, have remained pure at the age of sixty or seventy; and I boast that I could produce such people from every race. . . . and what shall I say of the innumerable multitude who have reformed intemperate habits?[25]

Justin mentions those in whom powerful compulsions—for example, for strong drink—have been broken. Many others, Justin says, "have changed their violent and tyrannical dispositions," overcome by the astonishing forbearance, patience, and unwavering honesty they have found in their Christian neighbors.[26]

Celebrating the new society formed by these "reborn" people,[27] Justin now sees the old society as evil—a society that, for example, abandons infants to die or to be raised by opportunists, who train them as prostitutes and sell them on the slave markets "like herds of goats or sheep."[28] As a privileged philosophy student, Justin might have displayed moral indifference; instead he is indignant about those abandoned children, and castigates moral relativists who pride themselves on their philosophical sophistication: "The worst evil of all is to say that neither good nor evil is anything in itself, but that they are only matters of human opinion."[29]

Justin's life now has a moral direction. He contrasts the natural life he once lived as passive prey to demons, with the spirit-infused life he lives now:

> We have learned to find God . . . and we believe it is impossible for the evil or envious person, or the conspirator, or for the righteous person—to escape God's notice; and every person goes to eternal punishment or salvation according to the value of his works.[30]

In his new life, Justin sees his role in the universe enormously enhanced; the stand he takes and the choices he makes not only decide his eternal destiny but engage him at present as an active combatant in the universal struggle between God's spirit and Satan.[31]

Yet Justin realizes the irony—and the terror—of his new situation: receiving divine illumination has ripped him out of all that was familiar, alienated him from his family and friends, and uprooted him from much of his culture. Most frightening, it has stripped him of all security. His baptismal exorcism placed him in opposition to the gods he had worshiped all his life and in potentially lethal conflict with virtually everyone he had ever known—above all, with governmental authorities. He now belongs to a group that the Roman majority and government magistrates regard with suspicion and contempt, despite all the evangelists' efforts to calm their fears.[32] Those publicly accused of allegiance to Christ are liable to arrest and interrogation, often under torture; to "confess" means immediate condemnation to death, by beheading, if one has the good fortune to be a Roman citizen, or, if not, by prolonged torture and public spectacle, including condemnation *ad bestias*—that is, being torn apart by wild animals in the public sports arena. Justin knows of cases in which believers or their slaves, including women and children, had been tortured until they "admitted" seeing Christians engage in atrocities, including ritual eating of human flesh and drinking blood from freshly slaughtered infants. Only thirty years earlier, even such a sober-minded official as Pliny, governor of Bithynia in Asia Minor, having satisfied himself by torturing Christians that they were not guilty of criminal acts, had decided that they deserved the death penalty, if only for their sheer "obstinacy."[33]

But why does the mere mention of the Christian name arouse such violent, irrational hatred? Reflecting on this question, Justin finds clues in what he calls the apostles' memoirs (which we call the gospels). There Justin reads that after God's spirit descended on Jesus at baptism, Satan and his demonic allies fought back, opposing Jesus, and finally hounded him to his death. So also now, Justin realizes, when the spirit descends on those who are baptized, the same evil forces that fought against Jesus attack his followers. The gospels show Justin how spiritual energies, demonic and divine, can dwell within human beings, often without their knowledge, and drive them toward destruction—or toward God. Now Justin understands the Pauline warning that

> our contest is not against flesh and blood, but against powers, against principalities, against the world-rulers of this present darkness, against spiritual forces of evil in heavenly places (Eph. 6:12).

The conviction that unseen energies impel human beings to action was, of course, nothing new; it was universally accepted throughout the pagan world. A thousand years earlier, Homer had described how such energies played upon human beings— how Athena had inspired Achilles to heroic warfare, and how Aphrodite had seized and possessed Helen of Troy, driving her into the adulterous passion that led her people into war. Recalling the death of Socrates, Justin realizes with a shock that Socrates himself had said the same thing the Christians are saying—that all the gods Homer praises are actually evil energies that corrupt people, "seducing women and sodomizing boys," and terrorizing people into worshiping them as gods.[34] It was for this reason, Justin says, that Socrates denounced traditional religion and was charged with atheism. These same demonic powers, furious with Socrates for threatening to unmask them, drove the Athenian mob to execute him. This universal demonic deception, Justin realizes, accounts for the irrational hatred that the mere presence of Christians arouses among pagans—not merely for the violent passions of the ignorant and unruly mob, but also for the criminalizing of Christians, approved even by the most enlightened emperors who ever ruled Rome.

Justin boldly addresses an open letter of protest to these rulers—the emperor Antoninus Pius and his two sons, the Stoic prince Marcus Aurelius, whom he calls "truest philosopher," and "Lucius the Philosopher"—appealing to them as fellow philosophers, hoping, he says, to open their eyes. Justin declares that he writes on behalf of "those people of every nation who are unjustly hated and slaughtered; I, Justin, son of Priscus and grandson of Bacchius, of Flavia Neapolis, myself being one of them."[35] By publicly identifying himself with those whom the demons seek to kill, Justin initiates a public challenge that will end not with amnesty but, as he admits he fears, with his own arraignment and execution.

Although Justin begins by honorifically addressing the emperor Antoninus Pius and his sons, he soon tells them bluntly that despite their philosophic aspirations, they are not even masters of their own minds. "Even now," Justin warns the rulers of the Roman world, "these demons seek to keep you as their slaves, by preventing you from understanding what we say."[36] Their irrational public hatred of Christians proves, Justin says, that their minds have been captured by the same evil spirits who incited the Athenians to kill Socrates; now, for the same reason, these spirits are driving them to kill Christians.

Not long after Justin wrote to the emperors (and apparently received no answer) he heard of a case involving the arrest of an aristocratic woman convert. Before conversion, Justin says, she had participated with her husband in drunken liaisons with their household slaves and other people; but after baptism, she became sober, refused to participate in such acts, and wanted to divorce him. Her friends persuaded her to stay with him, hoping for a reconciliation, and, Justin says, "she violated her own feeling and remained with him." But when she heard that her husband, on a trip to Alexandria, had behaved worse than ever, she demanded a divorce and left him. Her husband denounced her to the authorities as a Christian, and although she succeeded in delaying her own trial by appealing to the emperor, her husband turned in fury against Porphyry, her teacher in Christianity, and had him and several others summarily arrested and executed.[37]

Alarmed and distressed by this judgment, Justin wrote a second letter of protest, this time addressing himself to the "sacred Senate."[38] Sometime later Justin himself was accused, arrested, and interrogated. Rusticus, prefect of Rome, ordered Justin and those of his students who were arrested with him to "obey the gods and submit to the rulers." When he was offered acquittal from the death penalty if he sacrificed to the gods, Justin defiantly refused: "No person in his right mind turns from piety to impiety." Rusticus again warned the accused of the consequences, and then, finding them adamant, pronounced sentence:

> Let those who have refused to sacrifice to the gods and obey the commands of the emperors be beaten and led away to suffer the punishment of beheading, in accordance to the laws.[39]

Having lost their case in the Roman court, Justin and his companions walked toward the flagellation cell, consoling themselves that they had nonetheless won the decisive battle; they were triumphing over the demons, who wielded terror—fear of pain and death—as their ultimate weapon.

Had the rulers whom Justin addressed actually read his petitions (it is more likely that an imperial secretary deposited them in a government archive), they would have regarded Justin's vision of the spiritual world with contempt.[40] Marcus Aurelius, well known from the writings preserved in his private journal, probably would have detested Justin's "Christian philosophy" as obscenely grandiose—the opposite of what Marcus regarded as the hard-won truths he himself had gained from philosophy.[41] Marcus, revered during his reign as master of the civilized world (c. 161–180), valued more than his imperial wealth and honors the religious philosophy that helped him bear his responsibilities and sustained him through loneliness, disappointment, and grief. In his daily round of duties, Marcus constantly invoked philosophic reflection to remind himself that he, like everyone else, was subject to the forces that rule the universe.

Marcus was raised by his father, the emperor Antoninus Pius, to rule. Reluctantly Marcus gave up philosophy, his first love, to study such practical activities as martial arts, public speaking, riding, and building a character suitable for an emperor. Marcus praises his father as his greatest model of human character, and praises the gods for all the circumstances of his life, especially for his divinely given capacity "to imagine, clearly and often, a life lived according to nature," and for the "reminders—and, almost, the instructions—of the gods," who embody the forces of nature.[42]

Although Marcus often expresses himself in the language of traditional piety, he had adapted for himself the reflections of certain Stoic teachers such as Musonius Rufus, who had reinterpreted the "old gods"—Zeus, Hera, Aphrodite, Apollo—as elements of the natural universe. In the process of demythologizing the ancient myths, Stoic philosophers tended to diminish the uncanny, capricious, and hostile qualities that the ancient poets Homer, Sappho, and Hesiod attributed to the gods.[43] Marcus had come to believe that all gods and *daimones* ("spirit beings"), however chaotic or even conflicting they appear, are actually part of a single cosmic order.[44] Alone, at night, writing in his journal, perhaps in a tent encamped with his soldiers in the alien wilderness along a tributary of the Danube or on the Hungarian plain, Marcus often expresses awe mingled with a clear sense of the vulnerability of our fragile species. Yet he believes that piety consists in willingly submitting to *nature, necessity,* and *destiny,* terms Marcus regards as interchangeable. In his mind there is no question but that we all are subject to these cosmic forces; the only question is whether we can submit ourselves to them with equanimity.

Speaking as a man trying to tame the passions of anger and grief, Marcus continually reminds himself that "death, like birth, is a mystery of nature,"[45] each necessarily complementing the other:

> Everything that happens is as ordinary and predictable as the spring rose or the summer fruit; this is as true of disease, death, slander, and conspiracy as anything else. . . . So, then, if a person has sensitivity and a deeper insight into the things that happen in the universe, virtually everything, even if it be only a by-product of something else, will contribute pleasure, being, in its own way, a harmonious part of the whole.[46]

Recalling gladiatorial fights and shows featuring people being torn to death by wild animals, Marcus reflects that a true philosopher

> will look upon the actual gaping jaws of wild animals with no less pleasure than upon artistic representations of them; and will be able to appreciate, in old people, both men and women, the quality of age, and look with tempered wisdom on the erotic beauty of the young.[47]

Marcus speaks of "the gods" as the vast universal powers through which our own individual lives are woven into the fabric of existence, into which our elements eventually will dissolve:

> The human soul is most arrogant [*hybrystes*] when it becomes, so far as it can, a kind of abscess or tumor in the universe. For to complain at anything that happens is a rebellion against nature.[48]

Acutely aware that catastrophe and good fortune "fall without discrimination on those who are good and those who are evil," Marcus struggles to make sense of this fact. Does the universe simply function chaotically, "with no design and no direction"?[49] Does honesty require us to become atheists? But he rejects the idea that life is meaningless, and says instead,

> It is not a flaw in nature, as if nature were ignorant, or powerless, or making mistakes, that good and evil things fall without discrimination upon those who are good and those who are evil.[50]

On the contrary, this indiscriminateness shows that "living and dying, reputation and disgrace, pain and pleasure, wealth and destitution, actually are neither good nor evil"; instead, all alike are simply part of "nature's work." What *does* involve good and evil, however, is how we *respond* to what nature does:

> The only thing that makes the good man unique is that he loves and welcomes whatever happened, and what has been spun for him by destiny; and . . . does not pollute the divine *daimon* within . . . harmoniously following god.[51]

Intent on transcending his own natural responses to betrayal and loss—anger, self-pity, and grief—Marcus directs his whole moral energy toward the discipline of practicing equilibrium, often returning to what the ancients called "the unbearable grief," the loss of a child. Marcus and his wife, Faustina, like so many of their contemporaries, experienced this repeatedly; eleven of the fourteen children born to them had died in infancy or childhood. During one of these crises Marcus wrote to himself, "I see that my child is ill. I see. But I do not see that he is in danger"[52]—since his philosophy insists that dying is equivalent to living. Marcus chides himself harshly for his impulse to pray, "Let my child be spared"[53]; even to long that his child live and not die, Marcus believes, is to "complain against nature." Marcus consoles himself with the words of Epictetus, one of the great Stoic masters: "When you are kissing your child, whisper under your

breath, 'Tomorrow you may be dead.' " "Ominous words," others reproached Epictetus, but he replied, "Not at all, but only
indicating an act of nature. Would it be ominous to speak of harvesting ripe corn?"[54] Like Epictetus, Marcus ignores the obvious
objection that a child is hardly "ripe" for death's harvesting; he
muses only that every one of us will fall, "like grains of incense on
an altar, some sooner, some later."[55] So, he continues in his internal dialogue, instead of saying, "How unfortunate I am, that this
has happened to me," one should strive to say, "How fortunate I
am, that this has happened, and yet I am still unhurt, neither
crushed by the present, nor terrified of the future."[56] Reflecting
on reverses of fortune—emperors suddenly assassinated, slaves
freed—Marcus tells himself:

> Whatever happens to you, this, for you, came from destiny;
> and the interweaving of causes has woven into one fabric your
> existence and this event.[57]

Marcus's primary article of faith, then, involves the unity of
all being:

> All things are woven into one another, and the bond that
> unites them is sacred; and hardly anything is alien to any other.
> For they are ordered in relation to one another, and they join
> together to order the same universe. For there is one universe,
> consisting of all things; and one essence, and one law, one
> divine reason, and one truth; and . . . also one fulfillment of
> the living creatures that have the same origin, and share the
> same nature.[58]

Marcus perceives nature and destiny collapsed into one
divinely charged reality and strives to accept his own lot as a matter of religious obligation. He expects no less of everyone else—
certainly of anyone who aspires to philosophy.

Marcus was unique; few pagans tried to construct such a working synthesis of philosophy, ethics, and piety. Yet virtually all who
worshiped the gods would have agreed that these invisible ener-

gies preside over every element of life, giving or withholding fertility, fixing at birth each person's life span, allotting health and wealth to some, and to others poverty, disease, and slavery, as well as presiding over each nation's destiny.

Many pagans, perhaps the majority, performed rituals at temple festivals, participated in feasts, and poured out sacred libations, thus revering these supernatural powers as elements of "the divine." By Marcus's time, however, many worshipers would have agreed that all the gods and *daimones*, even those apparently in conflict with one another, must be part of a unified cosmic system, whether they called it the divine, nature, providence, necessity, or fate.

Belief in the universal power of fate, which Marcus struggled to accept, aroused in others a strong impulse to resist its all-pervading power. As Hans Dieter Betz and John Gager have shown, many people visited magicians who claimed to summon certain *daimones* and to bind them, for a fee, to improve one's health, or to guarantee success in love, horse races, or business.[59] Other people sought initiation into foreign cults, hoping to find in such exotic Egyptian gods as Isis and Serapis divine power that surpassed that of all the more familiar gods and could overturn the decrees of destiny. Lucius Apuleius, who may himself have undergone rigorous initiation into the mysteries of Isis, describes his ecstatic discovery that worshiping the Egyptian goddess could break the power of fate:

> Behold, here is Lucius, who rejoices in the providence of powerful Isis. Behold, he is released from the bonds of misery, and is victorious over his fate.[60]

Although many pagans had come to believe that all the powers of the universe are ultimately one, only Jews and Christians worshiped a single god and denounced all others as evil demons. Only Christians divided the supernatural world into two opposing camps, the one true God against swarms of demons; and none but Christians preached—and practiced—division on earth.[61] By refusing to worship the gods, Christians were driving a wedge between themselves and all pagans, between divine sanctions and Roman government—a fact immediately recognized by Rusticus, Marcus's teacher in Stoicism and his personal friend, who, in his public role as prefect of Rome, personally judged and sentenced Justin and his students to death.

After Justin's beheading, his young student Tatian, a zealous young Syrian convert, wrote a blistering "Address to the Greeks," which begins by attacking Greek philosophy and religion, and ends by denouncing Roman government and law. Tatian wants to show "the Greeks"—which Tatian takes to mean "pagans"—their demonically induced delusions. He asks the crucial question:

> For what reason, O pagans, do you wish to set the governmental powers against us, as in a wrestling match?[62]

Then he declares his spiritual independence:

> If I do not wish to comply with some of your customs, why am I hated, as if I were despicable? Does the governor order me to pay taxes? I do so willingly. Does he order me to do service? I acknowledge my servitude. For one must honor human beings in a way appropriate to humans; but one must fear God alone—he who is not visible to human eyes, nor perceptible by any means known to us.[63]

Tatian agrees with Justin that pagans cannot understand the violence of their own response to Christians until they begin to see that all the supernatural powers they worship are evil beings who are holding them captive. All the powers they worship are nothing more than the continuing fallout of a primordial cosmic rebellion. So Tatian, like Justin, begins at the beginning: "God is spirit," he explains, creator of supernatural and human beings alike. Originally, all supernatural beings were free, but, Tatian explains, drawing on Jewish accounts of the angels' fall, "the firstborn of these rebelled against God, and became a demon . . . and those who imitate him . . . and his illusions, become an army of demons."[64] This swarm of demons, enraged when punished for their apostasy, are nevertheless too weak to retaliate against God: "No doubt, if they could, they undoubtedly would pull down the very heavens themselves, together with the rest of creation."[65] Restrained from totally destroying the universe, they turned all their energies toward enslaving humanity. "Inspired by hostile malice toward humankind," they terrify people by images they send in dreams and fantasies. Tatian does not deny that these "gods" actually possess powers; he says they use their power to gain control over human minds. Nor do demons prey only upon the illiterate and superstitious. Philosophical sophisticates like Marcus Aurelius are no less vulnerable than the local shoemaker, for, as Marcus's own philosophy might show, *daimones* can turn philosophy itself into a means of subjugating people to their tyranny. Tatian ridicules the philosophers, calling Aristotle "absurd" for his famous statement that a human being is a mere "rational animal" (*logikon zoon*), part of the natural order.[66] Even elephants and ants, Tatian says, are "rational animals" in the sense that they "participate in the instinctive and rational nature of the universe," but to be human means much more. It means that one participates in *spirit*, having been created in the image of the God who is spirit.[67]

Deriding the philosophers, Tatian adamantly refuses to see himself as merely part of nature. Since baptism, Tatian says, his own sense of self has had virtually nothing to do with nature; "having been born again," he now identifies with the God who stands beyond nature. Tatian perceives his essential being as spirit, ultimately indestructible:

> Even if fire should annihilate my flesh, and the universe disperse its matter, and, although dispersed in rivers and seas, or torn apart by wild animals, I am laid up in the storehouse of a wealthy master . . . and God the king, when he pleases, will restore the matter that is visible to him alone to its primordial order.[68]

The power of destiny is not divine, as Marcus imagines, but merely a demonic conspiracy; for it was *daimones*, Tatian caustically explains, the offspring of fallen angels, who, having shown humans a map of the position of the stars, *invented destiny—an enormous injustice!* For those who judge and those who are judged are made so by destiny; the murderers and their victims, the wealthy and the destitute, are the offspring of the same destiny; and every human birth is regarded as a kind of theatrical entertainment by those beings of whom Homer says, "among the gods arouse unquenchable laughter" (emphasis added).[69]

Like the spectators who flock to the city amphitheater to amuse themselves, making bets while watching some gladiators win and others die in agony, so, Tatian says, the gods entertain themselves with human triumphs and tragedies. But those who revere the gods ignorantly "attribute events and situations to destiny, believing that each person's destiny is formed from birth"; and they "cast horoscopes and pay for oracles and divination" to find out what destiny has in store.

Tatian ridicules such superstitious people for failing to see that disease and other sufferings happen simply because of elements intrinsic to our physical constitution: surprisingly, he *secularizes* disease, accident, and death, removing them from the supernatural. Although everyone is vulnerable to these contingencies, Tatian says, they hold no real power over people who belong to God, since baptism breaks the bonds that once bound us to *destiny* and to *nature*. Now, he says,

we are superior to destiny, and instead of worshiping planets and *daimones,* we have come to know one Lord. . . . We do not follow the guidance of destiny; rather, we reject those [*daimones*] who established it.[70]

Tatian refuses to acknowledge any subjection to nature and refuses to submit to the demands of the culture and society into which physical birth delivered him:

I do not want to be a ruler; I am not anxious to be rich; I decline military command; I detest sexual promiscuity; I am not impelled by any insatiable love of money to go to sea; I do not contend for reputation; I am free from an insane thirst for fame; I despise death; I am superior to every form of disease; grief does not consume my soul. If I am a slave, I endure slavery; if I am free, I do not boast of my fortunate birth. . . . Why are you "destined" so often to grasp for things, and often to die? Die to the world, repudiating the insanity that pervades it. Live to God, and by apprehending God, apprehend your own nature as a spiritual being created in his image.[71]

Tatian rails against nature and culture—polemics that articulate the suspicion of both that will be woven into Christian theology for nearly two thousand years. The kind of attack Tatian launched would eventually transform Western attitudes toward Greek civilization. Classical civilization would become for Western Christendom virtually synonymous with paganism.[72] Like Justin, Tatian protests pagan indifference to human life:

I see people who actually sell themselves to be killed; the destitute sells himself, and the rich man buys someone to kill him; and for this the spectators take their seats, and the fighters meet in single-handed combat for no reason whatever; and no one comes down from the stands to help! . . . Just as you slaughter animals to eat their flesh, so you purchase people to supply a cannibal banquet for the soul, nourishing it with the most impious bloodshed. Robbers commit murder for the sake of loot; but the rich man buys gladiators to watch them being killed![73]

Tatian does not exaggerate here. The French scholar Georges Villes reports that spectators at the Roman amphitheater might watch as many as three hundred and fifty gladiators die before their eyes at a single day's entertainment.[74]

Declaring himself free from all worldly affiliations, Tatian openly defies pagan rulers: "I reject your legislation, along with your entire system of government." Only allegiance to the one true God "can put an end to the slavery that is in the world, and restore us from many rulers, and then from ten thousand tyrants"—freeing the believer from innumerable demonic tyrants and simultaneously from all the thousands of human rulers whom they secretly control.[75]

We know almost nothing about Tatian's life or what this conviction meant for him in practice; but we do know what it meant to the young Egyptian Christian named Origen, who was seventeen years old when he saw his beloved Christian father, Leonides, arrested and summarily executed for refusing to sacrifice to the gods. Thereafter Origen, later nicknamed Adamantius ("the adamant," or "the indomitable"), resolved to be a warrior on God's side against the forces of Satan. From childhood, as we shall see, Origen witnessed bitter conflict—and then the most astounding series of shifts and reverses—in the relationship between Christians and imperial power. He remained wary of those in power all his life. Though he believed that Christians benefited from the peace the Roman empire provided, he became the first Christian to argue publicly that people have an innate moral right to assassinate tyrants.

Born in the year 185 to a Roman father and an Egyptian mother, both baptized Christians, Origen was seven years old when the reigning emperor, Lucius Commodus, the sole surviving son of Marcus Aurelius, was murdered in his bath.[76] Rumor blamed a palace conspiracy involving Commodus's athletic trainer and Marcia, his concubine; but masses of people, hearing that the emperor was dead, poured into the streets to celebrate, for Commodus had rebelled against everything his distinguished father stood for. By the time he was strangled, Commodus was widely despised as a madman and a tyrant; he had shocked his constituents by pretending to be a gladiator, engaging in public combats in the arena, effectively abdicating his imperial responsibilities by playing the role of a slave. He had also neglected to persecute Christians: Marcia apparently favored Christians and had encouraged Commodus to leave them alone.

The battles of succession lasted three years. Septimius Severus emerged as victor, and seven years later, in 202 C.E., initiated new measures to purge his empire of Christians. It was then that Origen saw his father arrested along with others, charged with professing Christianity, and sentenced to beheading; apparently he was protected by Roman citizenship, as Justin had been, from slow torture and public execution.

While Leonides was in prison, Origen impulsively tried to join the group of martyrs and escaped death, it was said, only because his mother hid his clothes so that he could not leave the house. But Origen passionately urged his father not to lose heart out of concern for his wife and their seven children: "Be careful not to change your mind because of us."[77] His father stood firm; but his execution left the family destitute, since the state confiscated his property as that of a condemned criminal. Origen never forgot that imperial forces, however benign they later seemed to many Christians, might at any moment show their demonic origins.

Origen was rescued from destitution by the generosity of a rich Christian, who invited him into her household and supported him for several months while he continued studying literature and philosophy. The following year, already recognized, at the age of eighteen, for his brilliance and learning, Origen began to teach on his own, supporting himself, his mother, and her six younger children. The persecution that had cost Leonides his life continued in Alexandria under several changes of administration; several of Origen's own students were arrested and executed for professing Christianity, and he himself lived under suspicion. More than once, angry crowds threatened his life, especially when he ignored fears for his own safety and publicly embraced a condemned friend, a man named Plutarch, and attended his execution. So far, Origen himself escaped arrest and interrogation, probably because Severus's persecution had targeted upper-class converts, especially Roman citizens, like Origen's father and many of his students. Origen was protected, apparently, by having inherited from his Egyptian mother the low status Roman law accorded to native noncitizens.

When Origen was twenty-six, and still teaching, writing, and interpreting the Scriptures, Septimius Severus died and was succeeded by two sons, one of whom, Caracalla, promptly assassinated his brother Geta but left the Christians alone. For the moment the government seemed almost benign. One day in 215, during Caracalla's reign, soldiers arrived in Alexandria with a letter from the governor of Arabia (present-day Jordan), summoning Origen to appear at the palace. The governor had heard of Origen's brilliance and wanted to meet the young man; and Origen agreed. But after Caracalla had ruled for six years, he was assassinated by Macrinus, who reigned for only a year before he, too, was killed. He was succeeded by Heliogabalus, Caracalla's cousin, a reclusive, fanatical young worshiper of the sun god, a man whom many people regarded as insane.

Four years later, another cousin, Alexander Severus, replaced Heliogabalus on the throne, and now, for the first time in Roman history, members of the imperial house not only tolerated Christians but even favored them. Severus's mother, the empress Julia Mammea, who gathered many distinguished people at her court, sent soldiers to invite Origen to join them; when he arrived, she discussed with him, among other things, the possibility of reconciling Christians to Roman civilization. Christians of the time would have been astonished to hear a rumor circulating in the empire—whether true or not—that the emperor himself had set up statues of Abraham and Jesus along with those of Socrates and other holy men in his private palace sanctuary!

Hopes for a new age of tolerance were shattered, however, when Maximinus, a rough peasant from Thrace, assassinated Severus, took over the throne, and immediately renewed the persecution of the Christians. Origen followed with great concern the threatened arrest of several of his close friends and associates, including Ambrose, his rich and influential patron and friend, and the priest Protoctetus. Origen, who was not arrested, wrote to them in a passionate "exhortation to martyrdom," warning them not to waver, nor to be deceived by apparently genuine pleas to renounce their faith in order to save their lives. To give in, he said, would be to capitulate to Satan; for those arrested for Christ's sake, only death brings victory.[78]

In the struggle for the throne that followed Maximinus' death, the young emperor Gordian III prevailed, and he, too, left Christians alone. Assassinated by his own soldiers after ruling for four years, he was succeeded by his own chief general. The newly acclaimed emperor, Philip, the first Arab to achieve that position, immediately secured his rule by killing Gordian's young son.

Philip the Arabian may have been the first Christian emperor. At least three witnesses attest that he performed public penance for that murder in view of the astonished congregation, during the huge gatherings that attended the Easter vigil the following spring—penance imposed on the emperor by the Christian bishop of Antioch. During Philip's reign, thousands of new converts filled the churches. Now Origen complained in a sermon that conversion had become so common and even fashionable that it was no longer dangerous.

But Origen's suspicions of government power were confirmed when Decius killed Philip, seized power, and initiated a new and more aggressive persecution of Christians. This time, however, Origen, now in his mid-sixties and more renowned than ever, was arrested and brutally tortured; the governor hoped to gain a useful recantation from his most famous prisoner, but the attempt failed.

Origen knew that pagan opposition to Christianity was often based on more than superstition and prejudice. Years before his arrest, Origen had read a tract, "The True Word," which charged that Christian "atheism" masked a rebellion against everything society and government upheld. Only a few years before his arrest, Origen had decided to respond to these charges, for this was one of the most incisive and devastating attacks on Christians ever written.[79]

Celsus, who wrote the tract around 180 C.E., was a religiously inclined Platonic philosopher. He begins by charging that "the cult of Christians is a secret society, whose members hide together in corners for fear of being brought to trial and punishment." Citing their refusal of the magistrates' orders to sacrifice to the gods, Celsus says that if everyone adopted the Christians' attitude, there would be no rule of law.[80] Celsus lived at a time when the Christian movement was growing rapidly, especially among the illiterate. He writes that the Christians' refusal to obey certain laws and to cooperate with local or imperial officials threatens to "destroy legitimate authority, and return the world to chaos and barbarians"—even to "bring down the empire, and the emperor with it."

Origen's defiant reply opens by challenging the moral legitimacy of imperial rule:

> It is not irrational to form associations contrary to the existing laws, if it is done for the sake of the truth. For just as those people would do well who enter a secret association in order to kill a tyrant who had seized the liberties of a state, so Christians also, when tyrannized . . . by the devil, form associations contrary to the devil's laws, against his power, to protect those whom they succeed in persuading to revolt against a government which is barbaric and despotic.[81]

Origen stops short of identifying imperial law directly with the devil, and elsewhere he even praises the pax Romana for having providentially kept the peace during Jesus' lifetime. Nevertheless Origen characterizes as demon-inspired all laws and persons hostile to Christians. Christians, however, will triumph over their enemies; Jesus died, he explains, "to destroy a great *daimon*—in fact, the ruler of *daimones,* who held in subjection the souls of humanity."[82] Whoever considers empirical evidence will have to admit, he says, that the spread of Christianity, although unanimously opposed by human authorities, governmental and military, proves that some enormous, previously unknown power is now at work in the world:

> Anyone who examines the matter will see that Jesus attempted and successfully accomplished works beyond the range of human capacity. For everything opposed the spread of his teaching in the world—including the rulers in each period, and their chief military leaders and generals, everyone—everyone, to speak generally—who possessed even the slightest influence,

and in addition to these, the rulers of all the various cities, and the armies, and the people.[83]

Origen admits that the astounding success of the Christian movement has occurred principally among the poor and illiterate, but only because "the illiterate necessarily outnumber the educated." Yet "some persons of intelligence and education"— he might have mentioned Justin, Tatian, even himself—have committed their lives to the Christian faith. So, against all odds, Origen continues,

> our Jesus, despised for being born in a rural village—not even a Greek [that is, civilized] one, nor belonging to any nation widely respected; and being despised as the son of a poor laboring woman, [nevertheless] has been able to shake the whole civilized world.[84]

Jesus' impact surpasses that of "even Pythagoras or Plato, let alone that of any ruler or military leader in the world."

Astonishing turns of events in world history offer empirical proof that God's spirit, acting in Jesus, is conquering Satan. Origen agrees with Matthew and Luke that

> one fact which proves that Jesus is something divine and sacred is this: that the Jews have suffered because of him for a very long time such terrible catastrophes. . . . For what nation is exiled from its own capital city, and from the place sacred to the worship of its ancestors, except the Jews alone? . . . It was fitting, then, that the city where Jesus underwent sufferings should utterly perish, and the Jewish nation be overthrown. . . . And we can say with confidence it never will be restored to its former condition.[85]

If the suffering of the Jews proves that God is punishing them, what does that say about the suffering of Christians? And what about those innocent people who suffer disease, catastrophe, or human brutality? Here Origen chooses to be inconsistent. Such difficult problems, he says, are insoluble, "matters of deepest and most inexplicable insight into the whole administration of the universe."[86] Unlike many later Christians, Origen refuses to attribute the sufferings of the innocent simply to "God's will," for, he says, "not everything that happens happens according to God's will, or according to divine providence." Some things, he says, are "accidental by-products" of the works of providence; others occur when human beings—and, for that matter, supernatural beings as well—violate the divinely ordered administration of the universe and intentionally inflict harm. Many instances of human evil, as well as certain seemingly gratuitous natural catastrophes, like floods, volcanoes, and earthquakes, are instigated by "evil *daimones* and evil angels."[87]

Celsus would have found such suggestions profoundly disturbing, for as a Platonist philosopher he claims to revere "the one god who rules over all." Here the pagan Celsus argues for monotheism against what he sees—quite accurately—as the Christians' practical dualism:

> If one accepts that all of nature, and everything in the universe, operates according to the will of God, and that nothing works contrary to his purposes, then one must also accept that the angels and *daimones,* heroes—all things in the universe—are subject to the will of the one God who rules over all.[88]

Celsus urges Christians, too, to worship the one God and to revere everything that providence brings as manifestations of his goodness.

In advocating such monotheism, Celsus agrees not only with other philosophically minded intellectuals like Marcus Aurelius, but also with millions of people all over the empire—the vast majority of them illiterate—who worshiped the gods. The hymns that they heard intoned at the temples of Isis, the liturgies celebrated at the great altars of Serapis, the incantations chanted during processions honoring Helios or Zeus, and the prayers intoned at the festivals of Hecateten often identified the particular deity they had come to worship with the whole of the divine being. By the time of Marcus Aurelius, the classicist Ramsay MacMullen says, many took for granted the unity of all the gods and *daimones* in one divine source.[89]

What divided pagans from Christians, then, was not so much monotheism, since many pagans also tended toward monotheism, as the pagans' essential conservatism. Pagan worship binds one to one's place in the world, and asks the worshiper to fulfill whatever obligations destiny, fate, or "the gods" have decreed. As we have seen, Marcus continually reminds himself that piety means taking a reverent attitude toward his familial, social, and national responsibilities. Musing on whether the gods concern themselves with individual destiny, Marcus declares:

> If the gods took counsel together about me, then their counsel was good . . . and even if they have no special thought for me, at least they took thought for the universe; and I ought to welcome and accept everything that happens as a result. And even if the gods care nothing for human concerns, my own nature is a rational and political one; I have a city, and I have a country; as Marcus I have Rome, and as a human being I have the universe; consequently, whatever benefits these communities is the only good I recognize.[90]

We have seen how hard Marcus struggled to accept his obligations, aware as he was of his privileges and responsibilities, but many of his contemporaries found less incentive to do so. As the empire continued to expand and pressures of inflation and war increased, the advantages Roman citizenship had offered to millions of people diminished; furthermore, an increasing number of people found themselves excluded from its benefits while being enormously burdened by taxes and conscription. Emperor Caracalla, in 213, issued an edict that extended citizenship to all inhabitants of the empire, but what actual effect this had is difficult to determine.

The Christian movement offered a radical alternative—perhaps the only genuine alternative besides Judaism in the Roman empire. What the Roman senator Tacitus complained of in the Jews was doubly true of these breakaway sectarians:

> The first thing they do when they get hold of people is to teach them to despise their gods, neglect their cities, and hate their families; everything that we know as piety they neglect.[91]

We have seen that Christians did teach converts not only that the bonds of family, society, and nation are not sacred, but that they are diabolic encumbrances designed to enslave people to "Roman customs," that is, to demons.

What makes the Christians' message dangerous, Celsus writes, is not that they believe in one God, but that they deviate from monotheism by their "blasphemous" belief in the devil. For all the "impious errors" the Christians commit, Celsus says, they show their greatest ignorance in "making up a being opposed to God, and calling him 'devil,' or, in the Hebrew language, 'Satan.' " All such ideas, Celsus declares, are nothing but human inventions, sacrilegious even to repeat: "it is blasphemy . . . to say that the greatest God . . . has an adversary who constrains his capacity to do good." Celsus is outraged that the Christians, who claim to worship one God, "impiously divide the kingdom of God, creating a rebellion in it, as if there were opposing factions within the divine, including one that is hostile to God!"[92]

Celsus accuses Christians of "inventing a rebellion" (*stasis*, meaning "sedition") in heaven to justify rebellion here on earth. He accuses them of making a "statement of rebellion" by refusing to worship the gods—but, he says, such rebellion is to be expected "of those who have cut themselves off from the rest of civilization. For in saying this, they are really projecting their own feelings onto God."[93] Celsus ridicules Paul's warning that Christians must not eat food offered to the gods, lest they "participate in communion with *daimones*" (1 Cor. 10:20–22). Since *daimones* are the forces that energize all natural processes, Celsus argues, Christians really cannot eat anything at all—or even survive—without participating in communion with *daimones*. Celsus declares that

> whenever they eat bread, or drink wine, or touch fruit, do they not receive these things—as well as the water they drink and the air they breathe—from certain various elements of nature?[94]

Therefore, he adds,

> we must either not live, and indeed, not come into this life at
> all, or we must do so on condition that we give thanks and
> offerings and prayers to *daimones* who have been set over the
> administration of the universe; and we must do so as long as we
> live, so that they may be well disposed toward us.[95]

Celsus warns Christians that just as human administrators,
whether Roman or Persian, take action against subjects who
despise their rule, so these ruling *daimones* will surely punish
those who prove insubordinate. Celsus ironically agrees, then,
with Christians who complain that the *daimones* instigate persecution; he argues that they have good reason to do so:

> Don't you see, my excellent sir, that anyone who "witnesses"
> to your [Jesus] not only blasphemes him, and banishes him
> from every city, but that you yourself, who are, as it were, an
> image dedicated to him, are arrested and led to punishment,
> and bound to a stake, while he whom you call "Son of God"
> takes no vengeance at all upon the evildoer?[96]

Origen admits that this is true and concedes that at such
moments one might imagine that the evil powers have won. "It
is true," he says, "that the souls of those who condemn Christians, and those who betray them and enjoy persecuting them,
are filled with evil," being driven on by *daimones*.[97] Yet for martyrs, suffering and death are not the catastrophic defeat they
seem. On the contrary,

> when the souls of those who die for the Christian faith depart
> from the body with great glory, they destroy the power of the
> demons, and frustrate their conspiracy against humankind.[98]

The demons themselves, perceiving this, sometimes retreat,
afraid to kill Christians, lest they thereby ensure their own
destruction. It is for this reason, Origen says, that persecution

occurs only intermittently. But when the *daimones* recover their boldness and rage again at Christians, "then again the souls of the pious will destroy the army of the evil one." The *daimones'* awareness that Christians win by dying manifests itself, Origen declares, in the attitudes and actions of human judges

> who are distressed by those who endure the outrages and tor-
> tures, but glad when a Christian is overcome [and yields]. And
> it is not from any philanthropic impulse that this occurs.[99]

Origen had experienced this firsthand when he was arrested at Caesarea during Decius's persecution in 251. When he refused the judge's demands to renounce his faith, Origen endured repeated torture. He was chained in a dark cell. His torturers first wrenched his limbs apart and chained him into stocks; at other times they burned him and threatened him with terrible forms of execution. One of his grieved companions, moved by the old man's courage, writes that Origen's ordeal ended only after "the judge had tried him every way at all costs to avoid sen-tencing him to death,"[100] not out of compassion, but hoping to get him to publicly recant his faith. Failing this, the judge released him; but the torture and exposure Origen suffered in prison hastened his death.

Celsus warns that the "insanity" that impels Christians to "refuse their religious obligations, and rush headlong to offend the emperor and governors,"[101] actually may ruin the empire, eclipse the rule of law, and plunge the world into anarchy. Celsus demands that Christians do instead what all pious and patriotic citizens should,

> namely, help the emperor in his effort to provide for the com-
> mon good, and cooperate with him in what is right, and fight
> for him, if it becomes necessary.[102]

Origen dismisses such suggestions with contempt. He an-swers that Christians *do* help the emperor through their prayers, which "conquer all *daimones* who stir up war and . . . disturb the peace . . . so, although we do not believe in being fellow soldiers with him, we do fight on behalf of the emperor."[103] (Tertullian, writing in North Africa, declares that many Christians *do* serve in the army; such practices varied, apparently, from one circumstance to another.)[104] As for taking public office, Origen says, "we recognize in every land the existence of another national organization"—God's church. Origen knows that he is fighting over souls to help diminish the power of Satan; and he ends his polemic against Celsus by saluting his patron Ambrose, who ten years earlier had stood trial and endured prison and torture.

Persecuted Christians like Origen forged a radical tradition that undermined religious sanction for the state, claiming it instead for the religious conscience—a tradition that would enormously influence subsequent Western government and politics. Baptism opened access to vast new dimensions of reality—to the Kingdom of God, where God's people find their true home, and to the dominion of Satan, perceived as the ultimate moral reality underlying "this present evil age." Although unbelievers like Celsus ridiculed Christians for believing absurd and childish fantasies, many converts found in their vision of God's kingdom a place to stand, and new perspectives on the world into which they had been born.

This does not mean that Christians were the seditious conspirators that Celsus imagined. Justin and others staunchly insisted that most Christians were good citizens, most of whom, no doubt, wanted to avoid confrontation with the authorities, and attempted to follow the precepts expressed in New Testament letters like First Peter, which translates into Christian terms ancient conventions of civic virtue:

> For the sake of the Lord, accept the authority of every human institution, whether of the emperor, as supreme, or of governors, as those sent by him to punish those who do wrong and praise those who do not. . . . As slaves of God, live as free people. . . . Honor all people. Love the brotherhood. Fear God. Honor the emperor (1 Pet. 2:13–16).

What *was* revolutionary, however, was that Christians professed primary allegiance to God. Such allegiance could divide one's loyalties; it challenged each believer to do something most pagans had never considered doing—decide for oneself which family and civic obligations to accept, and which to reject.

Tertullian, for example, who lived in a world where what we call freedom of religion was alien or unknown, nevertheless claims such liberty for himself and censures the emperors for "taking away religious liberty [*libertatem religionis*] so that I may no longer worship according to my inclination, but am compelled to worship against it."[105] Origen, as we have noted, defending Christians against charges of illegality, dares argue that people constrained by an evil government are right not only to disobey its laws but even to revolt and to assassinate tyrannical rulers:

> It is not irrational to form associations contrary to the existing laws, if it is done for the sake of the truth. For just as those people would do well who enter a secret association in order to kill a tyrant who had seized the liberties of a state, so Christians also, when tyrannized . . . by the devil, form associations contrary to the devil's laws, against his power, to protect those whom they succeed in persuading to revolt against a government which is barbaric and despotic.[106]

Such convictions did not arise from a sense of the "rights of the individual," a conception that emerged only fifteen hundred years later with the Enlightenment. Instead they are rooted in the sense of being God's people, enrolled by baptism as "citizens in heaven," no longer subject merely to "the rulers of this present evil age," the human authorities and the demonic forces that often control them.

A hundred years after the gospels were written, then, Christians adapted to the circumstances of pagan persecution the political and religious model they found in those gospels—God's people against Satan's people—and identified themselves as allies of God, acting against Roman magistrates and pagan mobs, whom they see as agents of Satan. At the same time, as we shall see in the next chapter, church leaders troubled by dissidents *within* the Christian movement discerned the presence of Satan infiltrating among the most intimate enemies of all—other Christians, or, as they called them, heretics.

THE ENEMY WITHIN:
DEMONIZING THE HERETICS

During the second century Christianity's success in attracting converts raised new questions about what "being a Christian" required. Within provincial cities throughout the empire, Christian groups gained many thousands of new converts. Especially in the cities, conversion aroused conflict within households. When heads of wealthy households converted, they often required their families and slaves to accept baptism. More often, however, conversions occurred among the women of the household, as well as among merchants, traders, soldiers, and the hundreds of thousands of slaves serving in every capacity in Roman apartments, great houses, and palaces. Conversions may even have happened within the emperor's household. Tertullian, writing in the city of Carthage in North Africa (c. 180) boasts to his pagan contemporaries that "we are only of yesterday, and we have filled every place among you: city, islands, fortresses, towns, market places, the army camp, tribes, palace, senate, and forum."[1]

All converts understood, of course, that baptism washes away sins and expels evil spirits, and conveys to the recipient the spirit of God, the spirit that transforms a sinner into an ally of Christ and his angels. But then what? What does a Christian have to do to stand "on the side of the angels" in this world? What precisely is required if, for example, the baptized Christian is married to a pagan, or is a soldier, who has sworn allegiance to the emperor, or is a slave? Most pagans regarded the baptism of a family member or a slave as a calamity portending disruption within the household. Tertullian himself describes how pagans ostracized converts:

> The husband casts the wife out of his house; the father disinherits the son; the master, once gentle, now commands the slave out of his sight; it is a huge offense for anyone to be called by that detested name [Christian].[2]

Among themselves, Christians debated whether converts should maintain ordinary social and familial relationships or break them, as Jesus in the gospels required when he said, "Whoever does not hate his father and mother, wife and children, brothers and sisters, yes, even life itself, cannot be my disciple" (Luke 14:26). Such questions evoked many different answers as the movement increased in size and diversity throughout the empire. Sometimes in one city there were several groups, each interpreting "the gospel" somewhat differently and often contending against one another with all the vehemence ordinarily reserved for family quarrels. The apostle Paul himself, confronted two generations earlier by rival teachers, tried to prevent them from speaking, calling them Satan's servants,

> false apostles, deceptive workers, disguising themselves as apostles of Christ. And no wonder! Even Satan himself disguises himself as an angel of light. So it is not strange if his servants disguise themselves as servants of righteousness (2 Cor. 11:13–15).

"But," Paul adds ominously, "in the end they will get what they deserve." Christians dreaded Satan's attacks from outside—that is, from hostile pagans—but many of them believed that even more dangerous were Satan's forays among the most intimate enemies of all—other Christians, or, as most said of those with whom they disagreed, among heretics.

Within the movement, some people began to develop systems of organization to unify Christian groups internally, and to connect them with other Christian groups throughout the Roman world. The authority all Christians acknowledged, besides that of Jesus himself, was that of the apostles Peter, traditionally revered as the first leader of Christians in Rome, and Paul, founder of churches ranging from Greece to Asia Minor. Some Christians, two or three generations after Paul, wrote letters attributed to Peter and Paul, including First Peter and the letters of Paul to Timothy. These letters, later included in the New Testament and widely believed to have been written by the apostles themselves, attempted to construct a bridge between the apostles and Christians of later generations by claiming, for example, that Paul had "laid hands" on his young convert Timothy to ordain him as "overseer" or "bishop" of the congregation as Paul's successor. These letters are meant to show that, like Timothy, bishops legitimately exercise "apostolic" authority over their congregations.

Those who wrote First Peter and First Timothy were also concerned to deflect pagan hostility to Christians by modifying some of the more strident demands the gospels attribute to Jesus. Needing codes of conduct that offered moral guidance to those who were married and engaged in ordinary society and were not prepared to reject these commitments as, according to Luke, Jesus admonishes, these authors borrowed from pagan catalogues of civic virtue to construct new, "Christian" moral codes. As New Testament scholar David Balch has shown, these letters cast Peter and Paul in the unlikely role of urging believers to emulate conventional Roman behavior.[3] So, in First Peter, "Peter" urges believers, "For the sake of the Lord, accept the authority of every human institution" (2:13), specifically that of the emperor and his government. "Peter" also insists that believers carry out essential household responsibilities; wives must "accept the authority of your husbands, even if some of them do not obey the Word" (3:1); and husbands should "honor the woman, as the weaker vessel" (3:7). Slaves are to serve their masters as if serving the Lord himself, and masters, in turn, are not to mistreat their slaves; children are to show their parents appropriate deference and obedience (2:18–22; 5:5). In First Timothy, likewise, "Paul" offers Timothy similar moral advice, which he tells the young bishop, in turn, to enjoin upon his congregation.

But not everyone accepted these codes of conduct or the leaders determined to enforce them. Around 90 C.E., a famous letter attributed to Clement, a man regarded by many as the second or third bishop of Rome, after the apostle Peter, and written to Christians in the Greek city of Corinth, the site of a church originally founded by Paul himself, shows that the community was in an uproar over a matter of leadership.[4] In this letter, Bishop Clement expresses distress that those he calls "a few rash and self-willed people"[5] are refusing to accept the superior authority of the priests who he insists are their proper leaders. Such dissidents have initiated what Clement calls a "horrible and unholy rebellion"[6] within the church. They have rejected several priests set over them; apparently they also object that distinctions between "clergy" and "laity"—between those who claim to hold positions of authority and those they now call "the people" (in Greek, *laos*)—are not only unprecedented but unacceptable among Christians.

Denying the dissidents' charge that clerical ranks are an innovation, Clement, like the author of First Timothy, insists that the apostles themselves "appointed their first converts . . . to be bishops and deacons." Clement invokes the authority of the prophet Isaiah, making a farfetched claim that in ancient times Isaiah had already endorsed the "offices" of bishop and deacon. Clement cites Isaiah 60:17 ("I will make your *overseers* peace, and your *taskmasters* righteousness"), and interprets the key terms ("bishops" and "deacons," respectively), translated into Greek, to suit his argument.

Clement also appeals to the letters of Paul to Timothy to argue that "the apostles themselves appointed their first converts as 'bishops' and 'deacons.' " Although Clement writes at about the same time as the authors of Matthew and Luke, who depict the Jewish high priests as Jesus' enemies, Clement encourages Christians to imitate the Jewish priesthood. Among Christians, as formerly among Jews, Clement says, the high priests and the subordinate priests are divinely ordained for special duties, while "the layperson is bound by the order for laypeople."[7] Clement even urges his fellow Christians to emulate the Roman army:

Let us then serve in our army, brethren. . . . Let us consider
those who serve as our generals. . . . Not all are prefects, nor
tribunes, nor centurions, nor commanders, or the like, but
each carries out in his own rank the commands of the emperor
and of the generals.[8]

Later, Christians actually did adapt from Roman army administration the practice of organizing into districts (dioceses), each
administered by a central overseer (bishop), an organizational
strategy that persists to this day.

As bishop, Clement describes the dissidents' position as having
arisen from arrogance and jealousy. "Even the apostles," he
says, "knew that there would be strife over the title of bishop"
(1 Clement 14:1). The remedy, Clement continues, is for everyone to "submit to the priests," accepting the penance that the
priest will impose for their disobedience, "bending the knees of
your hearts, and bowing to [the priests'] superiority" (1 Clement
17:1). Perhaps hoping that those who had refused to obey would
now submit, Clement avoids associating them with Satan, as later
leaders would do with more entrenched dissidents.

We do not know the outcome of this dispute; none of the
opponents' responses survive. But during the second century, as
such controversies plagued churches throughout the empire,
church leaders who identified themselves with the proper "apostolic succession" widely copied Clement's letter and circulated it
throughout the Roman world, along with several other writings
they included in a collection called "the apostolic fathers of the
church." We know little about the process from which this collection emerged; but we can see that the writings it includes all
tend to emphasize the growing authority of the clergy and enjoin
adherence to detailed and practical moral codes.

Most Christians apparently accepted, along with the emerging
"canon" of the Scriptures, this second "canon" of church tradition. Several writings included in the "apostolic fathers" sought
to revise and, in effect, domesticate for the new influx of converts
such radical sayings of Jesus as these: "You cannot serve God and
money" (Matt. 6:24); "Give to whoever asks you" (Matt. 5:42);

"Sell all that you have and give . . . the money to the poor; then come, and follow me" (Luke 18:22). Included in the "apostolic fathers," for example, is a famous Christian handbook called the *Teaching of the Twelve Apostles*, which paraphrases Jesus' primary teaching as follows: "Love God and your neighbor; and whatever you do not want done to yourself, do not do to others."[9] Weaving together sayings from the Sermon on the Mount and canny advice, the *Teaching* qualifies Jesus' categorical command "Give to everyone who asks of you" by adding, "Let your money sweat in your hand until you know to whom you are giving it."[10] The *Teaching* adapts and expands some of the Ten Commandments, declaring that "the Second Commandment of the apostles' teaching is this: 'You shall not kill; you shall not commit adultery,' " and specifying that this means in practice that "you [masc.] shall not have intercourse with young boys; you shall not commit fornication; you shall not steal; you shall not procure abortions; you shall not kill newborns."[11]

Another writing included in the "apostolic fathers," the *Letter of Barnabas*, attributes similar moral teaching to Paul's companion and fellow preacher. *Barnabas*, like the *Teaching*, invokes a traditional Jewish teaching of the "two ways"—the "way of light," consisting of a list of actions that are good, and the "way of darkness," consisting of evil actions.[12] *Barnabas* interprets the Ten Commandments for Christians as requiring at least forty specific injunctions, including warnings against "arrogance of power" and "advocating in behalf of the rich" while denying justice to the poor, as well as the same sexual sins denounced in the *Teaching*: "[male] intercourse with boys," "fornication" (which probably means extramarital sexual activity of any kind), adultery, and abortion.[13] Thus *Barnabas* outlines a moral code that would dominate Christian teaching for generations, even millennia, to come.

Barnabas sets these contrasting ways of life in the context of God's spirit contending against Satan during "the present evil time."[14] Reminding Christians that "the spirit of God has been poured out on you from the Lord,"[15] *Barnabas* urges them to exercise moral vigilance, so that "the devil may have no opportunity to enter" the church, even though "the days are evil, and the evildoer is still in power."[16] While encouraging Christians to accept a modified version of Jewish ethical attitudes and practices, *Barnabas* warns Christians not to fall into the ways of the Jews, who, he says, "transgressed because an evil angel was leading them into error."[17] The new people of God are to "shun the way of darkness" and embrace the "way of light," since "over the one is set the light-bearing angels of God, but over the other, angels of Satan."

Although most converts accepted the bishops' instructions about what Christians must—and must not—do, some, probably a minority, questioned the authority of priests and bishops and rejected such practical moralizing. Around 180 C.E., Irenaeus, claiming the authority of apostolic succession as bishop of a congregation in Lyons, wrote a massive five-volume attack on deviant Christians—whom he called heretics—attacking them as secret agents of Satan.[18] In the opening of his enormously influential work, *Against Heresies,* Irenaeus acknowledges that "error is never put forth nakedly," as blatant folly, but only "dressed out in clever and ingenious disguises."[19] There are those, Irenaeus declares, who claim to be Christians, and are taken by all to be such, who actually teach "an abyss of madness and blasphemy against Christ."[20] Such false believers "use the name of Christ Jesus [only] as a kind of lure," in order to teach doctrines inspired by Satan, "infecting the hearers with the bitter and malignant poison of the serpent, the great instigator of apostasy."[21] Irenaeus suggests that those who resist the bishops' moral teaching do so because they themselves are driven by passion; some, he warns, "yield themselves up to the lusts of the flesh with utmost greed."[22]

For nearly two thousand years, most Christians have taken Irenaeus at his word, believing that many of those he called heretics were deceptive, licentious, or both. But after many writings by these so-called heretics were discovered in Upper Egypt in 1945, near the town of Nag Hammadi, those Christians whose works the bishops suppressed could speak for themselves, virtually for the first time in history.[23] When we read their writings, we find in some of them beliefs that sound bizarre; others seem to reflect intense, inquiring minds engaged on a variety of spiritual paths. One of the most extreme is the *Testimony of Truth,* a text that raises the primary question that Christian reformers have asked throughout two millennia, from the second century gnostic teacher Valentinus through Francis of Assisi, Martin Luther, George Fox, founder of the Society of Friends, and Mary Baker Eddy: What *is* "the gospel"? What is the "true testimony" about Christ and his message? Like other would-be reformers, the anonymous author of the *Testimony of Truth* begins by addressing "those who know how to listen, not only with their ears, but with their understanding."[24] Far from endorsing licentiousness, the *Testimony* insists that Christians practice asceticism. This author writes as a guardian of the true gospel; he believes that the great majority of Christians—those who accept the kind of leadership and domesticated morality advocated by the "apostolic fathers"—have fallen into moral error. "Many have sought the truth and have not been able to find it, because they have been taken over by the 'old leaven of the Pharisees and the teachers of the law.' "[25]

Most Christians, this teacher says, unthinkingly accept the Genesis account of creation, according to which the creator "commands one to take a husband or a wife and to beget, to multiply like the sands of the sea" (Gen. 1:28; 13:16).[26] But, this teacher objects, such Christians fail to realize that the gospel stands in diametric opposition to the law: "The Son of man came forth from incorruptibility,"[27] and came into the world to end the old order and initiate the new. He called on those who belong to him to be transformed: "This is the true testimony: when a person comes to know himself and the God who presides over truth, he will be saved."[28] But coming to know God requires that one renounce everything else: "No one knows the God of truth except the one alone who renounces all the things of the world."[29] Renunciation alone enables one to put off the old, false self, riddled with fear, greed, anger, lust, and envy, and to recover one's own true self in God. The true Christian follows a path shunned by most so-called Christians; such a person, this author says, thinks about the power which flowed over the whole universe, which comes upon him . . . and he is a disciple of his mind. . . . He begins to keep silent within himself . . . he rejects for himself argument and disputation . . . he is patient with everyone, makes himself equal with everyone, and he also separates himself from them.[30]

Christians like Justin Martyr, one of the fathers of the church, shared such aspirations for self-mastery. Justin wholeheartedly admired Christians who practiced renunciation and celibacy; he even singled out for special praise a young convert in Alexandria who had petitioned Felix, the governor,

asking that permission might be given to a surgeon to castrate him. For the surgeons had said they were forbidden to do this without the governor's permission. And when Felix absolutely refused to sign such a permission, the young man remained celibate.[31]

Origen, also revered as a father of the church, had been so determined to win his struggle against passion that as a young man he had castrated himself, apparently without asking anyone's permission, least of all the governor's.

The author of the *Testimony* never mentions castration, much less endorses it, but he insists nevertheless that only those who "renounce the whole world," beginning with sexual activity and commercial transactions, ever come to know God. The majority of Christian churches, from the second century to the present, have regarded such renunciation as a counsel of perfection, achieved only by a heroic few—in orthodox churches throughout the world by monastics, and in Roman Catholic churches by all priests and bishops, as well as monks and nuns. The author of the *Testimony* goes much further than Christians like Justin or Origen, however, when he declares that renunciation is not only admirable but essential for any true Christian. He knows, of course, that the great majority of Christians believe that God created male and female and commanded all his creatures, animal and human, to "be fruitful and multiply" (Gen. 1:28). But the author of the *Testimony,* reflecting on his own alienation from the majority of "worldly" Christians, suddenly believes he understands Jesus' warning to his disciples to "beware of the leaven of the scribes and Pharisees" (Mark 8:15). Jesus' words are not to be taken literally, as if they referred only to Jewish teachers; instead, taken symbolically, they warn against *Christian* teachers like the author of *Barnabas* or the *Teaching of the Twelve Apostles,* who invoke the Scriptures to sanction ordinary life.

According to the *Testimony,* the "scribes and Pharisees" and the "blind guides" against whom Jesus warns (Matt. 23) are none other than the majority of Christians—Christians who have been tricked into worshiping not God but supernatural "rulers" who are less than divine. The author of the *Testimony* takes Jesus' warning to mean that believers must shun the influence of the "errant desire of the angels and demons"[32]—the fallen angels who fell into error through their own lust. The *Testimony* even claims that the God whom most Christians worship, the God of the Hebrew Bible, is *himself* one of the fallen angels—indeed, the chief of the fallen angels, from whose tyranny Christ came to set human beings free: for, the *Testimony* declares, "the word of the Son of man . . . separates us from the error of the angels."[33]

What *Barnabas* says of the Jews—that they have been deceived by an "evil angel"—and what the majority of Christians say about pagans—that they unwittingly worship demons spawned by fallen angels—this author says about *other Christians.* This radical teacher does what millions of disaffected Christians have done ever since: regarding the majority of Christians as apostate, he reads them into the gospels as "Pharisees and scribes" (or at least as gullible disciples, susceptible to seduction by these teachers). Fourteen hundred years later, Martin Luther, for example, would come to see his former fellow Christians—Roman Catholics—as the "Pharisees and scribes" against whom Jesus warned his disciples. While most believers see in Christ and his message the power to overcome the forces of evil in the world, some dissenting Christians ever since the second century have claimed that the gospel itself has been co-opted by the forces of evil.

But the author of the *Testimony of Truth* goes far beyond the "protesting" Christians of the Reformation and later times. Convinced that Christ's message is precisely the opposite of "the law"—that is, the Hebrew Bible—this teacher raises radical questions:

> What is the light? And what is the darkness? And who is the one who created the world? And who is God? And who are the angels? . . . And what is the governance (of the world)? And why are some lame, and some blind, and some rich, and some poor?[34]

Approaching the Genesis story with questions like these, this teacher "discovers" that it reveals truth only when one reads it in reverse, recognizing that God is actually the villain, and the serpent the holy one! This teacher points out, for example, that in Genesis 2:17, God commands Adam not to eat from the fruit of the tree in the midst of Paradise, warning that "on the day that you shall eat of it, you shall die." But the serpent tells Eve the opposite: "You will not die, for God knows that when you eat of it your eyes will be opened, and you will be like God, knowing good and evil" (3:4–5). Who, asks the *Testimony*, told the truth? When Adam and Eve obeyed the serpent, "then the eyes of both were opened, and they knew that they were naked" (3:7). They did not die "on that day," as God had warned; instead, their eyes were opened to knowledge, as the serpent had promised. But when God realized what had happened, "he cursed the serpent, and called him 'devil' " (Gen. 3:14–15).[35] Now that Adam had attained godlike knowledge, God decided to evict him from Paradise, "lest he reach out his hand and eat of the tree of life and live forever" (Gen. 3:22), attaining eternal life along with knowledge.

"What kind of god is this god? . . . Surely he has shown himself to be a malicious envier,"[36] says the author of the *Testimony*. Not only is this god jealous of his own creation, he is also ignorant and vindictive. And what of the serpent, whom God cursed and called "devil"? According to the *Testimony of Truth*, the serpent who led Adam and Eve to spiritual enlightenment is actually *Christ,* appearing in this disguise in Paradise to release Adam and Eve from "the error of the angels"[37]—that is, error induced by malevolent supernatural "rulers," who masquerade as God in this world.

Another anonymous Christian teacher whose writing was discovered at Nag Hammadi was asked by one of his students what "the great apostle" Paul meant when he warned that "our contest is not against flesh and blood, but against the rulers of the universe and the spirits of evil" (Eph. 6:12). He replied by writing a secret revelation called the *Reality of the Rulers,* which, he says, "I have sent you since you have asked about the reality of the [cosmic] rulers."[38] The teacher explains that "their chief [the God of the Hebrew Bible] is blind; because of his power and his ignorance and his arrogance, he said, . . . 'It is I who am God, and there is none apart from me.' "[39] This teacher then says:

> When he said this, he sinned against the whole place. And a voice came forth from above the realm of absolute power, saying,
>
> "You are wrong, Samael," that is, "God of the blind." . . .
>
> And he said, "If anything else exists before me, let it become visible to me!"
>
> And immediately Wisdom stretched forth her finger and brought light into matter. . . .
>
> And he said to his offspring, "It is I who am the god of the whole."
>
> And Life, daughter of Faith-Wisdom, cried out and said, "You are wrong, Saklas!" (that is, "fool"). She breathed into his face, and her breath became for her a fiery angel; and that angel bound him and cast him down into Tartyros below the abyss.[40]

In the universe depicted by this teacher there is no devil, and no need for one, for "the Lord"—the God of Jews and most Christians alike—himself acts as chief of the fallen angels who seduce and enslave human beings. By declaring himself to be the supreme and unique God of the universe, he "sinned against the whole," refusing to recognize himself as part of a much larger divine reality. His boasts reveal him to be only a lesser, ignorant being whose power has led him into overweening pride (*hybris*) and into destruction.

According to the *Reality of the Rulers*, it is Samael and his fellow "rulers of the darkness" (Eph. 6:12), not the true God, who formed Adam's physical body (Gen. 2:7), set him to work in Paradise "to till it and cultivate it" (Gen. 2:15), then put him to sleep and fashioned his female partner out of his rib (Gen. 2:21–22). These same rulers commanded Adam not to eat from the fruit of the Tree of Knowledge, which could open his eyes to the truth, because they jealously wanted to keep control over him. When Adam and Eve, enlightened by the feminine spiritual principle who appeared to her in the form of the serpent, defied them, the rulers cursed the woman and the snake, and expelled Adam and Eve from Paradise:

> Moreover, they threw humankind into great distraction and into a life of toil, so that humankind might be occupied with worldly affairs, and might not have the opportunity of being devoted to the holy spirit.[41]

According to the authors of such teachings, the human condition, involving work, marriage, and procreation, does not reflect divine blessing, but demonstrates enslavement to cosmic forces that want to blind human beings to their innate capacity for spiritual enlightenment. Such radical Christians believe that most people, including most Christians, have fallen prey to the rulers of darkness and so, like most Jews and pagans, remain entangled in sexual, social, and economic bondage.

There are a few, however, among whom these authors number themselves, whose eyes have been opened, who have awakened to the divine source from which human beings come and to which they belong—a source deeply hidden in ordinary experience. The prototype of the spiritually awakened person is Eve's daughter, Norea. When the "rulers" try to seduce and deceive her, Norea cries out to God and receives divine help; the angel

Eleleth (whose Hebrew name means "understanding") reveals to her how these corrupt and limited powers have come to rule over the world, and assures her that she herself belongs not to them but to the powers above—the Father of the whole, and to his emanation and "daughter," Wisdom, and to divine Life:

> You, together with your offspring, are from above; these souls have come out of the imperishable light. Thus the rulers cannot approach her because of the spirit of truth present within her; and all who know this way live deathless in the midst of dying mankind.[42]

Those who have "the spirit of truth within them" refuse to enter into marriage, business, or any other worldly entanglements, in order to remain an "undominated generation," free "to devote themselves to the holy spirit."[43]

The *Secret Book of John,* another well-known "revelation" discovered at Nag Hammadi, offers another wildly mythological reading of Genesis intended to reveal the ties that bind people to futile and unsatisfying lives. The *Secret Book* explains that after Adam was created, the chief ruler and his allies carried out a series of three assaults intended to overpower and capture the children of Adam. First the chief ruler "seduced [Eve] . . . and begot in her two sons," Cain and Abel; thus from that time "up to the present day, sexual intercourse continued, because of the chief ruler," who "planted sexual desire" in Eve. Yet because certain people still eluded his domination despite the pressures of sexual desire,[44] the chief ruler next "made a plan together with his powers" to subdue even the strongest of human spirits: the rulers "committed adultery with Wisdom, and bitter fate was begotten by them."[45] From that time on, fate proved to be the most inescapable of bonds:

> For from that fate came forth every sin and every injustice and blasphemy and oblivion and ignorance, and every harsh condition, and serious violations, and great terrors. And the whole creation was blinded, so that they might not know God, who is above all of them.[46]

Since even the invention of fate left the rulers uneasy about their control over human beings, they planned a third conspiracy. The chief ruler "sent his angels to the daughters of men"[47] (cf. Gen. 6:2) to mate and procreate with them, and to share with them and to teach them how to mine gold and silver, iron and copper. Thus the *Secret Book* depicts the misery of ordinary human life, enmeshed in labor, driven by instinctive passion, dominated by fate, spent in getting money and trying to amass wealth. By all these devices the rulers kept human beings under their control:

> and they steered the people who followed them into great distraction; the people became old without having joy; they died without having found truth, and without knowing God. . . . And thus the whole creation became enslaved to them, from the foundation of the world until now.[48]

Certain Christians who stood with the majority responded to these extremists. Tertullian, a convert in the North African city of Carthage, and a contemporary of Irenaeus (c. 180 C.E.), agreed with Irenaeus in denouncing all who deviated from the majority consensus as "heretics." Both fathers of the church insist that what characterizes the true church is unanimity—agreement in doctrine, morals, and leadership. Christians, Tertullian says, quoting Paul, should "all speak and think the very same things."[49] Whoever deviates from the consensus is, by definition, a heretic; for, as Tertullian points out, the Greek word translated "heresy" (*hairesis*) literally means "choice"; thus a "heretic" is "one who makes a choice."[50] Tertullian notes that heretics actually pride themselves on the points at which they differ from the majority, regarding these as evidence of their own deeper insight. He says sardonically,

> Wherever they have hit upon any novelty, they immediately call their presumption a "spiritual gift," since they value not unity but diversity. . . . Consequently, most often they are in a divided state themselves, being ready to say—and indeed, quite

sincerely—of certain points in their belief, "This is not so," and "I take this in a different sense," and "I do not accept that."[51]

But Tertullian insists that making choices is evil, since choice destroys group unity. To stamp out heresy, Tertullian says, church leaders must not allow people to ask questions, for it is "questions that make people heretics"[52]—above all, questions like these: Whence comes evil? Why is it permitted? And what is the origin of human beings? Tertullian wants to stop such questions and impose upon all believers the same *regula fidei*, "rule of faith," or creed. Tertullian knows that the "heretics" undoubtedly will object, saying that Jesus himself encouraged questioning, saying, "Ask, and you shall receive; seek, and you shall find; knock, and it shall be opened to you" (Matt. 7:7). But Tertullian has no patience with such people: "Where will the end of seeking be? The point of seeking is to find; the purpose in finding, to believe."[53] Now that the church can provide a direct and simple answer to all questions in its rule of faith, Tertullian says, the only excuse for continuing to seek is sheer obstinacy:

> Away with the one who is always seeking, for he never finds anything; for he is seeking where nothing can be found. Away with the one who is always knocking, for he knocks where there is no one to open; away with the one who is always asking, for he asks of one who does not hear.[54]

The true Christian, Tertullian declares, simply determines to "know nothing . . . at variance with the truth of faith." But when people "insist on our asking about the issues that concern them," Tertullian says, "we have a moral obligation to refute them. . . . They say that we must ask questions in order to discuss," Tertullian continues, "but what is there to discuss?" When the "heretics" object that Christians must discuss what the Scriptures really mean, Tertullian declares that believers must dismiss all argument over scriptural interpretation; such controversy only "has the effect of upsetting the stomach or the brain."[55] Besides, Tertullian says, such debate makes the orthodox position look weak:

If you do discuss with them, the effect on the spectators will be to make them uncertain which side is right . . . the person in doubt . . . will be confused by the fact that he sees you making no progress, while the other side is on an equal basis with you in discussion . . . and *he will go away even more uncertain about which side to find heretical. . . . For, no doubt, they, too, have things to say; they will accuse us of wrong interpretation, since they, no less than we, claim that truth is on their side* (emphasis added).[56]

Instead of admitting heretics into debates over the Scriptures, Tertullian says, "straight thinking" (the literal translation of "orthodox") Christians must simply claim the Scriptures as their own exclusive property:

Heretics ought not to be allowed to challenge an appeal to the Scriptures, since we . . . prove that they have nothing to do with the Scriptures. For since they are heretics, they cannot be true Christians.[57]

But how do heretics come up with such ingenious and persuasive arguments from Scripture? Their inspiration comes, Tertullian says, from "the devil, of course, to whom belong the wiles that distort the truth."[58] Satan, after all, invented all the arts of spiritual warfare, including false exegesis. Paul's warning against "spiritual forces of evil in heavenly places," which the *Reality of the Rulers* turns against the biblical God and his angels, Tertullian takes in the opposite sense: Here, he says, Paul warns against the devil, who contrives false readings of the Scriptures to lead people into error.[59] In place of choices, questions, and discussions of scriptural interpretation, Tertullian prescribes unanimous acceptance of the rule of faith and, to ensure this, obedience to the proper ecclesiastical "discipline"—that is, to the priests who stand in proper succession from the apostles.[60] Tertullian's "prescriptions," if they had been enforced, might have proven effective against radical teachers like those who wrote the *Testimony of Truth*, the *Reality of the Rulers*, and the *Secret Book of John.* In any case, the groups these texts represented remained marginal among Christians; their appeal was limited to the few who were willing to heed a gospel that required one to break not only with the world but also with the Christian majority.

Others whom Tertullian and Irenaeus recognized as heretics were, however, far less radical—and, precisely for that reason, far more threatening to the emerging clerical authorities and their advocates. Prominent among them were followers of Valentinus, a Christian teacher from Egypt who had emigrated to Rome around the time Justin did, c. 140 C.E. Valentinus had no quarrel with clerical authority; in fact, if we can believe Tertullian on this point, Valentinus "expected to become a bishop himself, because he was an able man, both in genius and eloquence."[61] But Valentinus "broke with the church of the true faith,"[62] Tertullian says, because another man was made bishop instead; Tertullian, like Clement, attributes to those who challenge episcopal authority the motives of envy and frustrated ambition.

Valentinus had been baptized and had accepted the creedal statement of faith and participated in common Christian worship. But after his baptism he received a revelatory dream in which the Logos appeared to him in the form of a newborn child;[63] he took this vision as an impetus to begin his own spiritual explorations. Having heard of a teacher named Theudas who claimed to have received secret teaching from the apostle Paul himself, Valentinus eagerly learned from him all he could. Henceforth he became a teacher himself, amplifying what he had learned from Theudas with his own spiritual explorations, and encouraging his students to develop their inner capacity for spiritual understanding.

Valentinus intended to steer a middle course between two extremes—between those who claimed that the faith of the majority was the only true faith, and those, like the authors of parts of the *Testimony of Truth* and the *Reality of the Rulers,* who rejected it as false and debased. While he took for granted that accepting baptism and professing the common faith in God and Christ were necessary for those making a beginning in the faith, he urged his fellow believers to go beyond what Christian preachers taught and beyond the literal interpretation of the Scriptures to question the gospels' deeper meaning. By so doing, he believed, one could progress beyond faith to understanding, that is, to *gnosis*. This word is often translated "knowledge," but the translation is somewhat misleading, since *gnosis* differs from intellectual knowledge (as in phrases like "they *know* mathematics"), which is characterized in Greek by the word *eidein* (from which we derive the English word *idea*). English is unusual within its language group in having only one verb ("to know") to express different kinds of knowing. Modern European languages use one word to characterize intellectual knowledge and another for the knowledge of personal relationships: French, for example, distinguishes between *savoir* and *connaître,* Spanish between *saber* and *conocer,* Italian between *sapere* and *conoscere,* German between *wissen* and *kennen*. The Greek word *gignōsko,* from which *gnosis* derives, refers to the knowledge of personal relationships (as in "We *know* Christ" or, in the words of the Delphi oracle, "Know thyself"). The term might better be translated "insight," or "wisdom." One gnostic teacher encourages his students to seek *gnosis* within themselves:

> Abandon the search for God, and creation, and similar things of that kind. Instead, take yourself as the starting place. Ask who it is within you who makes everything his own saying, "my mind," "my heart," "my God." Learn the sources of love, joy, hate, and desire. . . . If you carefully examine all these things, you will find [God] in yourself.[64]

Another teacher says that *gnosis* reveals "who we were, and who we have become; where we are going; whence we have come; what birth is, and what is rebirth."[65] What the gnostic Christian finally comes to "know" is that the gospel of Christ can be perceived on a level deeper than the one shared by all Christians. One who takes the path of *gnosis* discovers that the gospel is more than a message about repentance and forgiveness of sins; it becomes a path of spiritual awakening, through which one discovers the divine within. The secret of *gnosis* is that when one comes to know oneself at the deepest level, one comes to know God as the source of one's being.

The author of the *Gospel of Philip,* a follower of Valentinus, describes *gnosis* as a natural progression from faith. Just as a harvest is gathered through the cooperative interaction of the natural elements, water, earth, wind, and light, so, *Philip* says,

> God's farming has four elements—faith, hope, love, and *gnosis.* Faith is our earth, in which we take root. And hope is the water through which we are raised; love is the wind through which we grow. *Gnosis,* then, is the light through which we ripen [or: "become mature"].[66]

Unlike the radical Christians of the *Reality of the Rulers* or the *Secret Book of John,* Valentinus and his followers did not reject the moral injunctions taught by priests and bishops; they did not despise or invert the Hebrew Bible, nor did they openly deny the authority of priests and bishops. Instead they accepted all these, but with a crucial qualification: they accepted the moral, ecclesiastical, and scriptural consensus as binding upon the majority of Christians, but not upon those who had gone beyond mere faith to *gnosis*—those who had become spiritually "mature."

Valentinus and his followers also accepted as necessary for beginners the moral order that the bishops enjoined, prescribing good works and proscribing bad ones. But Valentinus and his followers saw in the churches two different types of Christian.[67] Most Christians they call "ecclesiastic," or "psychic," Christians (that is, those who function on the level of *psyche,* or soul); "and they say," Irenaeus protests indignantly, "that we of the church are such persons."[68] But those who come to accept a second, secret initiation called "redemption" henceforth regard themselves as mature, "spiritual" Christians, who have advanced from mere faith toward spiritual understanding, or *gnosis.*

Because Valentinus and his followers publicly accepted baptism, attended common worship, and pronounced the same creed, most Christians considered them to be completely innocuous fellow believers, and they themselves insisted that this is what they were. But within a generation of Valentinus's teaching in Rome, the movement had won a considerable following throughout the Christian world, especially among the more educated members of the church. Tertullian complains that often it is "the most faithful, the most prudent, and the most experienced" church members "who have gone over to the other side."[69] Irenaeus, to his dismay, found Valentinian teachers active among members of his own congregation in Lyons, inviting believers to attend secret meetings, to raise questions about the faith and discuss its "deeper meaning."[70] In such meetings, unauthorized by the bishop, these Valentinians taught what Irenaeus regarded as blasphemy. They taught, for example, that the creator God described in Genesis is not the only God, as most Christians believe—nor is he the malevolent, degraded chief of the fallen angels, as the radicals imagine. According to Valentinus, he is an anthropomorphic image of the true divine Source underlying all being, the ineffable, indescribable source Valentinus calls "the depth," or "the abyss." When Valentinus does invoke images for that Source, he describes it as essentially dynamic and dyadic, the divine "Father of all" and "Mother of all."[71] Those who attended such meetings might also hear that the bishop—Irenaeus himself—although a good man, was a person of limited understanding who had not progressed beyond faith to *gnosis*.

Irenaeus acknowledges in *Against Heresies* that the followers of Valentinus think of themselves as people who are reforming the church and raising its level of spiritual understanding; but, he says, nothing good they accomplish could possibly compensate for the harm they inflict by "dividing in pieces the great and glorious body of Christ,"[72] the church. As bishop, Irenaeus saw that the very act of committing themselves to spiritual exploration set gnostic Christians apart from the rest, and effectively divided the community. Their presence as an insidious inner group threatened the fragile structures of organizational and moral consensus through which leaders like Irenaeus were attempting to unify Christian groups throughout the world.

While Valentinian Christians agreed that the bishops' moral instruction was necessary for psychic Christians, they tended to regard themselves as exempt, free to make their own decisions about acts that the bishops prohibited. Some Valentinian Christians, Irenaeus says, attend pagan festivals along with their families and friends, convinced that doing so cannot pollute them; others, he charges, go to gladiator shows, and are guilty of what he describes as flagrant sexual transgressions.[73] As an example, Irenaeus cites Marcus, a Valentinian teacher active "in our own district in the Rhone Valley." Irenaeus calls him a seducer who concocts special aphrodisiacs to entice the many women who "have been defiled by him, and were filled with passion for him," including "the wife of one of our deacons . . . a woman of remarkable beauty,"[74] who actually left home to travel with Marcus's group.

But when Irenaeus gets down to describing Marcus's actual techniques of seduction, we can see that he is speaking metaphorically. What concerns the bishop, among other things, is the enormous appeal that Valentinian teaching had for women believers, who were increasingly excluded during the second century from active participation in Irenaeus's church. Marcus, Irenaeus says, "seduces women" by inviting them to participate in celebrating the Eucharist, and by casting the eucharistic prayers in such "seductive words" as prayers to Grace, the divine Mother, along with the divine Father.[75] Worse, Marcus "lays hands" upon women to invoke the holy spirit to come down upon them, and then encourages them to speak in prophecy.[76] When Irenaeus accuses Marcus's followers of adultery, he is invoking a traditional biblical image for participating in "illicit" religious practices. The prophets Hosea, Isaiah, and Jeremiah, for example, often used the metaphors of adultery and prostitution to indict those they accused of being "unfaithful" to God's covenant.[77]

Several Valentinian works discovered at Nag Hammadi, including the *Gospel of Truth* and the *Gospel of Philip,* offer correctives to charges that the Valentinians were immoral. In one of the few remaining fragments of his teachings, Valentinus himself, commenting on Jesus' saying that "God alone is good," says that apart from God's grace, the human heart is a "dwelling place for many demons. But when the Father, who alone is good, looks upon it, he purifies and illuminates it with his light; thus the one who has such a heart is blessed, because he sees God."[78] The *Gospel of Truth,* which may also have been written by Valentinus, offers the following ethical instruction to gnostic Christians:

> Speak of the truth with those who seek for it, and of *gnosis* to those who have committed sins in their error. Secure the feet of those who have stumbled, and stretch out your hands to those who are ill. Feed those who are hungry, and give rest to those who are weary. . . . For you are the understanding which is drawn forth. If strength acts thus, it becomes even stronger. . . . Do not become a dwelling place for the devil, for you have already destroyed him.[79]

The *Gospel of Philip* proposes an alternative to the common Christian perception of good and evil as cosmic opposites.[80] In this gospel, unlike the New Testament gospels, Satan never appears. Instead, the divine Father and the holy spirit, working in harmony with each other, direct all that happens, even the actions of the lower cosmic forces, so that ultimately, in Paul's words, "all things work together for good" (Rom. 8:28). The *Gospel of Philip* offers an original critique of the way all other Christians, orthodox and radical alike, approach morality. Much as they disagree on content, both orthodox and radical Christians assume that morality requires *prescribing* one set of acts, and *proscribing* others. But the author of *Philip* wants to throw away all the lists of good things and bad things—lists that constitute the basis of traditional Christian morality. For, this author suggests, what we identify as opposites—"light and dark, life and death, good and evil"—are in reality pairs of interdependent terms in which each implies the other.[81]

Intending to transpose Christian moral discipline into a new key, the author of *Philip* takes the story of the tree of knowledge of good and evil as a parable that shows the futility of the traditional approach to morality. According to *Philip,* "the law was the tree"; the law, like the tree of knowledge, claims to give "knowledge of good and evil," but it cannot accomplish any moral transformation. Instead, it "created death for those who ate of it. For when it said, 'Eat this, do not eat that,' it became the beginning of death."[82]

To show that one cannot distinguish good from evil in such simple and categorical ways, *Philip* tells another parable, of a householder responsible for an estate that includes children, slaves, dogs, pigs, and cattle. The householder, who feeds each one the diet appropriate to its kind, is an image of the "disciple of God," who "perceives the conditions of [each person's] soul, and speaks to each one" accordingly, recognizing that each has different needs and stands at a different level of spiritual maturity.[83] Thus *Philip* refuses to argue over sexual behavior— whether, for example, Christians should marry or remain celibate. Posed as opposites, these choices, too, present a false dichotomy. This author admonishes, "Do not fear the flesh, nor love it. If you fear it, it will gain mastery over you; if you love it, it will devour and paralyze you."[84] *Philip* intends to follow Paul's insight that for one person marriage may be the appropriate "diet," for another, celibacy.

While rejecting the ordinary dichotomy between good and evil, this author does not neglect ethical questions, much less imply that they are not important. For him the question is not whether a certain act is "good" or "evil" but how to reconcile the freedom *gnosis* conveys with the Christian's responsibility to love others. Here the author has in mind a saying from the gospel of John ("You shall know the truth, and the truth shall make you free") and the apostle Paul's discussion of love and *gnosis* in 1 Corinthians, chapters 8 and 9. There Paul says that he considers himself, because of his own *gnosis*, free to eat and drink whatever he likes, free to travel with a Christian sister as a wife, and free to live as an evangelist at community expense. Yet, Paul says, "since not everyone has this *gnosis*" (1 Cor. 8:7–13), he willingly relinquishes his freedom for the sake of love, in order not to offend potential converts or immature Christians. The author of *Philip* follows Paul's lead, then, when he takes up the central question: How is the Christian to avoid sin? How can one act in harmony with *gnosis*, on the one hand, and with *agape*, or love, on the other?

The central theme of the *Gospel of Philip* is the transforming power of love: that what one becomes depends upon what one loves.[85] Whoever matures in love takes care not to cause distress to others: "Blessed is the one who has not caused grief to anyone."[86] Jesus Christ is the paradigm of the one who does not offend or grieve anyone, but refreshes and blesses everyone he encounters, whether "great or small, believer or unbeliever."[87] The gnostic Christian, then, must always temper the freedom *gnosis* conveys with love for others. The author says, too, that he looks forward to the time when freedom and love will harmonize spontaneously, so that the spiritually mature person will be free to follow his or her own true desires without grieving anyone else. Instead of commanding one to "eat this, do not eat that," as did the former "tree" of the law, the true tree of *gnosis* will convey perfect freedom:

> In the place where I shall eat all things is the tree of knowledge. . . . That garden is the place where they will say to me, "Eat this, or do not eat that, just as you wish."[88]

When *gnosis* harmonizes with love, the Christian will be free to partake or to decline, according to his or her own heart's desire.

The majority of Christians, by contrast, characterized spiritual formation as the Essenes had, as an internal contest between the forces of good and evil. The great Christian ascetic Anthony, who lived in Egypt c. 250–355 C.E. and became a pioneer among the desert fathers, taught his spiritual heirs in monastic tradition to picture Satan as the most intimate enemy of all—the enemy we call our own *self*. The *Life of Anthony,* written in the fourth century by Athanasius, bishop of Alexandria, describes how Satan tempts Anthony by speaking through his inner thoughts and impulses, through imagination and desire. *Philip,* on the other hand, interprets the human inclination to sin without recourse to Satan. But this does not mean, as some orthodox Christians suspected, that Valentinian Christians naïvely believed that they had no need to engage in moral struggle because they were "beyond good and evil," essentially incapable of sin. On the contrary, *Philip* teaches that within each person lies hidden the "root of evil." This is *Philip*'s interpretation of the traditional Jewish teaching of the *yetzer 'hara*, which the rabbis called the "evil impulse." So long as we remain unaware of "the root of evil" within us, *Philip* says, "it is powerful; but when it is recognized, it is destroyed." He continues,

> As for us, let each of us dig down to the root of evil within us, and pull out the root from the heart. It will be plucked out if we recognize it. But if we do not recognize it, it takes root in our hearts and produces its fruits in our hearts. It masters us, and makes us its slaves. It takes us captive, so that "we do what we do not want, and what we do not want to do, we do" [cf. Rom. 7:14–15]. It grows powerful because we have not recognized it.[89]

Essential to *gnosis* is to "know" one's own potential for evil. According to *Philip*, recognizing evil within oneself is necessarily an individual process: no one can dictate to another what is good or evil; instead, each one must strive to recognize his or her own inner state, and so to identify acts that spring from the "root of evil," which consists in such impulses as anger, lust, envy, pride, and greed. This teacher assumes that when one recognizes that a certain act derives from such sources, one loses the conviction needed to sustain the action. In order to do evil—whether to indulge in an angry tirade, commit murder, or declare aggressive war—one seems to require the illusion that one's action is justified, that one is acting for right reasons. This author holds, then, the optimistic conviction that "truth . . . is more powerful than ignorance of error."[90] Knowing the truth in this way involves more than an intellectual process; it involves transformation of one's being, transformation of one's way of living: "If we know the truth, we shall find its fruits within us; if we join ourselves with it, we shall receive our fulfillment."[91]

For the mature Christian, *Philip* suggests, the doctrine and moral strictures of the institutional church have become secondary, if not irrelevant. Yet unlike many later Protestant Christians, Valentinian Christians did not simply reject the ecclesiastical structures. Instead they claimed to build upon them as upon a foundation, just as Christians as a whole claimed to have built upon the foundations of Judaism. The author of *Philip,* in fact, like the author of the *Testimony,* at one point uses the terms "Hebrew" and "Christian" to compare the relationship between those who have received only the *preliminary* revelation, and those who have received the fuller understanding of *gnosis.*

Thus the author of *Philip* criticizes those he calls Hebrews and defines as "apostles and apostolic people," who fail to understand, for example, the meaning of the virgin birth. Many take it literally, as if Jesus' "virgin birth" referred to an actual conception and pregnancy. *Philip* ridicules such belief:

> Some said, "Mary conceived by the holy spirit." They are in error. They do not know what they are saying; for when did a female ever conceive through a female?[92]

As *Philip* sees it, Jesus, born of Mary and Joseph as his human parents, was reborn of the holy spirit, the feminine element of the divine being (since the Hebrew term for spirit, *Ruah,* is feminine) and of the "Father in heaven," whom Jesus urged his disciples to address in prayer ("Our Father, who art in heaven . . ."). Yet, the author adds, the very mention of a feminine spiritual power "is a great anathema to the Hebrews, who are the apostles, and apostolic people."[93]

Such people do see baptism as rebirth through the holy spirit, but they do not understand that they must be reborn from the heavenly Father as well. Thus, says *Philip,*

> when we were Hebrews, we . . . had only our mother; but when we became Christians, we had both father and mother.[94]

Baptism, then, differs for different people. Some, the author says, "go down in the water [of baptism] and come up without receiving anything,"[95] but nonetheless such a person says, "I am a Christian." For such people, according to *Philip,* the name

"Christian" is only a promise of what they may yet receive in the future. For others, however, baptism becomes a moment of transformation: "Thus it is when one experiences a mystery."[96] Whoever is reborn of the heavenly Father and heavenly Mother becomes a whole person again, receiving back a part of the human self that had been lost in the beginning of time—"the spirit, the partner of one's soul." Such a person becomes whole again, and "holy, down to the very body."[97] One can hardly refer to such a person as a Christian, "for this person is no longer a Christian, but a Christ."[98]

What about specific practical questions? This author's attitude recalls that expressed in the *Gospel of Thomas,* where Jesus' disciples ask him for specific directions: "Do you want us to fast? How shall we pray? Shall we give alms? What diet should we observe?" According to Matthew and Luke, Jesus offers specific answers to such questions. But according to the *Gospel of Thomas,* he says only, "Do not tell lies, and do not do what you hate,"[99] an ironic answer, for it turns one back upon one's own resources. Who but oneself can know when one is lying, or what one hates? The *Gospel of Philip,* too, while apparently expressing a preference for asceticism (obviously intended to mirror Paul's own preference for celibacy over marriage expressed in 1 Corinthians 7:1–40), refrains from offering specific instructions about sexual behavior. What matters, apparently, is not so much what one does but the quality of one's intention. Hence the *Gospel of Philip* remains nonprescriptive, but with two important provisos: first, the gnostic Christian must temper with love the freedom *gnosis* conveys; second, the believer must remain continually aware of his or her potential for doing evil, for only such awareness can free the Christian—even the gnostic Christian—from involuntary enslavement to sin.

Although Irenaeus and others charged that Valentinian Christians were dualists, the *Gospel of Philip* indicates the opposite. This author abandons even the modified dualism that characterizes the great majority of Christian teachings, based, as we have seen, on the conviction that God's spirit constantly contends against Satan. Instead of envisioning the power of evil as an alien force that threatens and invades human beings from outside, the author of *Philip* urges each person to recognize the evil within, and consciously eradicate it.

Bishop Irenaeus, determined to check the spread of the gnostic movement within the churches, realized that the measures Tertullian had suggested would not stop the Valentinians. It is not enough, Irenaeus says, to insist that all believers confess the same creed and accept the moral instruction provided by priests and bishops, for the wily "heretics" willingly do these things, at least in public. Nor is it enough simply to insist that Christians accept the authority of all priests and bishops. The Valentinians include within their own number many priests who are, so to speak, on their side; Irenaeus explains, "There are those who many believe are priests, but who . . . conduct themselves with contempt toward orders, . . . doing evil deeds in secret"[100]—like those who are actually initiated into *gnosis*. Rather, Irenaeus declares, believers must accept only *certain* priests—priests who not only are properly ordained but who clearly repudiate secret teaching and refuse to participate in private meetings unauthorized by the bishop. Therefore, Irenaeus concludes, "it is necessary to obey the priests who are in the church—those who, along with apostolic succession, have received the certain gift of truth." At the same time,

> it is also necessary to hold in suspicion other [priests] who depart from the primitive succession, and who assemble themselves in any place whatsoever, regarding these as heretics, or schismatics, or hypocrites . . . who cleave asunder and divide the unity of the church.[101]

These, Irenaeus warns, will receive divine punishment: fire from heaven will consume them.

Finally Irenaeus denounces Valentinian theology as the devious result of Satan's own inspiration. Irenaeus concludes his five-volume work *Against Heresies* by speaking, in God's place, the words of divine judgment:

> Let those persons, therefore, who blaspheme the creator, either by openly expressed disagreement . . . or by distorting

the meaning [of the Scriptures], like the Valentinians and all the falsely called gnostics, be recognized as agents of Satan by all who worship God. Through their agency Satan even now, and not earlier, has been seen to speak against God . . . the same God who has prepared eternal fire for every kind of apostasy.[102]

Just as in the beginning of time Satan led human beings astray by means of the serpent, "so now," Irenaeus declares, "do these people, filled with a Satanic spirit, seduce the people of God." Against "all heretics," Irenaeus helps construct for the Christian churches the structure that has sustained orthodox Christianity ever since, by claiming sole access to "the doctrine of the apostles, and the system of the church throughout the whole world, and the distinct manifestation of the body of Christ (that is, the church) according to the succession of bishops," together with "a very complete system of doctrine."[103]

CONCLUSION

This vision of cosmic struggle, forces of good contending against forces of evil, derived originally from Jewish apocalyptic sources and was developed, as we have seen, by sectarian groups like the Essenes as they struggled against the forces they saw ranged against them. This split cosmology, radically revising earlier monotheism, simultaneously involved a split society, divided between "sons of light," allied with the angels, and "sons of darkness," in league with the power of evil. Followers of Jesus adopted the same pattern. Mark, as we have seen, tells the story of Jesus as the conflict between God's spirit and the power of Satan, manifest in the opposition Jesus encountered from evil spirits and evil people alike. Each of the gospels in its own way invokes this apocalyptic scenario to characterize conflicts between Jesus' followers and the various groups each author perceived as opponents. We have seen, too, that as the movement became increasingly Gentile, converts turned this sectarian vocabulary against other enemies—against pagan magistrates and mobs engaged in bitter struggle with the growing Christian movement, and against various groups of dissident Christians, called heretics—or, in Paul's words, "servants of Satan."

Christians in later generations turned weapons forged in first-century conflict against other enemies. But this does not mean that they simply replaced one enemy with another. Instead, Christian tradition has tended to accumulate them. When pagan converts like Justin Martyr, for example, aimed vocabulary concerning Satan and the demons against Roman persecutors and against heretics, they often took for granted the hostile characterizations of the Jewish majority they found in the gospels. Justin himself praises those he calls Hebrews—that is, the ancient Israelites, revered ancestors of his own faith—but expresses condescension toward those of his contemporaries he calls not Hebrews but Jews for their "blindness" to God's revelation and their "misunderstanding" of their own Scriptures. Justin castigates the Jews in language largely drawn from Matthew's polemic against the Pharisees and often repeats for his Gentile audiences Luke's refrain in Acts that Jesus was "crucified by the Jews." Origen, too, although preoccupied primarily with struggles against Roman persecution and against "heretics"—and despite his own extensive conversations with Jewish teachers, whom he credited with teaching him a great deal about the Hebrew language and scriptural interpretation—nevertheless develops the views expressed in Matthew to characterize the Jewish people as divinely condemned for rejecting their Messiah.

The attitudes Justin and Origen express are not unique to them. They are readily recognized by most Christians from the second century through the twentieth because they draw upon a familiar source, the New Testament gospels. Throughout the centuries, Christians have turned the same polemical vocabulary against a wider range of enemies. In the sixteenth century, for example, Martin Luther, founder of Protestant Christianity, denounced as "agents of Satan" all Christians who remained loyal to the Roman Catholic Church, all Jews who refused to acknowledge Jesus as Messiah, all who challenged the power of the landowning aristocrats by participating in the Peasants' War, and all "protestant" Christians who were not Lutheran.

I am not saying that the gospel accounts are essentially Manichaean in the ordinary sense of the term, that they envision good and evil evenly matched against each other. Christian tradition derives much of its power from the conviction that although the believer may feel besieged by evil forces, Christ has already won the decisive victory. Anthony, one of the pioneers among the desert ascetics, a man famous for wrestling with demons, explains to his followers:

> Since the Lord dwelt among us, the Enemy has fallen, and his powers have been weakened. He does not submit quietly to his fall . . . but keeps on threatening like a tyrant.[1]

Describing how a great, towering figure once appeared to him, Anthony says he asked the intruder, "Who are you?" and was told, "I am Satan." Anthony boldly rebuked the Enemy, reminding him that

> "Christ has come and made you powerless. He has cast you down and stripped you." When he heard the Savior's name, he vanished, for he could not endure its burning heat. . . . If, then, even the devil admits that he is powerless, we ought to despise both him and his demons. . . .
> The Enemy with his hounds has only so many stratagems. . . . We should not be disheartened, nor succumb to cowardice of soul, nor invent terrors for ourselves. . . . We should take courage, and always be joyful as people who have been saved. Let us keep in mind that the Lord who defeated and vanquished him is with us.[2]

The faith that Christ has conquered Satan assures Christians that in their own struggles the stakes are eternal, and victory is certain. Those who participate in this cosmic drama cannot lose. Those who die as martyrs win the victory even more gloriously and are assured that they will celebrate victory along with all of God's people and the angels of heaven. Throughout the history of Christianity, this vision has inspired countless people to take a stand against insuperable odds in behalf of what they believe is right and to perform acts that, apart from faith, might seem only futile bravado. This apocalyptic vision has taught even secular-minded people to interpret the history of Western culture as a moral history in which the forces of good contend against the forces of evil in the world.

Philosophically inclined Christians such as Augustine of Hippo have often disparaged such mythological language and declared that, ontologically speaking, evil and Satan do not exist. On this level, orthodox Christianity does not diverge from monotheism. Yet Augustine himself, like many other philosophically sophisticated preachers, often speaks of Satan in sermons and prayers and acknowledges, when he is dealing with people confronted with obstacles, that Christians in this world still struggle against evil in ways that they experience as demonic attack.

So compelling is this vision of cosmic war that it has pervaded the imagination of millions of people for two thousand years. Christians from Roman times through the Crusades, from the Protestant Reformation through the present, have invoked it to interpret opposition and persecution in myriad contexts. To this day, many Christians—Roman Catholic, Protestant, Evangelical, and Orthodox—invoke the figure of Satan against "pagans" (among whom they may include those involved with non-Christian religions throughout the world) and against "heretics" (that is, against other Christians with whom they disagree), as well as against atheists and unbelievers. Millions of Muslims invoke similar apocalyptic visions and switch the sides, so that those who Christians believe are God's people become, for many Muslims, allies of "the great Satan."

Many religious people who no longer believe in Satan, along with countless others who do not identify with any religious tradition, nevertheless are influenced by this cultural legacy whenever they perceive social and political conflict in terms of the forces of good contending against the forces of evil in the world. Although Karl Marx's extreme and resolutely materialist version of this apocalyptic vision is now nearly defunct, a secularized version of it underlies many social and political movements in Western culture, both religious and antireligious.

So long as the Christian movement remained a persecuted, suspect minority within Jewish communities and within the Roman empire, its members, like the Essenes, no doubt found a sense of security and solidarity in believing that their enemies were (as Matthew's Jesus says of the Pharisees) "sons of hell," already, in effect, "sentenced to hell." This vision derives its power not only from the conviction that one stands on God's side, but also from the belief that one's opponents are doomed to fail. The words Matthew places in Jesus' mouth characterize his opponents as people accursed, whom the divine judge has already consigned "into the eternal fire prepared for the devil and his angels."

Yet among first-century Christian sources we also find profoundly different perceptions of opponents. Although Matthew's Jesus attacks the Pharisees and bitterly condemns them, and John at one point characterizes Jesus' opponents as Satan's progeny, the Q source that Matthew uses also suggests different ways of perceiving others, in sayings attributed to Jesus that urge reconciliation with one's opponents:

> If you are offering your gift at the altar, and there remember that your brother has something against you, leave your gift there before the altar and go; first be reconciled to your brother, and then come and offer your gift (5:23–24).

Or Matthew 5:43–44:

> You have heard that it was said, "You shall love your neighbor and hate your enemy." But I say to you, "Love your enemies and pray for those who persecute you, so that you may be children of your father in heaven."

To pray for one's enemies suggests that one believes that whatever harm they have done, they are capable of being reconciled to God and to oneself. Paul, writing about twenty years before the evangelists, holds a still more traditionally Jewish perception that Satan acts as God's agent not to corrupt people but to test them; at one point he suggests that a Christian group "deliver to Satan" one of its errant members, not in order to consign him to hell, but in the hope that he will repent and change (1 Cor. 5:5). Paul also hopes and longs for reconciliation between his "brothers," "fellow Israelites," and Gentile believers (Rom. 9:3–4).

Many Christians, then, from the first century through Francis of Assisi in the thirteenth century and Martin Luther King, Jr., in the twentieth, have believed that they stood on God's side without demonizing their opponents. Their religious vision inspired them to oppose policies and powers they regarded as evil, often risking their well-being and their lives, while praying for the reconciliation—not the damnation—of those who opposed them.

For the most part, however, Christians have taught—and acted upon—the belief that their enemies are evil and beyond redemption. Concluding this book, I hope that this research may illuminate for others, as it has for me, the struggle within Christian tradition between the profoundly human view that "otherness" is evil and the words of Jesus that reconciliation is divine.

NOTES

Introduction

1. Martin Buber, cited in discussion with Malcolm Diamond, professor of religion at Princeton University, May 1994.
2. Neil Forsyth, *The Old Enemy: Satan and the Combat Myth* (Princeton: Princeton University Press, 1987).
3. Walter Wink, *Unmasking the Powers: The Invisible Forces That Determine Human Existence* (Philadelphia: Fortress Press, 1986); C. G. Jung, *Answer to Job*, trans. R. F. C. Hull (London: Routledge and Kegan Paul, 1954).
4. Jeffrey B. Russell, *The Devil: Perceptions of Evil from Antiquity to Primitive Christianity* (Ithaca, N.Y.: Cornell University Press, 1970).
5. Robert Redfield, "Primitive World View," in Redfield, ed., *The Primitive World and Its Transformations* (Ithaca: Cornell University Press, 1953), 92.
6. Jonathan Z. Smith, "What a Difference a Difference Makes," in Jacob Neusner and Ernest S. Frerichs, eds., *To See Ourselves As Others See Us: Christians, Jews, "Others" in Late Antiquity* (Chico, Calif.: Scholars Press, 1985), 3–48.
7. William Scott Green, "Otherness Within: Towards a Theory of Difference in Rabbinic Judaism," in Neusner and Frerichs, eds., *To See Ourselves As Others See Us*, 46–69.
8. Even a well-known passage in the Talmud assumes that Jewish courts condemned and executed Jesus. See b. Sahn. 107b and parallel passages, b. Sotha 47a and j. Hag. 2.2., part of the Gemara on Sanh. 10.2. For discussion, see E. Bammel, "Christian Origins in Tradition," *New Testament Studies* 13 (1967): 317–35; see also David R. Catchpole, *The Trial of Jesus: A Study in the Gospels and Jewish Historiography from 1770 to the Present Day* (Leiden: E. J. Brill, 1971), for a fascinating and detailed discussion of the history of scholarship on this passage.

9. Barnabas Lindars, *New Testament Apologetic: The Doctrinal Significance of the Old Testament Quotations* (London: SCM Press, 1973).

10. James Robinson, *The Problem of History in Mark* (London: SCM Press, 1957; reprinted, Philadelphia: Fortress Press, 1982).

11. Albert Schweitzer, *The Quest of the Historical Jesus: A Critical Study of Its Progress from Reimarus to Wrede* (London: A. and C. Black, 1926).

12. Josef Jacobs, *Jesus as Others Saw Him* (New York: B. G. Richards, 1925); H. Danby, "The Bearing of the Rabbinical Code on the Jewish Trial Narratives in the Gospels," *Journal of Theological Studies* 21 (1920): 26–51; C. G. Montefiori, *The Synoptic Gospels* I, 2nd rev. ed. (London: Macmillan, 1927); Richard W. Husband, *The Prosecution of Jesus: Its Date, History and Legality* (Princeton: Princeton University Press, 1916); Josef Blinzler, *The Trial of Jesus: Jewish and Roman Proceedings Against Jesus Christ*, trans. I. and F. McHugh, 2nd rev. ed. (Westminster, Md.: Newman, 1959).

13. Simon Bernfield, "Zur ältesten Geschichte des Christentums," *Jahrbücher für Jüdische Geschichte und Literatur* 13 (1910): 117.

14. Hans Lietzmann, *Synopsis of the First Three Gospels,* trans. F. L. Cross, 9th rev. ed. (Oxford: Basil Blackwell, 1968); Martin Dibelius, *Die Formgeschichte des Evangeliums* (Tübingen: Mohr, 1919), trans. and reprinted in 1971; Dibelius, *From Tradition to Gospel* (New York: Scribner, 1965), 178–219; John R. Donahue, *Are You the Christ?* (Missoula, Mont.: Society of Biblical Literature, 1973).

15. Paul Winter, *On the Trial of Jesus,* 2nd ed. (Berlin: De Gruyter, 1974); see also M. Radin, *The Trial of Jesus of Nazareth* (Chicago: University of Chicago Press, 1931); J. Klausner, *Jesus von Nazareth, Seine Zeit, Sein Leben und Seine Lehre,* 2nd ed. (Berlin: Jüdischer Verlag, 1934); E. G. Hirsch, *The Crucifixion from the Jewish Point of View* (Chicago: Bloch Publishing & Printing, 1921).

16. Fergus Millar, "Reflections on the Trial of Jesus," in P. R. Davies and R. White, eds., *A Tribute to Geza Vermes: Essays on Jewish and Christian Literature and History* (Sheffield: JSOT Press, 1990), 355–81.

17. *The Trial of Jesus; the Jewish and Roman Proceedings Against Jesus Christ Described and Assessed from the Oldest Accounts* (Westminster, Md.: Newman, 1959), 290. See, for example, A. N. Sherwin-White, *Roman Society and Roman Law in the New Testament* (Oxford: Oxford University Press, 1983); T. A. Burkill, "The Condemnation of Jesus: A Critique of Sherwin-White's Thesis," *Novum Testamentum* 12 (1970):321–42; R. E. Brown, *The Death of the Messiah: From Gethsemane to the Grave* (New York: Doubleday, 1994).

18. See Winter; Lietzmann; Dibelius; G. Volkmar, *Die Evangelien* (Leipzig: Fues' Verlag, 1870), 588–91; J. Norden, "Jesus von Nazareth in der Beurteilung der Juden einst und jetzt," *Jüdische Literarische Zeitung* (June 18, 1930): 25; S. Grayzel, *A History of the Jews* (Philadelphia: Jewish Publication Society of America, 1947), 1337; J. Isaac, *Jésus et Israel* (Paris: A. Michel, 1948), 509; G. Bornkamm, *Jesus von Nazareth* (Stuttgart: Kohlhammer, 1956), 1504; E. P. Sanders, *Jesus and*

Judaism (Philadelphia: Fortress Press, 1985), states that "Jesus was executed by the Romans as would-be 'King of the Jews' " (p. 294) and also that internal conflict among Jews was "the principal cause of Jesus' death" (p. 296; cf. pp. 294–318). See also the important article reviewing recent scholarship by G. S. Sloyan, "Recent Literature on the Trial Narratives of the Four Gospels," in T. J. Ryan, ed., *Critical History and Biblical Faith: New Testament Perspectives* (Villanova: Villanova University Press, 1979), 136–76.

Chapter I

For a more technical discussion of the material in this chapter, see "The Social History of Satan, Part II: Satan in the New Testament Gospels," *Journal of the American Academy of Religions* 52/1 (February 1994): 201–41.

1. Josephus, *The Jewish War* 1.1, Loeb edition, vol. 2, trans. H. St. J. Thackery (London: Heinemann, 1926). For an excellent recent discussion of Josephus's works, see Shaye J. D. Cohen, *Josephus in Galilee and Rome: His Vita and Development as a Historian* (Leiden: E. J. Brill, 1979).

2. Josephus, *Life of Josephus* 4, Loeb edition, vol. 1, trans. H. St. J. Thackery (London: Heinemann, 1926).

3. Josephus, *War* 4.128.

4. *Ibid.,* 4.146.

5. *Ibid.,* 5.5.

6. *Ibid.,* 5.430.

7. *Ibid.,* 5.19.

8. For discussion of the dating of Mark, see Dennis E. Nineham, *The Gospel of Mark* (Baltimore: Penguin, 1963); Vincent Taylor, *The Gospel According to St. Mark,* 2nd ed. (London: Macmillan, 1966).

9. For discussion, see E. Pagels, *The Gnostic Gospels* (New York: Random House, 1979); for a summary edition and translation of the texts, see James M. Robinson, ed., *The Nag Hammadi Library in English* (New York: Harper, 1977); for Coptic texts, translation, and scholarly notes, see the series of over twenty volumes published in Leiden by E. J. Brill as *Nag Hammadi Studies.*

10. Tacitus, *Annals* 15.44, Loeb edition, trans. J. Jackson (Cambridge, Mass.: Harvard University Press, 1931).

11. Cited in the excellent discussion by Brent D. Shaw, "Bandits in the Roman Empire," *Past and Present* 165 (November 1984): 3–52. See also G. Humbert, "Latrocinium," in C. Davemberg and E. Saglio, eds., *Dictionnaire des antiquités greques et romaines* iii, 2 (1904): 991–92; R. MacMullen, "Brigandage," appendix B in *Enemies of the Roman Order: Treason, Unrest, and Alienation in the Empire* (Cambridge, Mass.: Harvard University Press, 1967), 255–68. E. J. Hobsbawm, *Bandits* (London: Penguin, 1969), singles out "social banditry"; Anton Block criticizes his view in "The Peasant and the Brigand: Social Banditry Reconsidered," *Comparative Studies in Society and History* 14 (1972): 494–504. See Richard A. Horsley, *Bandits, Prophets and Messiahs: Popular Movements in the Time of Jesus* (Minneapolis: Winston Press, 1985).

12. For discussion of the term *lēstēs* in Josephus, see Richard A. Horsley, "Josephus and the Bandits," *Journal for the Study of Judaism* 10 (1979): 37–63.

13. Most recently see Raymond E. Brown, *The Death of the Messiah* (New York: Doubleday, 1994).

14. Ched Myers has recently argued for an early date (68 C.E.) in *Binding the Strong Man* (Maryknoll, N.Y.: Orbis Books, 1981), 40–42.

15. The dating of the gospels is still a debated issue among New Testament scholars. I intend to follow the consensus, not to present any original arguments about dating.

16. For an excellent recent discussion of Jesus' sayings in Paul's writings, see H. Koester, *Ancient Christian Gospels: Their History and Development* (London: SCM Press, and Philadelphia: Trinity Press, 1990), 52–55.

17. Josephus, *Jewish Antiquities* 18.63 and 20.200, Loeb edition, vol. 9, trans. L. H. Feldman (Cambridge, Mass.: Harvard University Press, 1965).

18. See below, pp. 30–33.

19. Philo, *Embassy to Gaius,* 301–2, Loeb edition, vol. 10, trans. F. H. Colson (London: Heinemann, 1962).

20. James M. Robinson, *The Problem of History in Mark* (London: SCM Press, 1957).

21. *Ibid.,* p. 80: "The ministry of Jesus . . . consists in proclaiming the new situation (1:15) and in carrying through the struggle against Satan in the power of the spirit."

22. Mary Smallwood, *The Jews Under Roman Rule from Pompey to Diocletian* (Leiden: E. J. Brill, 1981), 164.

23. 1 Maccabees 2.

24. Robinson, *The Problem of History in Mark,* 63.

25. See, for example, G. Vermes, *The Dead Sea Scrolls: Qûmran in Perspective* (London: Collins, 1977), and the recent revisionist views of L. H. Schiffmann, *The Eschatological Community of the Dead Sea Scrolls* (Atlanta: Scholars Press, 1989).

26. The wording of the Greek text of Mark indicates that it was Jesus' family (*hoi peri autoû*) who went to seize him (3:21) and his family who were saying that he was insane (3:22). Many translators, however, apparently finding the obvious reading objectionable, have worded their translation in ways that avoid attributing such acts and beliefs to his family. The Revised Standard Version, for example, adds several words that suggest that his family intended to protect him from the hostile suspicions of outsiders: "When his family heard it, they went out to restrain him, for people were saying, 'He has gone out of his mind.' "

27. E. Best, "The Role of the Disciples in Mark," *New Testament Studies* 23 (1977):377–401; T. J. Weeden, *Mark: Traditions in Conflict* (Philadelphia: Fortress Press, 1971); Elizabeth Struthers Malbon, "Disciples/Crowds/Whoever: Mark on Characters and Readers," *Novum Testamentum* 28, 2 (1986): 104–30.

28. See Georg Bentram, *Die Leidengeschichte Jesu und der Christuskult,* FRLANT N.F. 22 (Göttingen: Vandenhoeck und Ruprecht, 1922), 55–71.

29. Dennis Nineham, on Mark 14:53–72, in *The Gospel of St. Mark* (Baltimore: Penguin, 1967), 398: "The proceedings which were the cause of Jesus' death . . . are shown as the work of the Jews. The Romans, in the person of Pilate, also played their part (15:25ff.) but the aim of this section is to show that the primary initiative and the real responsibility lay with the Jews, who, through their official representatives, solemnly rejected and destroyed the Messiah in full consciousness of what they were doing." Nineham discusses the reasons for doubting the historicity of Mark's trial narrative in 400–12; see also Rudolf Bultmann, *The History of the Synoptic Tradition*, trans. John Marsh, rev. ed. (New York: Harper and Row, 1968), 262–87; Eta Linnemann, *Studien zur Passionsgeschichte*, FRLANT 102 (Göttingen: Vandenhoeck und Ruprecht, 1970); John R. Donahue, S.J., *Are You the Christ? The Trial Narrative in the Gospel of Mark* (Missoula, Mont.: SBL Press, 1973). An opposite viewpoint is taken by David Catchpole in *The Trial of Jesus: A Study in the Gospels and Jewish Historiography from 1770 to the Present Day* (Leiden: E. J. Brill, 1971). Catchpole concludes that Luke's version of the Sanhedrin trial "plays a vital role in the historical reconstruction of the trial of Jesus" (p. 278). See also Raymond E. Brown, *The Death of the Messiah*, vol. 1, *From Gethsemane to the Grave* (New York: Doubleday, 1994), 516–60.

30. We do not know precisely what practices the Sanhedrin followed during the first century, since extant evidence comes from a later time; see David Goodblatt's article "Sanhedrin" in the *Encyclopedia of Religion*. I am also grateful to Professor Louis Feldman for his comments on this in a letter (May 1994), and for showing me a copy of an unpublished article, "Comments on the Physical Death of Jesus."

31. See the analysis in David Catchpole, *The Trial of Jesus*, and Raymond E. Brown, *Death of the Messiah*, vol. 1, 516–60.

32. Fergus Millar, "Reflections on the Trial of Jesus," in P. R. Davies and R. T. White, eds., *A Tribute to Geza Vermes: Essays on Jewish and Christian Literature and History*, JSOT Suppl. Series 100 (Sheffield: Academia, 1990), 355–81.

33. See bibliography in note 29. Typical is Nineham's comment that the trial before Pilate "is by no means an eyewitness report; indeed, it is not a report at all, so much as a series of traditions, each making some apologetic point about the trial" (*The Gospel of St. Mark*, 411).

34. Paul Winter, *On the Trial of Jesus*, 2d ed. (Berlin and New York: Walter de Gruyter, 1974), 33–34.

35. Bentram, *Die Leidengeschichte Jesu, passim*; John R. Donahue, *Are You the Christ?* (Missoula, Mont.: Society of Biblical Literature, 1973), 139–236.

36. Brown, *Death of the Messiah*, 696.

37. Philo, *Embassy to Gaius*, 301–2.

38. Smallwood, *The Jews Under Roman Rule*, 161–62.

39. E. Stauffer, "Zur Münzprägung des Pontius Pilate," *La Nouvelle Clio* 1–2 (1949–50), 495–514.

40. Brown, *Death of the Messiah*, 700.

41. See Smallwood, *The Jews Under Roman Rule,* 162, for discussion and references.
42. Josephus, *War* 2.176–77.
43. B. C. McGinny, "The Governorship of Pontius Pilate: Messiahs and Sources," *Proceedings of the Irish Biblical Association* 10(1986): 64.
44. Josephus, *Antiquities* 2.169–74.
45. Brown, *Death of the Messiah,* 703.
46. Josephus, *Antiquities* 18.85–87.
47. Winter, *On the Trial of Jesus,* 88.
48. See Howard C. Kee, *Who Are the People of God?* Forthcoming from Yale University Press, New Haven.

Chapter II

1. For a more detailed scholarly treatment of the material in this chapter, see E. Pagels, "The Social History of Satan, the 'Intimate Enemy': A Preliminary Sketch," *Harvard Theological Review* 84:2 (1991): 105–28.
2. See M. Hengel, *Judaism and Hellenism* (London, 1974), 209, which argues that apocalyptic writings are the work of a pious minority who segregated themselves from the official cult. See also M. Barker, "Some Reflections on the Enoch Myth," *Journal for the Study of the Old Testament* 15 (1980): 7–29; her article interprets *1 Enoch* as the work of a group protesting against Jerusalem cult practices, and suggests a link between such works as *Enoch* and the later development of Christian tradition.
3. See, in particular, the incisive essays by Jonathan Z. Smith, "What a Difference a Difference Makes," and William S. Green, "Otherness Within: Towards a Theory of Difference in Rabbinic Judaism," in Jacob Neusner and Ernest S. Frerichs, eds., *To See Ourselves as Others See Us: Christians, Jews, "Others" in Late Antiquity* (Chico, Calif.: Scholars Press, 1985), 3–48 and 49–69.
4. See Morton Smith, *Palestinian Parties and Politics That Shaped the Old Testament* (New York: Columbia University Press, 1971), especially 62–146; also Paul Hanson, *The Dawn of Apocalyptic* (Philadelphia: Fortress Press, 1975).
5. Jon D. Levenson, *Creation and the Persistence of Evil: The Jewish Drama of Divine Omnipotence* (San Francisco: Harper and Row, 1988). I am grateful to John Collins for referring me to this work.
6. *Ibid.,* 44.
7. Many scholars have made this observation; for a recent discussion see Neil Forsyth, *The Old Enemy: Satan and the Combat Myth* (Princeton: Princeton University Press, 1987), 107: "In the collection of documents . . . known to Christians as the Old Testament, the word [Satan] never appears . . . as the name of the adversary. . . . rather, when the satan appears in the Old Testament, he is a member of the heavenly court, albeit with unusual tasks." See also the article on *démon,* in *La Dictionnaire de Spiritualité* 3 (Paris: Beauschesne, 1957), 142–46; H. A. Kelly, "Demonology and Diabolical Temptation," *Thought* 46 (1965): 165–70.

8. M. Delcor, "Le Mythe de la chute des anges et l'origine des géants comme explication du mal dans le monde dans l'apocalyptique juive: Histoire des traditions," *Revue de l'histoire des religions* 190:5–12; P. Day, *An Adversary in Heaven: Satan in the Hebrew Bible* (Atlanta, Ga.: Scholars Press, 1988).

9. Forsyth, *The Old Enemy,* 113.

10. See discussion in Day, *An Adversary,* 69–106.

11. Forsyth, *The Old Enemy,* 114.

12. Note that 2 Samuel 24:1–17 tells a different version of the story, in which the Lord himself, not "the *satan*," incites David to take the census. For discussion, see Morton Smith, *Palestinian Parties and Politics That Shaped the Old Testament* (New York: Columbia University Press, 1971), 62–146; Forsyth, *The Old Enemy,* 119–20.

13. Pagels, "The Social History of Satan, the 'Intimate Enemy': A Preliminary Sketch," *Harvard Theological Review* 84:2 (1991): 112–14.

14. Paul D. Hanson, *The Dawn of Apocalyptic* (Philadelphia: Fortress Press, 1975), 125.

15. An excellent account of these events is to be found in Victor Tcherikover's *Hellenistic Civilization and the Jews* (New York: Atheneum, 1970).

16. 1 Maccabees, 2.

17. Tcherikover, *Hellenistic Civilization,* 132–74.

18. *Ibid.,* 253–65.

19. Such scholars as Knut Schäferdick, in his article "Satan in the Post Apostolic Fathers," s.v. "σατανᾶς," *Theological Dictionary of the New Testament* 7 (1971): 163–65, attributes this development to Christians. Others, including Harold Kuhn, "The Angelology of the Non-Canonical Jewish Apocalypses," *Journal of Biblical Literature* 67 (1948): 217; Claude Montefiore, *Lectures on the Origin and Growth of Religion as Illustrated by the Religion of the Ancient Hebrews* (London: Williams and Norgate, 1892), 429; and George Foote Moore, *Judaism in the First Centuries of the Christian Era,* vol. 1, *The Age of the Tannaim* (Cambridge, Mass.: Harvard University Press, 1927), rightly locate the development of angelology and demonology in pre-Christian Jewish sources, and offer different interpretations of this, as noted in Pagels, "The Social History of Satan, the 'Intimate Enemy,' " 107.

20. Which account is earlier—that in Genesis 6 or in *1 Enoch* 6–11—remains a debatable issue. See, for example, J. T. Milik, *The Books of Enoch: Aramaic Fragments of Qûmran Caves* (Oxford: Clarendon, 1976); George W. E. Nickelsburg, "Apocalyptic and Myth in *1 Enoch* 6–11," *Journal of Biblical Literature* 96 (1977): 383–405; Margaret Barker, "Some Reflections on the Enoch Myth," *JSOT* 15 (1980): 7–29; Philip S. Alexander, "The Targumim and Early Exegesis of the 'Sons of God' in Genesis 6," *Journal of Jewish Studies* 23 (1972): 60–71.

21. For a survey of this theme of rivalry between angels and humans, see Peter Schäfer's fine work *Rivalität Zwischen Engeln und Menschen: Untersuchungen zur rabbinischen Engelvorstellung* (Berlin and New York: de Gruyter, 1975). For a discussion of one strand of Muslim tra-

dition, see Peter Awn, *Satan's Tragedy and Redemption: Iblīs in Sufi Psychology* (Leiden: E. J. Brill, 1983).

22. Note scholarly debate cited in note 20 concerning the priority of Genesis 6. I am following those scholars who see *1 Enoch* 6–11 as amplifications of Gen. 6:1–4, including Philip S. Alexander and Paul Hanson, "Rebellion in Heaven, Azazel, and Euhemenistic Heroes in *1 Enoch* 6–11," *Journal of Biblical Literature* 96 (1977): 195–233.

23. George W. E. Nickelsburg, "Apocalyptic and Myth in *1 Enoch* 6–11," *Journal of Biblical Literature* 96 (1977): 383–405.

24. David Suter, "Fallen Angel, Fallen Priest: The Problem of Family Purity in *1 Enoch* 6–16," *Hebrew Union College Annual* 50 (1979): 115–35. Cf. George W. E. Nickelsburg, "The Book of Enoch in Recent Research," *Religious Studies Review* 7 (1981): 210–17.

25. John Collins, *The Apocalyptic Imagination: An Introduction to the Jewish Matrix of Christianity* (New York: Crossroad, 1984), 127.

26. This question dominated the concerns of many others as well; for discussion, see the forthcoming book by Howard C. Kee, *Who Are the People of God?*

27. George W. E. Nickelsburg, "Revealed Wisdom as a Criterion for Inclusion and Exclusion," in Neusner and Frerichs, eds., *To See Ourselves As Others See Us*, 76.

28. See the article by George W. E. Nickelsburg, "Riches, the Rich, and God's Judgment in *1 Enoch* 92–105 and the Gospel According to Luke," *New Testament Studies* 25 (1979), 324–49.

29. On the basis of the Watcher story in *1 Enoch* 6–16, Forsyth (*The Old Enemy*, 167–70) comments that it implies "a radically different theology" from that of the Genesis primordial history, in that "in Enoch we have heard nothing about a wicked humanity. Instead, all human suffering is attributed to the angelic revolt and the sins of their giant brood." Yet as I read the Enoch literature, its authors demonstrate awareness of the tension between—and correlation of—human and angelic guilt, or at least of the possibility of contradiction. The passage may be included as a corrective to any who exempt humans from responsibility by blaming the angels' transgressions. For a discussion, see Martha Himmelfarb, *Tours of Hell: An Apocalyptic Form in Jewish and Christian Literature* (Philadelphia: University of Pennsylvania Press, 1983).

30. This identification occurs commonly in later Jewish sources, often traced to the Septuagint translation of 1 Chronicles 16:26: οἱ τῶν ἐθνῶν θεοί δαίμωνες ἐίσιν.

31. Josephus, *Life*, 10.

32. Pliny the Elder, *Natural History*, Loeb edition, vol. 2, 5.15, 73. For discussion of Pliny's description of the Essenes, see J. P. Audet, "Qûmran et la notice de Pline sur les Esséniers," *Revue Biblique* 68 (1961): 346–87; D. F. Graf, "Pagan Witness to the Essenes," *Biblical Archaeologist* 40 (1977): 125–29.

33. L. H. Schiffman, *Archaeology and History in the Dead Sea Scrolls* (Sheffield: JSOT Press, 1989).

34. G. Vermes, *The Dead Sea Scrolls: Qûmran in Perspective* (Atlanta, Ga.: Scholars Press, 1989).

35. See F. F. Bruce, "The Romans Through Jewish Eyes," in M. Simon, ed., *Paganisme, Judaïsme, Christianisme* (Paris: E. de Boccard, 1978), 3–12; G. Vermes, *Post Biblical Jewish Studies* (Leiden: E. J. Brill, 1975), 215–24.

36. S. David Sperling, "Belial," forthcoming in Karel van der Toorn, *Dictionary of Deities and Demons* (Leiden: E. J. Brill).

37. See, for example, Matthew Black, *The Scrolls and Christian Origins* (New York: Scribner, 1961), 91–117.

38. Carol Newsome, *Songs of Sabbath Sacrifice: A Critical Edition* (Atlanta, Ga.: Scholars Press, 1985).

39. Yigael Yadin, who edited the *War Scroll,* commented that this text, like others from Qûmran, "considerably extends our knowledge of Jewish angelology—a subject of utmost importance in the Judaism of that time" (*Scroll,* 229). But Yadin did not tell us what constitutes its importance: Discernment of spirits, the capacity to recognize and understand the interrelationship of supernatural forces, both good and evil, is essential to the Essenes' sense of their own identity and the way they identify others. Having set aside, not so much as wrong but as inadequate, more traditional forms of Jewish identity, the Essenes articulate, through their accounts of the battle between angelic and demonic forces, on which side of the cosmic battle each person and each group of Jews stands.

40. Yigael Yadin assumes that the Prince of Light "is Michael, Prince of Israel": *The Scroll of the War of the Sons of Light Against the Sons of Darkness* (Oxford: Oxford University Press, 1962), 236. But this identification ignores the sectarianism that dominates the Qûmran texts. Instead, as John Collins observes, "In 1 QM Michael is no longer simply the Prince of Israel but leader of the Sons of Light. This designation may have been correlated in practice with members of the congregation, but in principle it was open to broader interpretations and freed from ethnic associations. Belial, too, is no longer the prince of a specific nation. . . . Rather, he represents evil at large, like Satan or Mastema in the book of *Jubilees.* . . . The adoption of this terminology in preference to the traditional, national, and social affiliations opens up considerably the range of application of the eschatological language. Specifically, it invites the correlation of the eschatological drama with the . . . moral conflict of good and evil within every individual" (*The Apocalyptic Imagination,* 128–31).

Chapter III

1. George W. E. Nickelsburg, "Revealed Wisdom as a Criterion for Inclusion and Exclusion: From Jewish Sectarianism to Early Christianity," in Jacob Neusner and Ernest S. Frerichs, eds., *To See Ourselves As Others See Us: Christians, Jews, "Others" in Late Antiquity* (Chico, Calif.: Scholars Press, 1985), 73.

2. *Ibid.*

3. Wayne A. Meeks, "Breaking Away: Three New Testament Pictures of Christianity's Separation from the Jewish Communities," in Neusner and Frerichs, eds., *To See Ourselves*, 94–115.

4. For a different perspective in Paul's view of Jews and Judaism, see John Gager, *The Origins of Anti-Semitism: Attitudes Toward Judaism in Pagan and Christian Antiquity* (Oxford: Oxford University Press, 1983), 193–264; Lloyd Gaston, "Paul and the Torah," in A. Davies, ed., *Anti-Semitism and the Foundation of Christianity* (New York: Paulist Press, 1979), 48–71.

5. K. Stendahl, *The School of St. Matthew* (Uppsala: C. W. K. Gleerup, 1954).

6. Wayne A. Meeks, *The First Urban Christians: The Social World of the Apostle Paul* (New Haven: Yale University Press, 1983).

7. For a discussion of this process, see H. Koester, *Ancient Christian Gospels: Their History and Development* (London: SCM Press, and Philadelphia: Trinity Press, 1990), 42–162.

8. See J. Kloppenborg, *The Formation of Q* (Philadelphia: Fortress Press, 1987), for a recent, revisionist view of the development of the Q source.

9. G. R. S. Mead, *Fragments of a Faith Forgotten* (reprint, New York: University Books, 1960), summarized what was known of such fragments at the turn of the century; see Morton Smith, *Clement of Alexandria and a Secret Gospel of Mark* (Cambridge: Harvard University Press, 1973).

10. For discussion of passages concerning women in gnostic sources, see Elaine Pagels, *The Gnostic Gospels* (New York: Random House, 1979), 48–69; Karen King, ed., *Images of the Feminine in Gnosticism* (Chapel Hill: University of North Carolina Press, 1986); Jorunn Jacobsen Buckley, *Female Fault and Fulfillment in Gnosticism* (Chapel Hill, University of North Carolina Press, 1986).

11. For a fuller discussion of some of the implications of this discovery, see Pagels, *Gnostic Gospels*.

12. For a discussion of the original language, see Bentley Layton, "Introduction to the Gospel of Thomas, NHC II.2," in B. Layton, ed., *Nag Hammadi Codex II. 2–7, together with Brit. Lib. Or. 4926 (1) and P. Oxy. 1, 654, 655* (Leiden: E. J. Brill, 1989), vol. 1, Nag Hammadi Series 20.

13. Koester, *Ancient Christian Gospels*, 49–172.

14. Irenaeus, *Libros Quinque Adversus Haereses*, ed. W. W. Harvey (Cambridge: Typis Academicis, 1857), vol. 1, 3.11.9. Hereafter cited as *Against Heresies*.

15. *Ibid.*, preface.

16. For assessment of Matthew's provenance, see the summary in Wayne A. Meeks, "Breaking Away," 108–14; Alan F. Segal, "Matthew's Jewish Voice," in David L. Balch, ed., *Social History of the Matthean Community* (Minneapolis: Fortress Press, 1991), 3–37; also, in the same volume: Anthony J. Saldarini, "The Gospel of Matthew and Jewish-Christian Conflict," 38–62; Robert H. Gundrey, "A Responsive Evaluation of the Social History of the Matthean Community in Roman Syria," 62–67; William R. Schoedel, "Ignatius and the Reception of the Gospel of

Matthew in Antioch," 129–77; Rodney Stark, "Antioch as the Social Situation for Matthew's Gospel," 189–210; also J. Andrew Overman, *Matthew's Gospel and Formative Judaism: The Social World of the Matthean Community* (Philadelphia: Fortress Press, 1990); Amy-Jill Levine, *The Social and Ethnic Dimensions of Matthean Salvation History:* "Go Nowhere Among the Gentiles" (Matt. 10:56) (Lewiston, N.Y.: Edwin Mellen, 1988).

17. Mary Smallwood, *The Jews Under Roman Rule from Pompey to Diocletian* (Leiden: E. J. Brill, 1981), 349.

18. Jacob Neusner's pioneering work has opened an understanding of this process; see, for example, *Formative Judaism: Religious, Historical, and Literary Studies,* Brown Judaic Studies, no. 91 (Chico, Calif.: Scholars Press, 1983).

19. See the incisive comments of Alan F. Segal, "Matthew's Jewish Voice," and J. Andrew Overman, *Matthew's Gospel and Formative Judaism.*

20. Alan F. Segal, *Rebecca's Children: Judaism and Christianity in the Roman World* (Cambridge: Harvard University Press, 1986); idem, "Matthew's Jewish Voice."

21. For discussion, see Raymond E. Brown, *The Birth of the Messiah: A Commentary on the Infancy Narratives in Matthew and Luke* (New York: Doubleday, 1977).

22. *Ibid.*

23. When Matthew retells the passion narrative, however, he drops his otherwise frequent references to the Pharisees. There, following Mark, he depicts the chief priests, scribes, and elders as Jesus' primary opponents.

24. George W. E. Nickelsburg, "The Genre and Function of Mark's Passion Narrative," *Harvard Theological Review* 73 (1980): 174.

25. For discussion, see, for example, Michael J. Cook, "Jesus and the Pharisees—The Problem As It Stands Today," *The Journal of Ecumenical Studies* 15 (1978): 441–60; D. Garland, *The Intention of Matthew 23* (Leiden: E. J. Brill, 1979); J. Andrew Overman, *Matthew's Gospel and Formative Judaism;* Klaus Pantle-Schieber, "Anmerkungen zur Auseinandersetzung von *ekklesia* und Judentum im Matthäusevangelium" *Zeitschrift für Neutestamentliche Wissenschaft* 80 (1989), 145–62.

26. Luke T. Johnson, "The New Testament: Anti-Jewish Slander and the Conventions of Ancient Polemic," *Journal of Biblical Literature* 108 (1989): 419–41.

Chapter IV

1. David B. Gowler, *Host, Guest, Enemy, and Friend: Portraits of the Pharisees in Luke and Acts* (New York: Lang, 1991); David A. Neale, *None But the Sinners: Religious Categories in the Gospel of Luke* (Sheffield: JSOT Press, 1991); Robert L. Brawley, "The Pharisees in Luke-Acts: Luke's Address to Jews and His Irenic Purpose," Ph.D. dissertation, Princeton Theological Seminary, 1978; Jack T. Sanders, *The Jews in Luke-Acts* (Philadelphia: Fortress Press, 1987); Joseph R. Tyson, *Images of Judaism in Luke-Acts* (Columbia: University of South Carolina Press, 1992).

2. See Susan Garrett, *The Demise of the Devil: Magic and the Demonic in Luke's Writings* (Minneapolis: Fortress Press, 1989).
3. David R. Catchpole, *The Trial of Jesus: A Study in the Gospels and Jewish Historiography from 1770 to the Present Day* (Leiden: E. J. Brill, 1971); Richard W. Husband, *The Prosecution of Jesus: Its Date, History and Legality* (Princeton: Princeton University Press, 1916); G. S. Sloyan, *Jesus on Trial: The Development of the Passion Narratives and Their Historical and Ecumenical Implications* (Philadelphia: Fortress Press, 1973); R. E. Brown, *The Death of the Messiah: From Gethsemane to the Grave* (New York: Doubleday, 1994).
4. Catchpole, *The Trial of Jesus*, 203.
5. Richard A. Horsley, "Josephus and the Bandits," *Journal for the Study of Judaism* 10 (1979): 37–63.
6. Alfred F. Loisy, *Les Évangiles Synoptiques* (Ceffons près Montieren Der: Chez l'Auteur, 1907–08), 787.
7. On the gospel of John, see J. Louis Martyn, *History and Theology in the Fourth Gospel*, 2nd ed. (Nashville: Abingdon, 1978); Norman R. Petersen, *The Fourth Gospel* (Valley Forge, Pa.: Trinity Press, 1993); C. H. Dodd, *The Interpretation of the Fourth Gospel* (Cambridge: Cambridge University Press, 1953).
8. Martyn, *History and Theology in the Fourth Gospel*; see also William Horbury, "The Benediction of the Minim and Early Jewish-Christian Controversy," *Journal of Theological Studies* 33 (1982): 19–61; T. C. G. Thornton, "Christian Understandings of the Birkath ha-Minim in the Eastern Roman Empire," *Journal of Theological Studies* 38 (1987), 419–31; Asher Finkel, "Yavneh's Liturgy and Early Christianity," *Journal of Ecumenical Studies* 18:2 (1981): 231–50; Alan F. Segal, "Ruler of This World: Attitudes About Mediator Figures and the Importance of Sociology for Self-Definition," in E. P. Sanders, ed., *Jewish and Christian Self-Definition*, vol. 2 (Philadelphia: Fortress Press, 1980), 245–68.
9. Wayne A. Meeks, "The Man from Heaven in Johannine Sectarianism," *Journal of Biblical Literature* 91 (1972): 50.
10. Gustave Hoennecke, "Die Teufelsidee in den Evangelien," *Neutestamentliche Studien: Für Georg Heinrici zu seinem 70* (Leipzig: J. C. Heinrichs, 1912), 208.
11. Raymond Brown, *The Gospel According to John*, Anchor Bible Commentary, vols. 29/29a (Garden City, N.Y.: Anchor Bible, 1966), 364–76.
12. *Ibid.*
13. Raymond Brown, "Incidents That Are Units in the Synoptic Gospels But Dispersed in St. John," *Catholic Biblical Quarterly* 23 (1961).
14. Rudolph Bultmann, *Das Evangelium Johannis* (Göttingen: Vandenhoeck und Ruprecht, 1941), trans. G. R. Beasley-Murray, *The Gospel of John: A Commentary* (Oxford: Basil Blackwell, 1971), 319.
15. *Ibid.*, 321.
16. See, for example, Robert Brachter, "The 'Jews' in the Gospel of John," *Practical Papers for the Bible Translator* 26/4 (1975): 365–409; R. Alan Culpepper, "The Gospel of John and the Jews," *Expository Times* 84 (1987): 273–88; C. J. Cuming, "The Jews in the Fourth Gospel," *Expos-*

itory Times 60 (1948–49): 290–92; Reginald Fuller, "The 'Jews' in the Fourth Gospel," *Dialog* 16 (1971): 37; Malcolm Lowe, "Who Were the 'Ioudaioi'?" *Novum Testamentum* 18/2 (1976):101–30; Massey Shepherd, "The Jews in the Gospel of John: Another Level of Meaning," *Anglican Theological Review Supplementary Series* 3 (1974): 96; John Townsend, "The Gospel of John and the Jews: The Story of a Religious Divorce," in Alan Davies, ed., *Anti-Semitism and the Foundations of Christianity* (New York: Paulist Press, 1979), 72–97; Urban C. von Wahlde, "The Johannine 'Jews': A Critical Survey," *New Testament Studies* 28 (1982): 33–60.

17. Rudolph Bultmann, 59.
18. Heinrich Schneider, "The Word Was Made Flesh: An Analysis of Revelation in the Fourth Gospel," 347–51.
19. Samuel Sandmel, *Anti-Semitism in the New Testament* (Philadelphia: Fortress Press, 1978), 115–17.
20. Rudolph Bultmann, 85–94, *passim.*
21. Fuller, "The 'Jews' in the Fourth Gospel," 20.
22. Fergus Millar, "Reflections on the Trial of Jesus," in P. R. Davies and R. White, eds., *A Tribute to Geza Vermes: Essays on Jewish and Christian Literature and History* (Sheffield: JSOT Press, 1990), 355–81.
23. Rosemary Reuther, *Faith and Fratricide: The Theological Roots of Anti-Semitism* (Minneapolis: Seabury Press, 1974).
24. Husband, *The Prosecution of Jesus,* 173–81.
25. Sandmel, *Anti-Semitism in the New Testament,* 115.
26. Dennis Nineham, *The Gospel of St. Mark* (Baltimore: Penguin Books, 1967), 412.
27. Dodd, *The Interpretation of the Fourth Gospel,* 97.
28. See, for example, Paul Winter, *On the Trial of Jesus,* 2nd ed. (Berlin: De Gruyter, 1974).
29. *Ibid.,* 88–89.
30. J. Andrew Overman, *Matthew's Gospel and Formative Judaism* (Minneapolis: Fortress Press, 1990).

Chapter V
1. See W. H. C. Frend, *Martyrdom and Persecution in the Early Church* (Oxford: Blackwell, 1965), on the persecution of Christians from 50 to 313 C.E.
2. Tacitus, *Annals* 15.44.
3. Robert L. Wilken, "Pagan Criticism of Christianity: Greek Religion and Christian Faith," in W. Schoedel, ed., *Early Christian Literature and the Classical Intellectual Tradition* (Paris: Éditions Beauchesne, 1979), 117–34. For an excellent discussion, see Wilken, *The Christians As the Romans Saw Them* (New Haven: Yale University Press, 1984).
4. Tertullian, *Apology* 1.
5. Georges Villes, *La Gladiature en Occident des origines à la mort de Domitien* (Rome: École française de Rome, 1981); Carlin Barton, *The Sorrows of the Ancient Romans: The Gladiator and the Monster* (Princeton: Princeton University Press, 1992).

6. Tacitus, *Annals* 15.44.
7. See *The Acts of the Christian Martyrs,* ed. and trans. H. A. Musurillo (Oxford: Oxford University Press, 1972).
8. See Justin Martyr, *Dialogue with Trypho,* chaps. 1–6, for Justin's own account of these events; see also L. Barnard, *Justin Martyr: His Life and Thought* (London: Cambridge University Press, 1967).
9. P. Hadot, *Exercices Spirituels et Philosophie Critique* (Paris: Études augustiniennes, 1981), 13–58.
10. Justin Martyr, *First Apology* 61.
11. See Ramsay MacMullen, *Christianizing the Roman Empire: A.D. 100–400* (New Haven: Yale University Press, 1984), 27–31, for a discussion of Justin Martyr's conversion to Christianity. This statement paraphrases and borrows from MacMullen's incisive discussion.
12. Justin Martyr, *Dialogue with Trypho* 7.
13. *Ibid.,* 8.
14. On baptism in early Christianity, see Peter Cramer, *Baptism and Change in the Early Middle Ages, c. 200–1150* (New York: Cambridge University Press, 1993).
15. Justin Martyr, *First Apology* 61.
16. *Ibid.*
17. A. H. Armstrong, "The Ancient and Continuing Pieties of the Greek World," in A. H. Armstrong, ed., *Classical Mediterranean Spirituality* (London: SCM Press, 1989), 66–101.
18. Felix Buffiere, *Les Mythes d'Homère et la pensée grecque* (Paris: Société d'édition, 1956), chap. 5, 136–54; for a fascinating discussion of later reinterpretation of Homer, see Robert Lamberton, *Homer the Theologian* (Berkeley: University of California Press, 1989).
19. Justin Martyr, *First Apology* 5, *passim.*
20. For an excellent discussion of Justin and the other apologists, see H. Wey, *Die Funktionen der bösen Geisten bei den griechischen Apologeten des zweiten Jahrhunderts nach Christus* (Wintermur: Keller, 1957), 3–32 (on Justin).
21. Justin Martyr, *First Apology* 25.
22. *Ibid.,* 43.
23. Justin Martyr, *Dialogue with Trypho* 8.
24. Justin Martyr, *First Apology* 14.
25. *Ibid.*
26. *Ibid.,* 16.
27. *Ibid.,* 61.
28. *Ibid.,* 27.
29. *Ibid.,* 28.
30. *Ibid.,* 12.
31. Elaine Pagels, "Christian Apologists and the 'Fall of the Angels': An Attack on Roman Imperial Power?," *Harvard Theological Review* 78 (1985): 301–25.
32. See P. de Labriolle, *La Réaction païenne: Étude sur la polémique antichrétienne du I^r au IVe siècle,* 2nd ed. (Paris, 1948); Ramsay MacMullen,

Enemies of the Roman Order (Cambridge, Mass.: Harvard University Press, 1966).

33. Pliny, *Epistle* 10.96. For discussion of Pliny's letter, see Wilken, *The Christians As the Romans Saw Them*, 15–17; A. N. Sherwin-White, *The Letters of Pliny: A Historical and Social Commentary* (Oxford: Oxford University Press, 1966).

34. Justin Martyr, *First Apology* 5.

35. *Ibid.*, 1.

36. *Ibid.*, 14.

37. Justin Martyr, *Second Apology* 2.

38. Justin Martyr, *Second Apology* 1.

39. Musurillo, *Acts of the Christian Martyrs,* chap. 5, "Martyrdom of Justin and His Companions."

40. Fergus Millar, *The Emperor in the Roman World, 31 B.C.–337 A.D.* (Ithaca: Cornell University Press, 1977).

41. P. A. Brunt, "Marcus Aurelius and the Christians." See also Brunt, "Marcus Aurelius and His Meditations," *Journal of Roman Studies* 64 (1974): 1–20, and Wilken, *The Christians As the Romans Saw Them*, 48–67.

42. Marcus Aurelius, *Meditations* 1.17.5; on Marcus Aurelius in general, see the biography by A. Birley, *Marcus Aurelius* (Boston: Little, Brown, 1966).

43. See note 18.

44. André-Jean Voelke, *L'Idée de Volonté dans le Stoïcisme* (Paris: Presses Universitaires de France, 1973), 109–12.

45. Marcus Aurelius, *Meditations* 4.5.

46. *Ibid.*, 4.44.

47. *Ibid.*, 3.2.

48. *Ibid.*, 2.16.

49. *Ibid.*, 12.14.

50. *Ibid.*, 2.11.

51. *Ibid.*, 3.16.

52. *Ibid.*, 8.49.

53. *Ibid.*, 9.40.

54. *Ibid.*, 9.34.

55. *Ibid.*, 4.15.

56. *Ibid.*, 4.49.

57. *Ibid.*, 10.5; see also 5.1.

58. *Ibid.*, 7.9.

59. Hans Dieter Betz, *The Greek Magical Papyri* (Chicago: University of Chicago Press, 1986); John G. Gager, *Curse Tablets and Binding Spells* (New York: Oxford University Press, 1992).

60. Marcus Aurelius, *Meditations* 11.15.

61. See Wayne Meeks, *The Moral World of the First Christians* (Philadelphia: Westminster Press, 1986).

62. Tatian, *Address to the Greeks* 4.

63. *Ibid.*

64. *Ibid.*, 7.

65. *Ibid.,* 16.
66. *Ibid.,* 15.
67. *Ibid.*
68. *Ibid.,* 6.
69. *Ibid.,* 8.
70. *Ibid.,* 9.
71. *Ibid.,* 11.
72. For a discussion of changing perceptions of Hellenism in the Eastern Empire, see Glen W. Bowersock, *Hellenism in Late Antiquity* (Ann Arbor: University of Michigan Press, 1990).
73. Tatian, *Address to the Greeks* 23.
74. Georges Villes, *La Gladiature en Occident des origines à la mort de Domitien,* 395–97; Alan Cameron, *Circus Factions: The Blues and the Greens at Rome and Byzantium* (Oxford: Clarendon Press, 1976); Carlin Barton, *The Sorrows of the Ancient Romans: The Gladiator and the Monster.*
75. Tatian, *Address to the Greeks* 28.
76. See Henri Crouzel, *Origen: The Life and Thought of the First Great Theologian,* trans. A. S. Worrall (San Francisco: Harper and Row, 1989); see also the discussion of Origen in Peter Brown, *The Body and Society: Men, Women, and Sexual Renunciation in Early Christianity* (New York: Columbia University Press, 1988), 160–77.
77. Quoted by Eusebius, *Historia Ecclesiae* 6.26, possibly from a letter. For discussion see Henri Crouzel, *Origen,* 6.
78. Origen, *Exhortation to Martyrdom.*
79. See Origen, *Contra Celsum.*
80. *Ibid.,* 8.68.
81. *Ibid.,* 1.1.
82. *Ibid.,* 1.31.
83. *Ibid.,* 1.27.
84. *Ibid.,* 1.29.
85. *Ibid.,* 4.22.
86. *Ibid.,* 7.68.
87. *Ibid.;* see also 8.31–32.
88. *Ibid.,* 7.68.
89. Ramsay MacMullen, *Christianizing the Roman Empire,* 21.
90. Marcus Aurelius, *Meditations* 6.44.
91. Tacitus, *Histories* 5.5.
92. Origen, *Contra Celsum* 6.42.
93. *Ibid.,* 7.2.
94. *Ibid.,* 8.28.
95. *Ibid.,* 8.33.
96. *Ibid.,* 8.39.
97. *Ibid.,* 1.43.
98. *Ibid.,* 1.44.
99. *Ibid.,* 8.44.
100. Eusebius, *Historia Ecclesiae* 6.34.
101. Origen, *Contra Celsum* 8.65.
102. *Ibid.,* 8.73.

103. *Ibid.*
104. Tertullian, *Apology* 42.
105. *Ibid.*, 24. See also *Apology* 28 and *To Scapula* 2.
106. Origen, *Contra Celsum* 1.1.

Chapter VI
1. Tertullian, *Apology*, chap. 37.
2. *Ibid.*, chap. 3.
3. David L. Balch, *Let Wives Be Submissive: The Domestic Code in 1 Peter* (Chico, Calif.: Scholars Press, 1981). See also John H. Elliott, *A Home for the Homeless: A Sociological Exegesis of 1 Peter, Its Situation and Strategy* (Philadelphia: Fortress Press, 1981). For a fascinating discussion of the various depictions of Paul, see Dennis Ronald MacDonald, *The Legend and the Apostle: The Battle for Paul in Story and Canon* (Philadelphia: Westminster Press, 1983).
4. For discussion, see Karlmann Beyschlag, *Clemens Romanus und der Frühkatholizismus* (Tübingen: Mohr, 1966); on 2 Clement, Karl Paul Donfried, *The Setting of Second Clement in Early Christianity* (Leiden: E. J. Brill, 1974).
5. *1 Clement*, chap. 1.
6. *Ibid.*
7. *Ibid.*, chap. 40.
8. *Ibid.*, chap. 37.
9. *Teaching of the Twelve Apostles* 1.2.
10. *Ibid.*, 1.6.
11. *Ibid.*, 2.2.
12. *Letter of Barnabas*, chap. 18.
13. *Ibid.*, chap. 22.1–2; 19.
14. *Ibid.*, 18.2; cf. 2.1; 4.9.
15. *Ibid.*, chap. 2.
16. *Ibid.*
17. *Ibid.*, chap. 9.9.
18. *Ibid.*, chap. 18.
19. Irenaeus, *Against Heresies*, ed. W. W. Harvey (Cambridge: Typis Academicis, 1857), vol. 1, preface.
20. *Ibid.*
21. *Ibid.*, 1.27.4.
22. *Ibid.*, 1.6.3.
23. For discussion, see Elaine Pagels, *The Gnostic Gospels* (New York: Random House, 1979).
24. *Testimony of Truth* (NHC IX, 3) 3.29.6.
25. *Ibid.*, 29.9–10.
26. *Ibid.*, 30.2–4.
27. *Ibid.*, 30.18–19.
28. *Ibid.*, 44.30–45.4.
29. *Ibid.*, 41.4–7.
30. *Ibid.*, 43.29–44.16.
31. Justin, *First Apology* 29.

32. *Testimony of Truth* (NHC IX, 3) 29.15–17.
33. *Ibid.*, 41.3–4.
34. *Ibid.*, 41.28–42.14.
35. *Ibid.*, 47.5–6.
36. *Ibid.*, 47.14–30.
37. *Ibid.*, 41.4.
38. *Hypostasis of the Archons* (NHC II,4) 86.26–27.
39. *Ibid.*, 86.27–31.
40. *Ibid.*, 86.31–87.4; 94.22–95.13.
41. *Ibid.*, 91.7–11.
42. *Ibid.*, 96.17–27.
43. On the "undominated generation," see Michael Williams, *The Immoveable Race: A Gnostic Designation and the Theme of Stability in Late Antiquity* (Leiden: E. J. Brill, 1985).
44. *Apocryphon of John* (NHC II, 1) 24.15–27.
45. *Ibid.*, 28.11–14.
46. *Ibid.*, 28.21–29.
47. *Ibid.*, 29.17–20.
48. *Ibid.*, 29.32–30.7.
49. Tertullian, *Prescription Against Heretics*, chap. 5.
50. *Ibid.*, chap. 6.
51. Tertullian, *Against the Valentinians*, chap. 4.
52. Tertullian, *Prescription*, chap. 7.
53. *Ibid.*, chap. 8.
54. *Ibid.*, chap. 11.
55. *Ibid.*, chap. 16.
56. *Ibid.*, chap. 18.
57. *Ibid.*, chap. 37.
58. *Ibid.*, chap. 40.
59. *Ibid.*, chap. 18.
60. *Ibid.*, chap. 39.
61. Tertullian, *Against the Valentinians*, chap. 4.
62. *Ibid.*
63. Walther Völker, ed., *Quellen zur Geschichte der Christlichen Gnosis* (Tübingen: J. C. B. Mohr, 1932), "Die Fragmente Valentins," Fragment 7, p. 59.
64. Hippolytus, *Refutation of All Heresies* 8.15.1–2.
65. Theodotus, cited by Clement of Alexandria, *Excerpts from Theodotus* 78.2.
66. *Gospel of Philip* (NHC II, 3) 79.22–31.
67. For discussion, see Pagels, *The Johannine Gospel in Gnostic Exegesis* (Nashville, Tenn.: Abingdon Press, 1993), 83–97.
68. Irenaeus, *Against Heresies* 1.6.2.
69. Tertullian, *Prescription*, chap. 3.
70. Irenaeus, *Against Heresies* 3.15.2.
71. *Ibid.*, 1.11.1; I.21.3.
72. *Ibid.*, 4.33.7.
73. *Ibid.*, 1.6.2–3.

74. *Ibid.*, 1.13.7, 1.13.5.
75. *Ibid.*, 1.13.3.
76. *Ibid.*, 1.13.3.
77. See, for example, Jeremiah 2:1–3:5; Hosea 2:1–4:19; Isaiah 60:1.
78. Völker, *Quellen*, Fragment 2, p. 58.
79. *Gospel of Truth* (NHC I, 3)32.35–33.21.
80. For a fuller discussion, see Pagels, "The Mystery of Marriage in the Gospel of Philip, Revisited," in Birger A. Pearson, ed., *The Future of Early Christianity: Essays in Honor of Helmut Koester* (Minneapolis: Fortress Press, 1991).
81. For an excellent discussion, see Klaus Koschorke, "Die 'Namen' in Philippusevangelium: Beobachtungen zur Auseinandersetzung zwischen gnostischem und kirchlichem Christentum," *Zeitschrift für Neutestamentliche Wissenschaft* 64 (1973): 307–22.
82. *Gospel of Philip* (NHC II, 3) 74.5–12.
83. *Ibid.*, 80.23–81.14.
84. *Ibid.*, 66.5 5–7.
85. *Ibid.*, 78.24–79.14.
86. *Ibid.*, 79.34–35.
87. *Ibid.*, 80.10.
88. *Ibid.*, 73.33–74.2.
89. *Ibid.*, 83.13–30.
90. *Ibid.*, 84.1–6.
91. *Ibid.*, 84.11–14.
92. *Ibid.*, 55.23–26.
93. *Ibid.*, 55.26–30.
94. *Ibid.*, 52.21–25.
95. *Ibid.*, 64.22–24.
96. *Ibid.*, 64.29–30.
97. *Ibid.*, 77.2–3.
98. *Ibid.*, 67.26.
99. *Gospel of Thomas* (NHC II, 2) 33.19–20.
100. Irenaeus, *Against Heresies* 4.26.3.
101. *Ibid.*, 4.26.2.
102. *Ibid.*, 5.26.2.
103. *Ibid.*, 4.33.8.

Conclusion

1. Athanasius, *Life of Anthony* 28.
2. *Ibid.*, 41.

I discovered John Dominick Crossan's incisive book *Who Killed Jesus? Exposing the Roots of Anti-Semitism in the Gospel Story of the Death of Jesus* (San Francisco: HarperCollins, 1995) only after I had completed my work on this book and so was not able to refer to it in the text.

INDEX

Abel, 162
abortion, sin of, 154
Abraham, 35–36, 37, 51, 54, 59, 78, 137
Acts of the Apostles, 97–98, 113, 180
Adam and Eve, 49
    in Nag Hammadi texts, 159–60, 161, 162–63
"Address to the Greeks" (Tatian), 131–35
adultery, sin of, 154, 170
Against Heresies (Irenaeus), 155, 169, 177–78
agape ("love"), 172
Agrippa II, 108
Ahriman, xviii
Akkad, xviii
Albinus, 108
Alexander the Great, 9, 44, 45, 50
Alexandria, 8, 10, 29–30, 69, 136, 137, 157, 173
almah ("young woman"), 77
Ambrose, 137, 146
Ammonites, 36
Amos, 38
Ananus II, 108
Andrew, 17, 24, 67
angelology, 59–60
angels, xv, xvi–xvii, 12, 13, 36, 90, 149, 155, 162–63, 181
    adversarial role of, 39–43
    demonic offspring of, 49, 50, 54, 132–33, 158
    derivation of term, 39
    Essenes and, 59–60
    fallen, xv–xvii, 47–55, 58, 85–86, 118, 131–33, 141, 143, 158–63, 165, 169
    mating of, with human women, 48–49, 50–51, 163
    metallurgy introduced by, 50, 163

    as "sons of God" (*benē 'elōhīm*), 39, 41, 48, 50
    "watcher," 50–53
Annas, 107
Anthony, 173, 180–81
Antioch, 65, 75, 138
Antiochus Epiphanes, 45–46
Antipas, 4
anti-Semitism, 34, 104–5
Antoninus, Marcus Aurelius, *see* Marcus Aurelius, Emperor of Rome
Antoninus Pius, Emperor of Rome, 124–25, 126
Aphrodite, 120, 126
apocalyptic literature, 13, 51, 56, 179
apocrypha, 35, 48–55, 56
    Book of the Watchers, 49–52, 54, 55, 56, 58, 60
    First Book of Enoch, 50, 52–53, 56
    Jubilees, 53–55, 56, 59, 60
    I Maccabees, 14, 45–46
Apollo, 119, 120, 126
"apostolic fathers of the church, the," collected writings of, 153–55, 156
aposynagoge, 99
Apuleius, Lucius, 130
Ares, 120
Aristotle, 132
Armstrong, A. H., 119
assimilation, conflicts over, 38, 45–46, 53, 55, 57, 60
Athanasius, 173
Augustine of Hippo, 182
Azazel, 47, 50, 51, 55

Babylonian exile, 43, 45
Balaam, story of, 40–41
Balch, David, 151